NEGOTIATING MIGRATION IN THE CONTEXT OF CLIMATE CHANGE

Global Migration and Social Change series

Series editors: **Nando Sigona,** University of Birmingham, UK and **Alan Gamlen**, Monash University, Australia

---

The Global Migration and Social Change series showcases original research that looks at the nexus between migration, citizenship and social change. It advances new scholarship in migration and refugee studies and fosters cross- and inter-disciplinary dialogue in this field. The series includes research-based monographs and edited collections, informed by a range of qualitative and quantitative research methods.

Out now in the series:

Belonging in Translation:
Solidarity and Migrant Activism in Japan
Reiko Shindo, August 2019

Borders, Migration and Class in an Age of Crisis:
Producing Immigrants and Workers
Tom Vickers, July 2019

Time, Migration and Forced Immobility:
Sub-Saharan African Migrants in Morocco
Inka Stock, June 2019

Home-Land: Romanian Roma, Domestic Spaces and the State
Rachel Humphris, March 2019

The Politics of Compassion:
Immigration and Asylum Policy
Ala Sirriyeh, June 2018

Find out more at

bristoluniversitypress.co.uk

NEGOTIATING MIGRATION IN THE CONTEXT OF CLIMATE CHANGE

International Policy and Discourse

Sarah Louise Nash

With a Foreword by
Andrew Baldwin

BRISTOL
UNIVERSITY
PRESS

First published in Great Britain in 2019 by

Bristol University Press
University of Bristol
1-9 Old Park Hill
Bristol
BS2 8BB
UK
t: +44 (0)117 954 5940
www.bristoluniversitypress.co.uk

North America office:
Policy Press
c/o The University of Chicago Press
1427 East 60th Street
Chicago, IL 60637, USA
t: +1 773 702 7700
f: +1 773-702-9756
sales@press.uchicago.edu
www.press.uchicago.edu

British Library Cataloguing in Publication Data
A catalogue record for this book is available from the British Library

Library of Congress Cataloging-in-Publication Data
A catalog record for this book has been requested

ISBN 978-1-5292-0126-0 hardcover
ISBN 978-1-5292-0128-4 ePub
ISBN 978-1-5292-0127-7 ePdf

Cover design by Andrew Corbett
Front cover image: 123RF/Milosh Kojadinovich
Printed and bound in Great Britain by CPI Group (UK) Ltd,
Croydon, CR0 4YY
Bristol University Press uses environmentally responsible
print partners

Dedicated to the memory of Jim Bell
My teacher, mentor and friend

Contents

List of Figures and Tables

Figures

Tables

List of Abbreviations

ADP	Ad Hoc Working Group on the Durban Platform for Enhanced Action
CAT	Convention against Torture and Other Cruel, Inhuman and Degrading Treatment or Punishment
CMA	Conference of the Parties serving as the meeting of the Parties to the Paris Agreement
COP	Conference of the Parties
COST	European Cooperation in Science and Technology
EACH-FOR	Environmental Change and Forced Migration Scenarios
GHG	Greenhouse gas
ICCPR	International Covenant on Civil and Political Rights
ICESCR	International Covenant on Economic, Social and Cultural Rights
IDMC	Internal Displacement Monitoring Centre
IDP	Internally displaced person
IEO	International epistemic organisation
ILO	International Labour Organization
IOM	International Organization for Migration
IPCC	Intergovernmental Panel on Climate Change
LDC	Least developed country
MECLEP	Migration, Environment and Climate Change: Evidence for Policy
MRFCJ	Mary Robinson Foundation – Climate Justice
NAP	National Adaptation Plan
NDC	Nationally Determined Contribution
NRC	Norwegian Refugee Council
OHCHR	Office of the High Commissioner for Human Rights
PDD	Platform on Disaster Displacement
SBI	Subsidiary Body for Implementation
SBSTA	Subsidiary Body for Scientific and Technological Advice
SDG	Sustainable Development Goal

UDHR	Universal Declaration of Human Rights
UKCCMC	United Kingdom Climate Change and Migration Coalition
UNDP	United Nations Development Programme
UNFCCC	United Nations Framework Convention on Climate Change
UNHCR	United Nations High Commissioner for Refugees
UNISDR	United Nations Office for Disaster Risk Reduction
UNU-EHS	United Nations University Institute for Environment and Human Security
WIM	Warsaw International Mechanism for Loss and Damage associated with Climate Change Impacts
WMO	World Meteorological Organization

About the Author

Sarah Louise Nash is a postdoctoral researcher in the Institute of Forest, Environment, and Resource Policy at the University of Natural Resources and Life Sciences in Vienna, Austria. She holds a PhD in Political Science from the University of Hamburg, as well as degrees in Human Rights and International Politics (University of Glasgow), German and Politics (University of Edinburgh) and Political Science (University of Vienna). Her work is concerned with the politics and policy of climate change, with a particular focus on the issue complex of climate change and migration. Born and raised in Scotland, Nash is a multiple migrant, having studied in Austria and Germany. She worked for a year in Istanbul, Turkey, as a MERCATOR-IPC fellow at Istanbul Policy Centre before returning to her chosen home of Vienna.

Series Preface

The editorial team of this Bristol University Press book series on Global Migration and Social Change are delighted to bring you Sarah Louise Nash's new book, *Negotiating Migration in the Context of Climate Change: International Policy and Discourse.*

The aim of the series as a whole is to spur new discussions among a diverse disciplinary audience by publishing migration and refugee studies research that is at once academically ground-breaking and engaged with the most pressing policy issues. The series was conceived during the unfolding of the Eurozone and migration crises of 2016, coverage of which helped drive the Brexit referendum result in Britain and the election of Donald Trump in the USA; we wanted the series to examine migration through the lens of the crises and the broader changes of our era.

It is hard to imagine a more pressing policy issue than climate change. A good deal of the topic's salience derives from its relationship with issues of human migration. Nash's aim is to study what has become known as the climate change and migration nexus: a discourse in which climate change and migration are interrelated issues, both requiring urgent policy responses. Nash's contribution to the series is therefore extremely relevant and timely.

The book also highlights links between the European crises – which formed the context to our launch of this series – to the fraught politics and policy surrounding climate change. For example, the so-called European migration crisis coincided with the United Nations Framework Convention on Climate Change (UNFCCC) negotiations in Paris, where questions of migration were already on the agenda, not least because of the way fears of future 'climate change refugees' were sometimes being leveraged to motivate climate action in troubling ways.

This is an exceptionally well-written, thoughtful and novel book. It thoroughly and chronologically details the evolution of global climate change and migration policy making: a topic that is already at the top of the international policy-making agenda and which is certain to become increasingly important in coming decades. As well as a guide to current commentators, this book will stand as a historical record of a key moment in the evolution of the global regimes for both environment and migration.

The book identifies key actors, documents and events which continue to shape the global policy-making landscape. Readers will appreciate its theoretical and methodological uniqueness, as well as its first-hand perspective on high-level processes. The book provides a strong and attention-grabbing introduction to the topic and establishes links between local climate action, which everyone reading the news knows well, and global policy making, which is obscure to all but a few experts.

This book starts a conversation that invites a lot more research. Naturally, Nash's book emphasises the period 2010 to 2015/2016 – her study period – and so we look forward to ongoing research that probes developments both before and after these dates. We are keen to see future research expand to a greater range of case studies to provide a stronger sense of connection between local and global policy making concerning climate change and migration.

In sum, this is a timely and decisive contribution to a topic of strong and growing importance that relates directly to the central themes of the current series. We will most definitely be using this book for our own work, and we recommend it to you.

Alan Gamlen and Lakshmin Mudaliar
Melbourne and Geneva
2019

Foreword

Andrew Baldwin

Of all the crises that mark our contemporary world, none are as worrying to me as the outpouring of support for white nationalism and white supremacy across Europe and the West. Climate change is a close second. Of course, the former has always been a feature of capitalist modernity. From slavery to colonialism to postcoloniality in the metropole, race and whiteness are constitutive features of the worlds we inhabit, not just the unfortunate by-products of those worlds. What is different today, however, is just how freely white supremacy is articulated and felt in the public domain in the West. What I find most worrying about this development is the way in which white supremacy's governing affects of injury, resentment, betrayal and nostalgia all seem to be underpinned by a populism that repudiates fact, reason and argumentation in favour of fealty and immediate experience. What seems to matter most to those in thrall to this populism is the retention of white power at all costs, regardless of the way populism cynically undermines contemporary institutions, such as science and law. I have never before in my life believed in false consciousness to the extent I do now. It worries me no end that those in power in Britain and America shamelessly exploit the legitimate grievances brought about by four decades of neo-liberal globalisation to service their own will to power.

But I also worry about climate change. I worry about the worlds it stands to unleash. I worry for those who stand to experience its effects most sharply. And I worry for my kids. But mostly I worry about what will happen when the violence of climate change meets with the populist violence of white supremacy. Climate denialism has long been a hallmark of right-wing populism. There is nevertheless a long tradition of right-wing environmentalism, one of the features of which is anti-immigration. Garett Hardin stands as an emblematic figure in this respect. Not only was Hardin one of the twentieth century's most influential environmentalists, he was also virulently anti-immigrant. He stands as a powerful reminder that 'saving the environment' is never innocent and that always beneath the veneer of environmental discourses are powerful political projects that rest on appeals to 'nature'. I worry that someday this ugly anti-immigrant environmentalism will enter the climate change mainstream. Maybe it already has.

This brings to me to the marvellous book you now hold in your hand. Sarah Louise Nash does not confront issues of race and climate change in *Negotiating Migration in the Context of Climate Change*. She does, however, provide a much-needed avenue for thinking about the international political context in which climate change is more and more articulated as a problem of migration. Her concern in the book is to trace the emergence of the climate-migration nexus as an object of international climate change governance precisely in order to call attention to the boundaries erected around it. Such boundaries, for Nash, are worthy of our consideration because they tell us something about the process by which 'legitimacy' is constructed in international fora. They become emblems of the possible, demarcating not only legitimate and illegitimate speech, but, more importantly, defining the terms of political possibility. When we trace the emergence of these boundaries, what Nash reveals is a curtailed political imaginary that forecloses the possible. Migration becomes reaffirmed as an object of managerial expertise. The nation state becomes reaffirmed principally as a political container of migration. Migration becomes merely adjunct to markets. Migration becomes, in the words of my long-time collaborator and co-author, Giovanni Bettini, depoliticised.

But what kind of fate is this for a social process as ancient as the human story itself? At a world-historical conjuncture that demands radical new ideas and revitalised political awareness, depoliticising migration seems to be moving in a direction that diminishes the efficacy of migration as a powerfully transformational phenomenon. There is always a risk, of course, that the promise of migration can be overstated and that the figure of the migrant can become overburdened, even romanticised, as the privileged site of change. For most of the world's migrants, migration is a struggle. But equally to take a diminished view of migration as merely the state's constitutive outside delimits the horizons of the political imagination. When we follow Nash through international negotiation of the climate-migration nexus, we bear witness to the political work that is being done in the name of 'climate change and migration', whereby the complex socio-political life of migration becomes reduced to just another object of technical expertise. But the reward that comes from reading this book is that Nash also invites us to think beyond this boundary object, to think in ways that take the future seriously and that locate the true political act as one that holds the future open to all possibilities. She reminds us that in the face of mounting right-wing populism, our political moment requires not closure, control and containment but debate and contestation as the pre-condition for bringing new worlds into being.

Migration and Climate Change: The Construction of a Nexus

The idea that people are being forced to move because of climate change, and that in the future even more people will be forced to do so, has captured imaginations globally. Cinema screens have been filled with the stories of people whose homes, and indeed entire communities, towns and nation states, are unlikely to withstand rising sea levels; photo exhibitions have created powerful visualisations of what climate change might mean for people across the world; protesters have brandished banners festooned with slogans such as 'Act Now Or Swim Later!'; artists have set up tents under the signage 'Climate Refugee Camp'; politicians have held cabinet meetings under water in full diving gear; journalists have brought the idea further into the public consciousness within the pages of a range of newspapers; and entire bookshelves can be filled with the books, not to mention dissertations and university essays, that have been dedicated to the subject.

The majority of these representations of lives touched by climate change are expressions of outrage that the actions of a few will affect the lives of so many, that climate change will have consequences so grave that people will be forced to leave their homes. These contributions to the discourse, infused with sentiments of climate justice and undertones of a fear of people on the move, are the facets of the discourse most often visible to wider society. They have also led to impassioned calls for action to be taken at the global level, where these vibrant, raw and often emotional pleas are transformed into the dry, bureaucratic, technocratic world of international policy making. Here, vocabulary, definitions, punctuation and the allocation of competencies become part of the same discourse. Policy briefings, draft negotiating texts, meetings of people in suits in Bonn, Geneva and New York, initiatives and task forces become entwined with the films, photographs, protests and literature.

At a time when the fear of migration is etched on global society, it is no surprise that different media have tried to make sense of (changing) mobility patterns. Here, actual mobility – the experienced movements of people into and away from different societies – indeed plays a role; however, the perceptions of these movements, the constructions of migrants, and the different stories that accompany movements of people are without a doubt even more important for shaping these cultural goods. At the time of writing, Donald Trump is the incumbent President of the United States of America. The anti-migrant rhetoric that marked his election campaign and many of the practical measures that have been implemented against migrants during his time in office have had a tangible impact on the way migration is understood. Whether or not a wall is eventually built along the southern border of the US, the populist sentiment that has been whipped up will most likely be a lasting legacy of his presidency. Combined with the withdrawal of the US from the Paris Agreement of the United Nations Framework Convention on Climate Change (UNFCCC), which came into force just four days before Trump was elected President, the chances for transformative visions of migration and climate change coming from this side of the Atlantic are minimal.

Crossing the ocean, migration has also moved into the spotlight in European politics since the events of 2015, when large numbers of people crossing Europe's external borders and heading north prompted an unprecedented opening of borders and large numbers of people heading for Germany in particular. The reactions to these events, that were dubbed the 'refugee crisis' or 'migration crisis', are still reverberating around the European Union (EU). With asylum applications more than doubling between 2014 and 2015 across the EU, some member states have faced challenges: the bureaucratic challenge of processing larger number of asylum applications, the linguistic challenge of supporting new arrivals to learn the language of their host country, the service provision challenge of ensuring that necessary infrastructure is in place, and the integration challenge of ensuring harmony between people who have just arrived and the communities in which they are now living. However, another challenge has been the anti-migrant rhetoric that has been echoing around European politics, stoking the fires of the Brexit campaign for the United Kingdom to leave the EU and contributing to the election of right-wing governments in a not insignificant number of EU member states. The crisis has thus become one of European politics, of the need to find solutions that allay fears and prevent further migration into the EU. The growth of the border security industry of the EU, and dubious events such as the inability of search and rescue ships operating in the Mediterranean to find harbours in which to dock and allow their passengers, people they have plucked from the sea, to disembark.

But what does this crisis of European politics have to do with climate change? The timing of the peak of the crisis as perceived by the EU, in terms of a period where high numbers of people were continuing to arrive at the union's external borders, coincided with the Paris negotiations of the UNFCCC, where a global climate change agreement was being thrashed out by negotiators. Migration was already present as a topic in the negotiations, and the simultaneous attention that was being paid to climate change and to migration in the media led to increased attention on the phenomenon of migration in the context of climate change, frequently employing a crisis framing drawing on the idea of the 'refugee crisis' or 'migration crisis' that was being played out vividly across Europe's borders.

The policy-making discourse on migration and climate change is therefore anything but straightforward. A wide variety of ideas are flowing into policy spaces that have their own procedures, languages and conventions, regulated by both written and unwritten rules of behaviour, and while issues are being negotiated, people are also negotiating their way through these spaces. Migration in the context of climate change is a construct, shaped by these ideas, the people who are presenting them, the moments in which they are being discussed, and the (institutional and geographical) spaces in which this is playing out. In this sense, this book is then about two parallel sets of negotiations: the official, technical and bureaucratic negotiations of policy spaces, and the personal journeys of people working on migration and climate change who have been negotiating a path through meetings, conferences, documents, discussions and debates.

A plethora of different policy 'solutions' has been proposed as a response to the issue complex of migration and climate change, following an instrumentalist perspective on policy making that designates migration and climate change as a problem and policy responses as a solution. These proposals, none of which has been put into practice, have encompassed amending the 1951 Refugee Convention (UN General Assembly, 1951) to include people displaced due to climate change (Republic of Maldives Ministry of Environment, Energy and Water, 2006), creating a new separate legal regime to protect 'climate refugees' as a Protocol on Recognition, Protection, and Resettlement of Climate Refugees (Biermann and Boas, 2010) or a regionally oriented regime (Williams, 2008) anchored in the UNFCCC or modelled on the Convention against Torture and Other Cruel, Inhuman and Degrading Treatment or Punishment (CAT) (Falstrom, 2001). Compelling counterarguments have been made against these proposals. The 1951 Refugee Convention is widely regarded as an inappropriate avenue for several reasons: first, because people moving in the context of climate change are not necessarily experiencing persecution with their state willing but unable to provide protection against a problem created elsewhere (McAdam, 2011b); second, because it might lead to competition between political refugees already covered by the convention and the new category of 'climate refugees' (Biermann and Boas, 2010); third, because it does not address the root causes of displacement, only the resulting movements of people (Falstrom, 2001); and fourth, because it may lead to a devaluation of current refugee protection (Keane, 2004). The proposal for a new treaty has also faced criticism because it would come up against the 'near impossibility' of identifying those to protect, due to the multi-causality of decisions to move (Geddes et al, 2012: 961), and the practical obstacles standing in the way of creating such a treaty (McAdam, 2011b) in addition to its ratification, implementation and enforcement (McAdam, 2011b; Geddes et al, 2012).

Others pin hope on organisations to take up the mantel of filling the perceived 'governance gap' on migration in the context of climate change (Simonelli, 2016). The starring roles are usually awarded to the United Nations High Commissioner for Refugees (UNHCR) and the International Organization for Migration (IOM), due to their positions in the international governance regime and their status as UN agencies. Given that a degree of mandate creep has been identified in both organisations, which have been autonomously engaging with the topic of climate change despite not always being sanctioned by member states (Hall, 2016), this is not really a surprise. At the same time, Andrea Simonelli argues that neither organisation has 'sought to expand their mandates into the area of climate induced displacement', with 'inaction' on their part leading to the governance gap instead being filled by a sub-entity of the UNFCCC (Simonelli, 2016: 138).

However, the rejection of grand proposals for an overarching, normative framework and the ambiguous positioning of the two main UN agencies working on human mobility does not mean that the policy-making world has been silent on migration and climate change. Instead, policy makers have adopted a piecemeal approach, chasing the recognition of the links between migration and climate change in a number of fora and pointing to the relevance of other existing treaties or international regimes for this issue complex without the need for amendments. There are manifold reasons why this approach has been taken, from legal challenges to lacking political will, and very low chances of implementation have all made a grand solution unappealing. However, continuing conceptual difficulties also make the nexus between migration and climate change difficult to pin down, making it in turn incredibly difficult to address precise but wide-reaching policies. At the same time as making policy, policy makers have been occupied with chasing the shadows of the 'phenomenon' of migration and climate change and the people who are at its heart.

These challenges suggest that an instrumental approach to policy making that is based around proposing new policy 'solutions' is not necessarily the most promising for scholars, and that as a result not enough is known about the possibilities (and the limits) of policy making. It is therefore important not to neglect perspectives that aim to advance understanding of the (shifting) dynamics of this (socially constructed) emerging policy-making arena. One of the aims of this book is therefore to provide an in-depth analysis of what is happening in policy making on migration and climate change, differentiating this contribution from work that proposes new policy responses (compare Simonelli, 2016). The perspective favoured in this book forces us to ask basic questions such as what exactly the relation between migration and climate change looks like, but also to invest time into considering how this relation is being understood, the influence of the social and political processes of policy making, how power and knowledge are influencing these processes, and how, ultimately, we, as a global society, are choosing to make rules that might further down the line have concrete impacts on people's lives. This expressly critical approach can uncover established assumptions that are proving formative for the young area of policy making on migration and climate change, allowing for these assumptions to be disrupted and potentially newly constelled.

This perspective is accompanied by one necessary caveat: I do not deny the existence of climate change, or indeed people who may be on the move as a result. The claim that the relation between migration and climate change, as well as the constituent parts of this relation, are socially constructed does not have to logically lead to a denial of their existence or importance for humanity. Following Andrew Baldwin and Giovanni Bettini, 'climate change is a real, material circumstance with potentially dire consequences for much of the world's population, especially those already living on the fringes of capital' (Baldwin and Bettini, 2017: 2). Some of these dire consequences will also be tied up with the complexities of (im)mobility. The significance (and violence) of these consequences is made no lesser by the recognition of the social construction of the nexus between migration and climate change.

Set against this background, the aim of this book is to examine the distinct policy debate surrounding the climate change and human mobility nexus, in particular the construction of these two related concepts as a distinct phenomenon that requires policy responses. The discussion is guided by two questions: first, how have attempts at policymaking on the migration and climate change nexus become possible?; and second, how do the ways advocacy actors think and talk about the migration and climate change nexus influence the policies proposed to address it?

Understanding the migration and climate change nexus

The recognition of a relation between migration and climate change is foundational for the construction of a policy-making discourse, for if no relation exists and is widely recognised as existing, why is a policy response called for? Policy making on migration and climate change is therefore built on the recognition of a link between the two phenomena. The logic is that climate change will affect the places that people live and their livelihoods to such an extent that they will be forced (or choose) to move. In many quarters, attempts to understand this link have manifested as a 'quest for numbers' (Jakobeit and Methmann, 2012: 301), with ever-increasing numbers being cited as predictions of how many people will be on the move in the coming decades. Such quantification may give the illusion of a deeper understanding of the links between migration and climate change; however, the 'quest for numbers stretches the predictive capacity of the social sciences beyond its limits' (Jakobeit and Methmann, 2012: 302). Estimates have been on shaky ground methodologically, and fail to recognise both the multi-causality of migration and the climate change adaptation efforts that people may undertake where they live (Gemenne, 2011). The (well-founded) critiques of this approach to understanding migration and climate change do, however, provide a challenge to those working towards a more nuanced approach. The standpoint that climate change and migration are linked, but in a complex, contextual way, influenced by a multitude of different factors, is much more difficult to explain and distil in a catchy headline than a large number and an assurance that this many people will move due to climate change. Despite this, a shared foundation has emerged that climate change and migration are linked, however multifaceted, complex and contextual this link may be.

This shared foundation does not, however, render the discourse free of contestation, with movements of people that are happening or are predicted to happen in the context of climate change being characterised in a number of different ways (Bettini et al, 2017). One strand of the discourse, that which urges us to 'Act Now Or Swim Later!', is a humanitarian plea to help vulnerable people, often labelled as 'climate refugees', whose lives are being plunged into disarray by the impacts of climate change. This is often combined with a securitised strand of discourse that presents people who might move in the context of climate change as a security threat that will, without efforts to do something in response, result in uncontrolled mass movements of people resembling 'waves' or a 'flood' arriving at the borders of states in the Global North (Bettini, 2013). The fear that this argument generates has been mobilised as an argument for climate change mitigation and adaptation measures, as well as humanitarian assistance, but has also fed into calls for increased border security and has been linked to calls for military responses (Martin, 2010; White, 2011). A response to these discursive strands has been labelled 'migration as adaptation'. A core argument behind this phrase is that human mobility is not inherently negative, but, when it occurs in a more managed way, can be a strategy that is used by people in order to increase their resilience in the face of climate change and, as such, can be classed as an adaptation strategy (Foresight, 2011b). Rather than flight, movement is characterised as labour migration, idealised as temporary or circular migration by individuals, with financial remittances sent back to family members who have not moved and therefore increasing the resilience of households and communities overall (Bettini and Gioli, 2016).

All of these strands of discourse have been subject to critique; the discourse around 'climate refugees' is critiqued for portraying people as victims who have no agency and as such no influence over their fate (Bettini et al, 2017). The securitised strand of this discourse has been critiqued for the border practices such as controls, militarisation and hostility that it can feed into and reinforce, intentionally or otherwise, as well as for being highly racialised (Telford, 2018). As Gregory White so eloquently outlines,

> 'Getting tough' – responding in a militarized fashion – is an easy, cynical step in a warming world. It may be politically successful with anxious electorates. It may tap into the public's fears about climate change and the prospect of desperate hordes of 'refugees' inundating North Atlantic borders. And it may be more politically palatable than policies that mitigate greenhouse gas (GHG) emissions. Building a fence is easier than changing lifestyles. Yet the injection of security impetus into climate-induced migration is unethical and unworkable. (White, 2011: 7)

In *Storming the Wall*, Todd Miller joins the dots between climate change and increasing border militarisation, where fear of the person who finds themselves mobile in the context of climate change is the link in the train of logic between climate change and the need for increased border security. Miller chronicles 'the way a massive system of social and economic exclusion militarizes divisions not only between the rich and the poor, but between the environmentally secure and the environmentally exposed' (Miller 2017: 31). Climate justice concerns lay therefore not only in the adverse effects of climate change, but in the responses that these effects elicit.

Despite these concerns, Benoît Mayer, in his analysis of advocacy on migration and climate change, argues that his 'cold analysis … suggests that the security argument for the "management" of environmental migration is most likely to succeed' in provoking policy responses (Mayer, 2014: 36). The question must then be asked whether the price of policy responses steeped in a securitised discourse, and the potential impacts this may have on the actions that are taken, is worth paying.

Although avoiding these pitfalls, the strand of the discourse that is built up around 'migration as adaptation' has been critiqued for being inherently neoliberal, with the labour of the migrant being the essential ingredient for surviving in a changing climate (Felli, 2013; Bettini, 2014). Therefore, although the concept of resilience (as an antonym of vulnerability) affords agency to people affected by climate change, it also transfers the responsibility for surviving these impacts on to their shoulders and does not retain any kernel of climate justice (Bettini et al, 2017). As argued by Daniel Faber and Christina Schlegel, this position, which they describe as a 'neoliberal minimalist position, ignores the contradictions and structural inequalities that (re)produce socio-ecological vulnerabilities impeding the mobility of some while forcing others into displacement' (Faber and Schlegel, 2017: 12).

This contestation and critique serves to highlight that the nexus between migration and climate change is an essentially contested phenomenon (White, 2011, chapter 1), which quite simply means that 'people cannot agree on how to define the phenomenon but nevertheless acknowledge that it is a phenomenon worth speaking about' (Baldwin, 2014: 518). It becomes clear when reading the literature that no accepted definition of 'climate migration' or the people affected by the phenomenon (under whatever label, be it 'climate migrant' or 'climate refugee') actually exists. Part of this difficulty in defining either the phenomenon or the people affected by the migration and climate change nexus is the multi-causality of the vast majority of decisions to move. More critical scholars have raised concerns that a tight focus on climate change may serve to downplay other structural factors that cause people to move (and indeed some of which will also be responsible for climate change), thus depoliticising discussions on drivers of migration (Baldwin and Bettini, 2017).

This difficulty with identification and definition of a phenomenon is a problem for policy making, for if policy making is to provide 'solutions', a known phenomenon must be present to be solved. In a connected observation, 'the discourse on climate change and migration is written almost exclusively in the future-conditional tense' (Baldwin, 2012: 628). What we may be forgiven for viewing mainly as a quirky observation, mainly of grammatical interest, is actually of great importance for how the migration and climate change nexus is conceptualised and discursively reproduced. The 'speculative and future-conditional' (Faber and Schlegel, 2017: 8) problematisation of the migration and climate change nexus as a theoretical possibility or a predicted outcome of climate change (however high the likelihood) rather than an easily identifiable group of people follows one common temporal structure: the migration and climate change nexus is a problem set in the future but playing out in the present. Grounds to support governance of the nexus have thus been built on the basis of scientific knowledge and prediction, academic research, future-scenario planning and even speculation.

It is surprising that this cocktail of conceptual difficulties has not impeded the emergence of a distinct area of policy making surrounding the migration and climate change nexus. Indeed, it is the stubborn presence of the nexus on policy agendas despite such high levels of contestation and conceptual uncertainty that makes policy making on migration and climate change so intriguing. Policy making is not simply concerned with working out what policy solutions could be implemented in order to address a predefined problem and negotiating the politics of their implementation; rather, the question of what it *is* that policy is actually being designed to govern is ever present, and policy responses that do emerge will be inherently linked to the answers, which may be multiple and contradictory.

In examining the emergence of this area of policy making, this book will concentrate particularly on one group of actors that are active in policy making, termed here as advocacy actors. For the purposes of this book, the term refers to actors of various types that are actively making systematic efforts to further specific policy goals related to migration and climate change. Sometimes goals converge and a high degree of coordination exists between these actors, but at the same time these actors are not conceptualised as a tight network or grouped entity, with different actors also acting individually and with varying degrees of synchronisation. The term 'actors' is used purposely here (as opposed to, for example, 'organisations') to allow for a broad spectrum of different entities, including organisations from the UN family, non-governmental organisations (NGOs), very loose (and difficult to classify) entities such as 'initiatives', academic networks and individuals. In addition, many of the advocacy actors analysed will straddle more than one of these different types.

These advocacy actors are embedded in a broader epistemic community that surrounds the migration and climate change nexus. The term epistemic community, coined by Peter Haas, can be understood following Noel Castree's definition as communities of professionals from various disciplines and backgrounds, which 'gain their distinctiveness, and sense of self-identity, through a mixture of their value-set, ontological beliefs, questions of interest, objects/domains of concern, methods of inquiry, the criteria favoured for determining worthy ideas, knowledge or information, and their chosen genre of communication' (Castree, 2014: 42). These communities are important, because they draw boundaries around specific areas of knowledge and play a role in creating the rules for legitimate ways to conceptualise and speak about the issues central to the community. The epistemic community surrounding migration and climate change has already been identified as highly relevant by Andrew Baldwin and Giovanni Bettini, who argue that this epistemic community matters:

> … because insofar as it configures migration in the context of climate change as exceptional and thus in need of expert management, it negates the more fundamental notion that migration is not exceptional but central to the multiplicities of human existence. And this, we would suggest, has the effect of prohibiting more fundamental questions from being asked about, for example, what migration might come to mean in the context of climate change, how it relates to democratic and public life, and what it can tell us about humanness today. (Baldwin and Bettini, 2017: 6)

Related to policy making, the epistemic community is important for normalising the area of work of migration and climate change, as well as legitimising the bureaucratic and technocratic work towards policy 'solutions'. However, it also adds to covering over many of the conceptual difficulties that this chapter has already highlighted. Advocacy actors play a significant role within, but are not tantamount to, an epistemic community. Epistemic communities also contain actors that are not actively or systematically attempting to influence policy, although of course they frequently do so through other work. The embeddedness of advocacy actors within this epistemic community, a dynamic particularly prevalent in the community surrounding migration and climate change, has also affected the development of advocacy positions and strategies.

Interpreting the migration and climate change nexus

The opening pages of this book have alluded to its theoretical positioning, but before proceeding it is important to explicitly set out some of the premises on which the analysis contained in the remaining pages is based, a task that will be addressed in the next three sub-sections. The approach taken in this book can be classed as an interpretivist approach to political science that 'focuses on the meanings that shape actions and institutions, and the ways in which they do so' (Bevir and Rhodes, 2016: 3). Research agendas are as such typically less concerned with uncovering 'truths' about a single objective reality than with revealing the meaning of human experience (Lynch, 2014: 2). As a consequence, this book is interested in how meanings are multiple and unstable, existing in parallel and also changing. It is also interested in how knowledge is constructed and how knowledge, together with power, make meaning. This also leads to an interest in the performative effects of different meanings – the concrete effects that they may have on the world. All of these themes are woven throughout this book.

In relation to climate change, Chris Methmann, Delf Rothe and Benjamin Stephan have set out the general character of an interpretive research agenda, arguing as follows:

> [I]n very general terms, what sets apart interpretive analysis from a more traditional perspective on climate change can be boiled down to one formula: the latter takes global warming as a simply existing thing-in-the-world, and analyses how actors (at all different social and political levels) respond to this phenomenon. An interpretive perspective, by contrast, investigates the 'problematization' (Foucault 1994) of climate change: how global warming is rendered as an object and problem to be acted upon, how different meanings of climate change (e.g. as a global environmental threat, as an economic problem or as a security risk) emerge and become dominant, how the different meanings affect the toolkit of feasible political solutions, and what the effects of such practices are. (Methmann et al, 2013: 4)

Following this understanding of climate change, the impacts of climate change, including potential changes in human mobility, cannot be explained purely by physical, material changes, but also by their discursive representations. This also applies to understanding human mobility; while it is not to be disregarded that people are moving, it depends on the discursive representation whether people are considered as victims of displacement due to climate change, as heroes of adaptation, or as masses of 'illegal migrants', with each of these representations framing people with individual biographies, ideas and personalities (see Andersson, 2014).

Knowing the migration and climate change nexus

Interpreting the migration and climate change nexus requires interrogating how the relation between migration and climate change is being *known*, an interrogation that is also highly significant if it is going to be possible to understand how the essentially contested nature of the migration and climate change nexus is influencing how it is understood in policy-making circles. This is a pressing research agenda that has already been identified by Andrew Baldwin, Chris Methmann and Delf Rothe as in need of interrogation, with them setting out the following set of epistemological questions that 'has largely been ignored':

> How has this knowledge come into existence? What are the techniques, assumptions and values that underpin it? And what are the politics of this knowledge? How does the way we think about climate-induced migration influence the way we propose to govern it? (Baldwin et al, 2014: 122)

A core tenet of interpretivist political science that affects how knowledge is conceptualised is an epistemological position that rejects the possibility of pursuing objective analysis of the 'real world'. In this perspective, knowledge cannot be taken to be a singular true representation of a social phenomenon. Rather, particular knowledge may take on truth effects, where certain knowledge is privileged and taken to be particularly legitimate, giving it the impression of depicting a true, objective reality (Foucault, 1980: 93). This has implications for the kind of research that is presented in this book; rather than searching for knowledge on a 'true' representation of migration and climate change, interpretations and meanings, as well as the productive implications of these meanings, become the focus. This should not be read as a rejection of scientific standards, and the aim is not, through rejection of objective analysis of the real world, to fall into a relativist quagmire. In using the concept of knowledge, this book therefore aims, following Donna Haraway, to 'have simultaneously an account of radical historical contingency for all knowledge claims and knowing subjects … and a no-nonsense commitment to faithful accounts of a "real" world, one that can be partially shared' (Haraway, 1988: 579). To achieve this, knowledge is approached as 'situated and embodied knowledges' (Haraway, 1988: 583), 'where partiality and not universality is the condition of being heard to make rational knowledge claims' (Haraway, 1988: 589). Singular knowledge claims therefore provide a partial picture on migration and climate change. They stem from a particular context and background and can as such never be neutral. They can, however, be valid, especially strengthened by making the context of knowledge visible and recognising its partiality.

This is an interesting lens through which to view the 'knowledge dependence' (Gottweis, 2003: 256) that is so often a core component of policy-making processes. In an approach to knowledge that is concerned with situated knowledges, this dependence is, however, not a dependence on a single, true, objective representation of a phenomenon, but rather on a number of (sometimes contradictory) situated knowledges. As Herbert Gottweis further argues, 'as the legitimacy of policymaking relies often on technical and scientific arguments, power becomes intertwined with knowledge: the exercise of power is predicated upon the deployment of knowledge' (Gottweis, 2003: 256).

Indeed, it is not just the reliance on knowledge alone that brings power into the analysis. Following Michel Foucault, power and knowledge always exist in a relation (Foucault, 1980: 93). An important aspect of this conceptualisation of power is that power is not a resource, 'it is never localised here or there, never in anybody's hands, never appropriated as a commodity or piece of wealth' (Foucault, 1980: 98) and as such, it cannot be owned by anyone and is instead imbued in all social relations. The omnipresence of power in social relations is not necessarily sinister, as power is also normatively neutral, acting not only as a constraining but also a productive force (Foucault, 1980: 109). In scholarship on migration and climate change, knowledge and power relations are relatively neglected, with Andrew Baldwin and Giovanni Bettini noting that 'the empiricist conceit running through the discourse on climate change and human migration leaves little room for conceiving of the intricacies of knowledge and power' (Baldwin and Bettini, 2017: 5). The migration and climate change nexus, 'overwhelmingly represented as a crisis that demands technical and expert solutions' (Baldwin and Bettini, 2017: 5) therefore privileges expert knowledge, which is rarely problematised.

One particularly useful avenue for understanding the power–knowledge relations that are at play in policy making on migration and climate change is through the concept of performativity, following Judith Butler, 'that reiterative power of discourse to produce the phenomena that it regulates and constrains' (Butler, 1993: xxi). It is not only the content of knowledge on migration and climate change, but also the language employed to talk about the issue, the visuals used in knowledge products, the adherence to strict rules of conduct in particular settings, the institutional affiliation of the speaker and even the display of a UN agency lanyard that can cause power and knowledge to continue to reverberate.

Deconstructing the migration and climate change nexus

In order to answer the questions set out towards the beginning of this chapter, this book traces the emergence of the migration and climate change nexus as an object of policy making. This analysis can be described as a history of the present, following the genealogical discourse analysis tradition of Michael Foucault, which provides a frame for analysis of the historical construction of often taken-for-granted phenomena by scrutinising the formation of particular problematisations or rationalities. Genealogy, as employed here, is 'an attempt to renew an acquaintance with the strangeness of the present against all the attempts to erase it under the necessary dialectic of reason in history or to mark it as a final denouement or irreversible loss' (Dean, 2010: 56).

At this point, it is useful to take a brief step back to the Nietzschean inspiration for Foucault's genealogy, in particular, the differentiation between origin (*Ursprung*) and emergence (*Entstehung*). Foucault, following Nietzsche, challenges 'the pursuit of the origin' and its attempt to 'capture the exact essence of things, their purest possibilities, and their carefully protected identities' (Foucault, 1977: 142). Therefore, rather than pursuing the *origin* of policy making on migration and climate change, this book looks at the emergence of the area of policy making by deconstructing the way in which it has emerged throughout time. In reconstructing the emergence of a phenomenon, the attempt is not 'to trace the gradual curve of their evolution, but to isolate the different scenes where they engaged in different roles' (Foucault, 1977: 140).

In order to achieve this, 'genealogy is gray, meticulous, and patiently documentary. It operates on a field of entangled and confused parchments, on documents that have been scratched over and recopied many times' (Foucault, 1977: 139). Therefore, shifts, dislocations and contradictions come into focus. This meticulous approach is most apparent in Chapters 2, 3 and 4 of this book, which painstakingly document and deconstruct different episodes of policy making on migration and climate change. As well as focusing on the emergence of phenomena, genealogy focuses on the silences; in other words, on what is excluded from the discourse (Foucault, 1977: 140), an element that is the focus of chapter seven.

Using this form of deconstruction (Lynch, 2014: 21), this book picks apart the policy-making discourse on migration and climate change, charting how the nexus is discursively constituted over time, and the different situated knowledges that are part of this constitution come into focus; this brings with it scepticism of timeless truths and an openness to change. Genealogy therefore explicitly questions knowledge that appears authoritative or 'naturalised' and is a method of critique through its 'questioning of the historical conditions of existence' (Mahon, 1992: 104). Power, and the relations of power and knowledge that structure social (and political) relations, are an essential part of this critique.

To add analytical vocabulary to the genealogy, this book borrows from the work of Ernesto Laclau and Chantal Mouffe, on the creation of fixation of meaning (Laclau and Mouffe, 1985). According to their approach, it is impossible to permanently fixate meaning, but is something that is constantly strived for, with the purpose of discourse analysis being to map these struggles for meaning. The first concept utilised in this book from Laclau and Mouffe's discourse analysis is 'hegemonic closures', which refers to apparent fixations of meaning by which a meaning appears natural or non-contingent. Deconstruction of these hegemonic closures is a vital aspect of discourse analysis and a form of critique. Points of hegemonic closure are often also 'nodal points' within a discourse, particularly privileged signs in a discourse around which other signs are ordered. It is from this relationship to the nodal point that other signs acquire their meaning, making nodal points vital for 'the temporary fixation of meanings, the construction of a discursive center' (Nabers, 2015: 115).

In order for discourse to be open for new meanings, these meanings need to come into contact with other discourses, allowing struggles for meaning to take place. These meanings can be found in the 'field of discursivity', plains of discourse that are home to a 'surplus of meaning' that is 'the necessary terrain for the constitution of social practice' (Laclau and Mouffe, 1985: 111).

Speaking about the migration and climate change nexus: a note on terminology

The terminological alphabet soup that distinguishes work on migration and climate change, both within academia and policy making, necessitates a note on the terminology used in this book. The first point to be made here is that this book actively avoids utilising terminology that internalises the relation between migration and climate change as a causal relationship, such as 'climate migration' or 'climate displacement'. This has two main reasons. First, the use of such terms provides further legitimisation to the phenomenon itself, although one of the purposes of this book is actually its deconstruction. Avoiding using terms such as 'climate migration' therefore makes it easier to practise critique and expand the boundaries of how the relation between migration and climate change is contemplated. Second, avoiding reinforcing a causal relationship between migration and climate change is recognition of the other factors that lead to migration, and should not be pushed into the shadows by a focus on climate change. As argued by Ethemcan Turhan and Marco Armiero,

> [I]t must be clear that migration is often an externality of military interventions, proxy wars, imposition of structural economic reforms, multi-causal destruction of livelihoods both by rapid and slow violence through environmental change, establishment of enclosures, and corporate imperialism that have dispossessed and continue to dispossess people in different corners of the world. (Turhan and Armiero, 2017: 2)

Phrases such as 'relation between migration and climate change' and the 'migration and climate change nexus' or 'migration in the context of climate change' will therefore be used throughout this book, signalling the climate change component in the discussion but hopefully avoiding simplification to a singular causal relationship between climate change and migration.

Despite not wishing to put a sole focus on a causal relationship between migration and climate change, this book does expressly use the term 'climate change' rather than 'environment' or 'environmental degradation', which are sometimes used when the relationship to climate change is deemed to be too complex. This is part of a recognition of the 'real, material circumstance' of climate change (Baldwin and Bettini, 2017) and the real, material consequences that it will have for a large part of the world's population, in part made visible through changes in human mobility. Furthermore, explicitly talking about climate change makes an opening for examining the policy making that is taking place under the auspices of global climate change politics, which has so far been the most prominent forum for international policy making on the migration and climate change nexus. It also opens the door for thinking about the causes not just of migration that may be connected to climate change, but also of the phenomenon of anthropogenic climate change, and the climate justice implications that this might bring with it.

A final point of terminology is related to the vocabulary that is selected to talk about movements of people and the people who are on the move.

It should be noted that I have not found satisfactory terminology to talk about movements that are occurring in the context of climate change, as all terms referring to movements of people are heavily loaded, have contested definitions, and are mobilised in policy making on climate change and migration in a variety of different ways. However, the term 'migration' was selected for use because it is freed from the multitude of legal connotations (and problems) that surround 'refugee' terminology, and is the most commonly used noun in the discourse when talking about human mobility that is occurring in the context of climate change. Having said this, I also on occasion use the term 'human mobility'; this term is useful as it is often perceived as being more neutral than the 'migration' term, and it is also used as an umbrella term to refer to different types of movement. This term is mainly employed when analysing the 'migration' term itself in relation to language when a synonym is necessitated in order to create clarity.

Who, where and when? The method behind the book

Two methods have been employed in this book: first, document analysis, and second, semi-structured interviews. For the document analysis, a corpus of documents was put together, consisting of advocacy documents on the topic of migration and climate change, produced by advocacy actors working on the issue with the aim of contributing to policy discussions. In addition to standard policy briefings and evidence submitted to negotiations, this corpus includes opinion pieces published in fora such as online blogs, podcasts and magazines, press releases, newspaper articles, and transcripts of speeches.

Initially, the time frame for this analysis was December 2010 to December 2015, the time period between international climate change negotiations in Cancun and Paris. This initial time frame was refined during the research process, particularly because of insights gained during the expert interviews conducted, where great importance was placed on both of these sets of negotiations. The analysis was subsequently expanded to include January 2016 to December 2018, also to encompass some of the effects of this period on the continuing policy-making discourse on migration and climate change in the analysis.

The analysis covers 207 documents that were published in the course of policy processes such as negotiations of the UNFCCC, as well as by organisations, entities and coalitions carrying out policy work on migration and climate change during this period. This document analysis was supported by 18 semi-structured interviews with individuals who are active in advocacy on migration and climate change (see Table 1). Initial interview partners were identified from being referenced in or having authored documents contained in the document corpus. Following this, a snowball sampling method was used, with initial interview partners suggesting other people to interview. Interview partners are drawn from

Table 1: Interviews

Interview	Reference	Organisation	Date
1	IDMC Interview, 2015	Internal Displacement Monitoring Centre	25/03/15
2	IOM Interview 1, 2015	IOM (Staff Members 3 and 4)	23/03/15
3	IOM Interview 2, 2015	IOM (Staff Member 1)	24/03/15
4	IOM Interview 3, 2015	IOM (Staff Member 5)	26/03/15
5	IOM Interview 4, 2016	IOM (Staff Members 1 and 2)	21/01/16
6	IOM Interview 5, 2016	IOM (Staff Member 2)	17/11/16
7	Kälin Interview, 2016	Walter Kälin, Nansen Initiative	20/01/16
8	Knox Interview, 2016	John Knox, Special Rapporteur on Human Rights and the Environment	10/02/16
9	Nansen Initiative Interview, 2015	Nansen Initiative	24/03/15
10	OHCHR Interview, 2016	Office of the High Commissioner for Human Rights (Staff Member 1)	22/01/16
11	OHCHR Interview, 2018	OHCHR (Staff Member 1)	15/08/18
12	PDD Interview, 2018	Platform on Disaster Displacement	12/09/18
13	UKCCMC Interview, 2015	United Kingdom Climate Change and Migration Coalition	01/07/15
14	UNHCR Interview 1, 2015	UNHCR (Interviewee 1)	25/03/15
15	UNHCR Interview 2, 2016	UNHCR (Interviewee 1)	21/01/16
16	UNHCR Interview 3, 2016	UNHCR (Interviewee 2)	15/11/16
17	Warner Interview, 2015	Koko Warner, United Nations University Institute for Environment and Human Security	01/07/15
18	Warner Interview, 2016	Koko Warner, UNFCCC	16/11/16

mainstream organisations working on migration and climate change and selected because of their prominent presence in the field. This was partly a practical consideration of accessibility, but also a conscious decision, as it reflected the mapping of the field being interrogated in this book. Five particular interviewees were interviewed twice, in order to gain perspectives on changing policy dynamics.

After collection, the documents and transcribed interviews were coded by hand, using codes that were drawn from the documents themselves and constantly updated throughout the coding process. The purpose of this coding process was to establish the nodal points of the discourse, the privileged signs around which other signs are ordered, as well as points of hegemonic closure, apparent fixations of meaning by which meaning appears natural or non-contingent (Laclau and Mouffe, 1985). Both semiotic and ideational components were addressed and therefore this analysis went beyond a content analysis concerned with counting frequently used terms, examining both the linguistic and social context of terms used. Linguistically, markers such as tense, (modal) verbs, syntax, and active and passive voice were analysed, with attention being paid to how these markers influenced the meanings attached to signs. Socially, intertextuality (relationships between different texts, including explicit references but also shared ideas and phrases) between different documents and interviews was analysed. Furthermore, links to particular events, people, or perceived shared understandings (explicit and implicit) were included in the analysis.

The outcome of this coding exercise was a database of signs with notes on the different meanings that have been attached to them (also, conversely, the different signs that are attached to one idea), as well as remarks from the linguistic and social analysis. Cross-references were made between almost every document and transcribed interview in the corpus.

Why this analysis? The contribution of the book

The analysis conducted in this book is designed to contribute to the academic field in two distinct ways. First, the book traces the emergence and establishment of a policy field via a detailed empirical analysis of the ways in which the topic has been discussed in the context of the UNFCCC and beyond by a series of crucial advocacy actors. It does this by zooming into a series of key episodes. This first strand of analysis creates a resource for readers looking for a detailed account of the evolution of the policy field surrounding migration and climate change. Second, the book combines the empirical analysis with a critical analysis that problematises the power–knowledge dynamics, following in the footsteps of critical scholarship on migration and climate change. This second strand of analysis will appeal to readers interested in problematisation of the underlying forms of knowledge, and normative implications of policy making on the issue complex of migration and climate change. The combination of these two strands, which build on each other and are both developed from the theoretical foundations detailed in this chapter, is a unique contribution to the literature.

What's next? Introducing the rest of the book

This chapter has set the scene for the forthcoming chapters, in particular orienting the coming discussions in existing academic literature and setting out the theoretical and conceptual premises that have shaped this analysis. The rest of this book is dedicated to laying bare the policy-making efforts that have emerged on migration and climate change. The first part of the book, contained in Chapters 2, 3 and 4, give detailed accounts of the central episodes of policy making across different policy domains that have been formative for the emergence of a distinct area of policy making on migration and climate change and the development of an improvised policy framework. Chapter 3 provides an interlude to the charting of episodes, with an in-depth analysis of the Paris negotiations in December 2015, which was a seminal episode of policy making that has shaped work on migration and climate change both leading up to and since the negotiations. The second part of the book, contained in Chapters 5, 6 and 7, deconstructs particular aspects of the policy-making discourse identified in Part I. Chapters 5 and 6 should ideally be read in conjunction, and deconstruct both the 'phenomenon' of migration and climate change and the representations of the people whose lives are being affected by it, respectively. Chapter 7 turns to a notable silence in the policy-making discourse on migration and climate change (at least in the pre-2015 period) – human rights. Finally, Chapter 8 is a concluding chapter that draws out particular points of interest and critique from the analysis, offering a thought-provoking impulse for studies of policy making on migration and climate change moving forward.

PART I

Episodes of Policy Making on Migration and Climate Change 2010–18

From Cancun to Paris: The Coming of Age of a Policy Field

This chapter is concerned with the 'meticulous, and patiently documentary' (Foucault, 1977: 139) element of genealogy, giving an overview and detailed analysis of the central episodes of policy making on migration and climate change between 2010 and 2015. The term 'episode' is drawn here from the lexicon associated with the genealogical approach to discourse analysis and can be seen as synonymous with 'historical series, epochs, events or moments' and 'are meant to perioditise the history of an object under study' (Vucetic, 2011: 1301). The term 'episodes' is also selected here, rather than any of the synonyms listed in the previous chapter, to emphasise the intertwining nature of the episodes; like episodes of a television programme, they build on each other and cross-references can be established between them, without the episodes necessarily being situated on a linear trajectory or culminating with a grand finale.

Unusually for a genealogy, episodes are arranged here chronologically; this is to enable the chapter to also be easily used as a reference tool and set different policy-making processes in their temporal context. Especially with long negotiation processes, this is not always clear. The hope is that despite being arranged in this way, the links between different episodes, the interconnections, and the influences they have had on later policy making will become apparent.

The selection of episodes in this chapter deserves to be subjected to a critical glance in its own right, for these key episodes closely mirror the mainstream development of the field. It could indeed legitimately be argued that by looking away from these events and shining a light on other less mainstream developments, a different analysis may have been possible. The episodes analysed in this chapter have nevertheless been selected for two interrelated reasons. First, these episodes were gathered during the research process itself; they were referenced in documents, reported in newspaper articles and discussed by interview partners, and were at times even part of my own personal journey of working in this research area. Second, this book interrogates the status quo, the research and policy establishment on migration and climate change with the very direct intention of disturbing it, and the approach that has been selected to do so is the deconstruction of many of its component parts. The exclusion of key moments or junctures in the development of the policy-making field (albeit in favour of highlighting other, perhaps overlooked, moments) would make the tracks they have left in the policy-making discourse very difficult to detect and follow.

Episode 1: COP16 of the UNFCCC in Cancun (December 2010) – ushering in a new era for the migration and climate change nexus

The 16th Conference of the Parties (COP) of the United Nations Framework Convention on Climate Change (UNFCCC) that took place in Cancun in December of 2010 marked the first inclusion of the issue of human mobility in the context of climate change in a text agreed at the global level (Warner, 2012). The now infamous paragraph 14(f) of the Cancun Adaptation Framework, the provision relating to human mobility, invites Parties to undertake 'measures to enhance understanding, coordination and cooperation with regard to climate change induced displacement, migration and planned relocation, where appropriate, at national, regional and international levels' (UNFCCC, 2010: paragraph 14(f)) and has been a defining feature of policy making that has followed.

The symbolic value of this short piece reverberates throughout all of the episodes to follow, with the community working on the migration and climate change nexus now having a sentence that wields considerable clout on the international stage at its disposal. This special status is consistently emphasised by those carrying out advocacy on the issue, with the decision being described as a 'landmark decision' (UNHCR, 2014: 17) or a 'significant breakthrough' (IOM, 2014d: 66) that is used to legitimise further work, by providing 'a basis for further action to address human mobility prompted by disasters and climate change' (UNHCR, 2014: 17), with advocacy work frequently described as 'anchored in' this decision (Advisory Group on Climate Change and Human Mobility, 2015a: 2), or as work that 'builds on' this paragraph (Nansen Initiative, 2015a: 15).

This identification of Cancun as a 'basis' for work that follows has the effect of setting Cancun as a starting point for work on migration and climate change or at the very least ushering in a new era where work is backed up by being anchored in an international agreement. This perceived legitimacy is important for shifting the tone of the debate, and the post-Cancun era is characterised by a move towards working out *how* to talk about the migration and climate change nexus rather than *whether* it should be talked about. Therefore, from 2010 onwards, the main role of advocacy actors shifted from purely agenda setting to working on actual content of provisions. In early 2011, reflecting on engagement by the United Nations High Commissioner for Refugees (UNHCR) on climate-induced displacement, Koko Warner foresees this role for advocacy organisations:

> Now that the issue is part of the Cancun Adaptation Framework, Parties are more likely than ever to seek specific types of information about migration, displacement, and planned relocation. UNHCR and its partners have a unique chance to help frame issues, articulate questions and their responses, share experience from their operations on the ground, etc. (Warner, 2011: 16)

The inclusion of the text on human mobility within the Cancun Adaptation Framework is important for the development of this nexus not only because of its legitimising function but also because of the area within which it establishes the issue, anchoring it within adaptation. By framing the issue in this manner, a whole range of narratives become possible that conceptualise mobility in a positive manner as a potential facet of climate change adaptation (Black et al, 2011; Foresight, 2011b; Warner et al, 2012; IOM, 2014d), with the inclusion of human mobility concerns under adaptation policy now being a standard advocacy recommendation made in the context of climate change negotiations (Advisory Group on Climate Change and Human Mobility, 2015a; IOM, 2015b).

Perhaps the most obvious impact of paragraph 14(f) is the tripartite differentiation between climate change-induced 'displacement, migration and planned relocation' (UNFCCC, 2010: paragraph 14(f)) that has become a set phrase, with IOM for example identifying that 'a tendency towards the adoption of language on "human mobility" seems to gather consensus', using this phrase to highlight different types of mobility that are identified as coming under the umbrella term (IOM, 2014d: 48). The explanation of this terminology given in advocacy documents is overwhelmingly neutral, conveying a feeling that this terminology is correct and uncontroversial: for example, '"human mobility" *is* an umbrella term that encompasses displacement of populations, migration and planned relocation' (Advisory Group on Climate Change and Human Mobility, 2015a: 2, emphasis added). Given the complexity of human mobility and the lively debates that take place in relation to terminology, whether among policy makers, advocacy actors or academics, this apparent consensus needs to be interrogated further.

The inclusion of human mobility concerns within the Cancun Adaptation Framework has also been marked by organisations approaching the issue from a human mobility standpoint beginning to explicitly use the term 'climate change' (rather than 'environment' or 'environmental degradation', which had previously been favoured):

> 'I think you can see also a shift. At the beginning we were speaking of migration, environment and we were staying a bit away from climate change. And I think you can see since 2011, or 2010 at the Cancun Agreement, where there was migration in the climate negotiations in the Adaptation Framework … we have moved towards more and more inclusion of climate change language.' (IOM Interview 2, 2015)

The inclusion of human mobility concerns in the text of the Cancun Adaptation Framework has also had an impact on knowledge creation surrounding the nexus. This is perhaps not surprising given that the text of the agreement specifically concerns knowledge creation through the requested 'measures to enhance understanding' (UNFCCC, 2010: paragraph 14(f)). The paragraph has subsequently been drawn on as 'indicative of the importance the international climate change community now places on the issue of climate change and migration' and as committing 'national governments and their constituencies to begin the difficult task of coming to terms with this phenomenon' (European Cooperation in Science and Technology Secretariat, 2011), in this instance being mobilised to make the case for a scientific network on the subject of climate change and migration.

This is an example of the mutually constitutive nature of knowledge and power, with the legitimising power of the paragraph endorsed by the international community being mobilised in order to make the creation of knowledge on a specific issue (here the nexus between migration and climate change) possible. This is knowledge that then feeds back into legitimisation of the nexus as a 'problem' requiring further scientific enquiry and responses from global governance. This gives weight to the somewhat self-perpetuating claim that the issue is one requiring more and more research to furnish the international community with the knowledge it needs to create instruments or policies to govern it (Nash, 2018c).

Although the Cancun Adaptation Framework is now not the only instance of the migration and climate change nexus being anchored in a text agreed at the global level, it is still deemed relevant. "Cancun is not dead" (UNHCR Interview 2, 2016) as it has not been subsumed but merely added to by subsequent decisions and agreements made by the UNFCCC. In addition, paragraph 14(f) is still being mobilised in order to justify work that is being carried out on the nexus, albeit now as part of a longer list of instances where the international community has recognised the issue.

Episode 2: 60th anniversary of the 1951 Refugee Convention – a foiled attempt to follow up on 14(f)

One of the first attempts to follow up on Cancun was when UNHCR made climate change-induced displacement one of the topics to be investigated during the 60th anniversary of the 1951 Refugee Convention, which opportunely fell on 28 July 2011. In speeches (Guterres, 2011b) and press releases (UNHCR, 2011e) to mark the anniversary, climate change as an emerging driver of displacement is mentioned on numerous occasions, with António Guterres (then High Commissioner for Refugees) arguing that 'a growing number of people are uprooted by natural disasters or lose their livelihoods to desertification, with climate change now found to be the key factor accelerating all other drivers of forced displacement' (Guterres, 2011b).

To consider the issue, an expert roundtable on Climate Change and Displacement: Identifying Gaps and Responses was held from 22 to 26 February 2011, the stated aims of which were as follows:

- Identifying existing gaps in the protection of populations displaced as a result of climate-related events;
- Assessing legal options to address these protection gaps;
- Exploring practical arrangements with respect to the specific case of so-called 'sinking island' States;
- Considering strategies to secure commitment on climate-related displacement; and
- Discussing a set of common understandings on responses to climate-related displacement. (UNHCR, 2011b: 3–4)

In a briefing that was prepared for this roundtable, Koko Warner suggests that UNHCR 'in partnership with research and other partners, has the chance to provide sound practice-based and evidence-based responses to Party questions' (Warner, 2011: 19). The same briefing, however, questions the capacity of UNHCR to undertake this role, arguing that

> [A] challenge will be to keep a consistent and visible presence in the UNFCCC and other relevant policy processes, given the constant 'normal' burden of managing humanitarian crises worldwide (a trend which could be exacerbated by climate variability and longer term change). Ideally one person should be dedicated to attending each climate session to talk with delegates in collaboration with IASC sub-group members. (Warner, 2011: 16)

This recommendation bears an uncanny similarity to the strategy that UNHCR has since gone on to pursue in relation to its work on human mobility and climate change. However, it is also relevant because it suggests a role for UNHCR, despite the fact that this work technically falls outside of the tight mandate of the organisation (McAdam, 2012; Hall, 2013).[1]

The recommendations given in this briefing (Warner, 2011) and the others prepared for the meeting (McAdam, 2011a; Park, 2011; Zetter, 2011), as well as the fact that this topic is being considered by UNHCR so soon after the conclusion of the Cancun COP, suggests an attempt to both establish UNHCR as a relevant actor for work on this issue and legitimise the organisation working on climate change. This meeting was also on the radar of the human rights community, being referenced for example in a thematic section on climate change in the Special Rapporteur on the Human Rights of Internally Displaced Persons' annual report to the UN General Assembly (Beyani, 2011b: paragraph 28).

The involvement of UNHCR also signals a move to include a perspective based on expertise in human mobility in discussions that were largely playing out in the context of climate change negotiations, where other expertise on climate science is (understandably) dominant. As explained by Walter Kälin, "the question for the High Commissioner was how to follow up on Paragraph 14(f) of Cancun" because it was clear that while climate change negotiations and ministries involved have significant expertise in adaptation and migration, they did not have this expertise with regard to population movements (Kälin Interview, 2016).

In June 2011, the Nansen Conference on Climate Change and Displacement was hosted by the Government of Norway (Norwegian Refugee Council, 2011), the purpose of which 'was to facilitate multidisciplinary dialogue to improve our understanding of the challenges at hand and conclude with a set of recommendations for action'

(Norwegian Refugee Council, 2011: 6). Although the event was hosted by the Government of Norway rather than UNHCR, the latter was involved in the event. The very naming of the conference as the Nansen Conference after Fridtjof Nansen, who was the first High Commissioner for Refugees under the League of Nations between 1920 and 1930, establishes an important link. During the event itself, the then High Commissioner for Refugees, António Guterres, spoke in support of a set of principles being recommended at the event and, importantly, linked the conference to the forthcoming UNHCR Ministerial Meeting, which was taking place in December 2011:

> [I]t would be particularly apt, I believe, if this conference were to recommend a set of principles, which could perhaps be known as the Nansen Principles, for the protection of people who have been forced to leave their own country as a result of catastrophic environmental trends and events. The articulation of such principles, underlining the need for displacement responses to be guided by the fundamental notions of humanity, human dignity and human rights, would be a valuable contribution to the ministerial meeting that is planned for December. (Guterres, 2011a)

The High Commissioner got his wish and ten Nansen Principles were recommended at the culmination of the conference, which, 'while not formally adopted, reflect the outcome' of the conference (Kälin, 2012: 48). The Principles themselves are not particularly radical, in that they do not propose the creation of new frameworks, norms or tools of international law. Rather, they emphasise the use of existing norms of international law (Principle VII), including the Guiding Principles on Internal Displacement (Principle VIII), and the primary role of states to protect their populations (Principle II), as well as the importance of actions that are informed by adequate knowledge (Principle I). The importance of other players, particularly local governments, communities, civil society and the private sector (Principle III), and a role for regional frameworks and international cooperation (Principle IV), is also recognised. Furthermore, activities involving the strengthening of prevention and resilience (Principle V), capacities to respond to disasters (Principle VI) and participatory approaches to planned relocation (Principle X) are all explicitly mentioned (Norwegian Refugee Council, 2011: 5).

Interestingly, among these principles one particular gap requiring a more 'coherent and consistent approach at the international level' (Norwegian Refugee Council, 2011: 5) is identified. This gap involves meeting 'the protection needs of people displaced externally owing to sudden-onset disasters' (Norwegian Refugee Council, 2011: 5). This is interesting as the gap identified contains no mention of climate change, being simultaneously broader (disasters not related to climate change may also be included) and narrower (only impacts of climate change qualifying as disasters come under this label).

The Nansen Conference should have served as 'the next step which should have led to states making a commitment to address the issue at the December 2011 UNHCR Ministerial Meeting' (Kälin, 2012: 49). It was envisaged by UNHCR that 'States will use this meeting to make forward looking and specific commitments to undertake activities which will concretely improve protection and assistance for refugees and stateless people' (UNHCR, 2011a: 1), including displacement related to climate change. In order to aid this process and influence potential pledges, UNHCR had already released a Guidance Note in May 2011, before the Nansen Conference had taken place, in which it suggested potential topics for the state pledges, one of which was 'providing legal migration opportunities for people who may be forced to leave their countries of origin owing to slow-onset environmental degradation and/or the effects of climate change, such as sea-level rise or desertification' (UNHCR, 2011a: 8).

This Ministerial Meeting took place in December 2011, but states were not particularly enthusiastic for the inclusion of this topic and the Ministerial Communiqué adopted at the meeting did not contain any reference to climate change-induced displacement (UNHCR, 2011c). According to Kälin, 'this was no accident but rather the expression of a lack of willingness by a majority of governments, whether from reasons of sovereignty, competing priorities or the lead role of UNHCR in the process' (Kälin, 2012: 49).

However, the Ministerial Communiqué does not rule out the possibility of work on emerging displacement scenarios, including those connected to climate change. The document states that 'we will reinforce cooperation with each other and work with UNHCR and other relevant stakeholders, as appropriate, to deepen our understanding of evolving patterns of displacement and to agree upon ways to respond to the challenges we face in a changing global context' (UNHCR, 2011c: 10).

In particular, this opens up a role for UNHCR to cooperate with states in the creation of knowledge in order to increase understanding of the relationship between climate change and displacement, echoing Principle I of the Nansen Principles and Cancun's paragraph 14(f).

Despite this potential opening, UNHCR's organisational set-up means that states control whether it takes up new lines of work beyond its mandate and, despite the concerted efforts of the organisation to promote the issue during the anniversary year commemorations, "at the end of the year ministers were not ready to give him [the High Commissioner] the green light to continue the process" (Kälin Interview, 2016). This effectively foiled the attempt made by UNHCR to take ownership of the follow-up to Cancun. 'In sum, UNHCR has not gained a mandate to expand its activities into protection for those displaced across international borders by climate change sudden events or slow onset events' (Hall, 2013: 102).

Although this particular attempt to follow up on paragraph 14(f) did not result in institutionalisation of the issue within UNHCR or in any states directly pledging to provide legal migration opportunities to those moving because of environmental degradation or climate change, it did provide the impetus for the governments of Norway and Switzerland to pledge in their statements made during the Ministerial Meeting (Government of Norway, 2011; Swiss Confederation, 2011) that they would support an initiative to look more closely at the issue of cross-border disaster-induced displacement, based on the Nansen Principles.

> [T]he Norwegian government calls for a more coherent and consistent approach at the international level to meet the protection needs of people displaced externally owing to sudden-onset disasters, including where climate change plays a role. We therefore pledge, along with the Swiss government, to cooperate with interested states and other relevant actors, including UNHCR, with the aim of obtaining a better understanding of such cross border movements at relevant regional and sub-regional levels, identifying best practices and developing consensus on how best to assist and protect the affected people. (Government of Norway, 2011)

In his speech to mark the closing of the Ministerial Meeting, António Guterres particularly welcomed the exploration of this topic:

> … States signalled their readiness to engage in a timely debate about the new challenges of forced displacement. Four countries pledged to move this debate forward with us and to explore initiatives at regional and sub-regional levels to assess the protection gaps created by new forms of displacement, especially environmentally-related cross-border displacement. (Guterres, 2011c)

In this same speech, Guterres responds to the reluctance of states to endorse work on the migration and climate change nexus in what, given the amount of engagement UNHCR has had with the issue during 2011, may appear to be backpedalling:

> Let me repeat that UNHCR is not seeking an extended mandate in this area, but it is encouraging that States now recognize the need for the international community to come together and find solutions to fill these protection gaps. (Guterres, 2011c)

Notably, the term 'climate change' has also been dropped in this speech, with Guterres switching to talk of 'environmentally related' displacement. This is obviously a departure from Cancun, which is firmly anchored in climate change politics, but is perhaps more palatable for states and less of a shift for the migration community. Importantly, this wording is also less controversial and less closely linked to the concept of historical responsibility for climate change.

The link between this initiative of the Norwegian and Swiss governments and processes that originated within UNHCR is important, as it has had an impact on the way in which human mobility is framed. With the UNHCR being focused on forced forms of mobility, forced movement was at the heart of discussions on climate change happening in the context of the 60th anniversary of the Refugee Convention (as opposed to more voluntary forms of mobility).

Episode 3: Foresight report – consolidating the 'migration as adaptation' narrative

While institutional developments in 2011 were concentrated around UNHCR, the close interaction between academia and policy making was also being strengthened with the publication of the Foresight report entitled *Migration and Global Environmental Change* (Foresight, 2011b). The report was initiated and funded by the United Kingdom Government Office for Science, with a lead expert committee made up of six professors spread across the disciplines of geography, economics, climate system research and politics.

Gaining legitimacy as expert knowledge as a result of being led by scientists and adopting a positive tone dramatically different from the apocalyptic, securitised tones that had haunted much of the work carried out in the early 2000s, the Foresight report has been received overwhelmingly positively. It is perfectly conceivable that this particular direction in tone may have been down to securitisation-weary academics involved in the report's production. In part because of the tone it takes, but also because of its content, the report indicates a shift in the discourse, rooting it squarely in development (Bettini and Gioli, 2016). In terms of content, Foresight is best known for arguing that 'migration can represent a "transformational" adaptation to environmental change, and in many cases will be an extremely effective way to build long-term resilience' (Foresight, 2011b: 10), an argument that is now widely used by advocacy organisations (IOM, 2014d; UKCCMC, 2014; Advisory Group on Climate Change and Human Mobility, 2015a) and academics alike (Black et al, 2011; McLeman, 2014; Warner and Afifi, 2014b).

Alongside the report itself is an archive comprising a further 75 documents, such as reviews, case studies, workshop reports and working papers (Foresight n.d.), that fed into the final document. This evidence-heavy contribution therefore takes the debate firmly in the direction of knowledge. Furthermore, the one-year review of the report's impacts has highlighted a take-up of this knowledge by advocacy actors, with the 'thinking' of both UNHCR and IOM (among others) being influenced by the report (Foresight, 2011a: 2–3). The Foresight report therefore represents an early example of the tight relationship between academic research and policy making on the migration and climate change nexus.

Although the Foresight report was initiated in October 2009 (Foresight, 2011a: 23) before the Cancun Adaptation Framework came into being, the narrative advanced in the report is highly compatible with the framework. Not only does the focus on adaptation tie into the anchoring of human mobility concerns into this particular domain of climate change politics, but the use in the report of migration to refer to (more or less) voluntary movements as per the understanding of migration projected by the tripartite distinction of mobility set out in Cancun fits with the understanding of categories of mobility that have become dominant through it.

The Foresight report was also pivotal for bringing into discussions the concept of resilience, which the report defines as 'the ability of people, communities or systems to absorb shocks and regenerate after a disturbance' (Foresight, 2011b: 234). Resilience is an essential ingredient of the migration as adaptation narrative, where resilience plays the role of a positive aspirational characteristic that can be increased through (labour) migration thanks to the diversification in livelihoods that this allows. A further frequently touted positive consequence of this form of human mobility is that it decreases instances of displacement because people and communities are more resilient to shocks. The Foresight report is therefore also one of the first examples of human mobility in the context of the nexus being clearly divided into 'positive' and 'negative' mobilities, and even goes beyond this to also consider non-mobility.

Episode 4: COST action on climate change and migration (2011–15) – solidifying the academic community

Perhaps the most concrete example of a distinct research community coming together around the migration and climate change nexus is the European Cooperation in Science and Technology (COST) research action 'COST Action IS 1101 Climate change and migration: knowledge, law and policy, and theory'. This brought together the following:

> … a diverse ensemble of established and early-stage social scientists to build upon and extend existing social science research into climate change and migration across three interrelated fields of investigation: knowledge; law and policy; and theory. (European Cooperation in Science and Technology Secretariat, 2011: 3)

The creation of this network was a response from academics to calls from the international community (for example, in the Cancun Adaptation Framework) for more research on the topic.

However, the most interesting aspect is not the creation of the network itself (although of course this does suggest a certain level of interest in the topic on the part of the European Union, which funded the network and is therefore also relevant to some extent). Instead, the effects of the collaboration of academics working on the issue are of interest. The network (of which I was an active participant) provided the opportunity for scholars to meet at workshops and conferences, to network, and to collaborate. The relationships between scholars that have emerged from this network have contributed to the development of a distinct research community surrounding the climate change and migration nexus.

Furthermore, the network solidified relationships not only between different members of the academic community but also between the academic community and advocacy actors, with many of the events also involving representatives of these advocacy actors and as a result making both communities more accessible. Therefore, as well as enabling individuals to forge personal relationships, the network facilitated the sharing of research findings, new theoretical perspectives and advocacy work. At times, this blurred the boundaries between the two communities, with networking events resulting, for example, in publications containing work by authors from academia and advocacy organisations between the same covers (for example, see Rosenow-Williams and Gemenne, 2016).

Such a clear manifestation of a formalised epistemic community developing around the migration and climate change nexus is especially interesting from the power–knowledge perspective. It is questionable whether, without significant interest from the international community, such a network would have been possible. But the involvement of powerful actors in the issue and their desire to know more about it in order to inform their decisions opens doors to acquiring funding and working to meet the demand for creating scientific knowledge. Therefore, power is not simply in the hands of scientists as possessors of knowledge that they disseminate to policy makers; rather, the gatekeepers of funding whose interests are set by an issue's perceived societal or political relevance are extremely powerful in terms of what makes it on to research agendas.

Episode 5: Launch of the Nansen Initiative – the governments of Norway and Switzerland follow through on their pledge

The Nansen Initiative, launched in October 2012, is inextricably linked to the Nansen Conference of the previous year (as the very name of the initiative suggests) and to the processes that had been ongoing under the auspices of UNHCR. The initiative grew from pledges made by the governments of Norway and Switzerland (Government of Norway, 2011; Swiss Confederation, 2011) to cooperate with other states and actors

> ... with the aim of obtaining a better understanding of such cross border movements at relevant regional and sub-regional levels, identifying best practices and developing consensus on how best to assist and protect the affected people. (Government of Norway, 2011)

In addition to the events that took place surrounding the 60th anniversary of the Refugee Convention commemorations (in particular, the expert roundtable in February 2011, the Nansen Conference, and the UNHCR Ministerial Meeting in December 2011), an Information Note introducing the Nansen Initiative identifies 'the Climate Negotiations (UNFCCC) and the Cancún Agreement' as the origins of the initiative (Nansen Initiative, 2013: 2).

The initiative is described as a 'state-led, bottom-up consultative process' that is aimed at building consensus. Given the reluctance of states to endorse work on climate change by UNHCR, this has been a very important exercise. Norway and Switzerland, as funders of the initiative, play a prominent role. These two states were joined in the of the initiative by Australia, Bangladesh, Costa Rica, Germany, Kenya, Mexico and the Philippines (Nansen Initiative, 2013), to which UNHCR and IOM were also standing invitees (Nansen Initiative, 2014a). Other actors were included in and were able to inform the process through the consultative committee, which was made up of representatives from international organisations, researchers, think tanks and non-governmental organisations (Nansen Initiative, 2014a).

In order to emphasise its role as a forum for building consensus among states rather than striving to create new international norms to impose upon them, the Nansen Initiative frequently explicitly set out what it did *not* intend to do: 'The initiative does not aim at creating new legal standards' (Nansen Initiative, 2013: 1). Again, Walter Kälin, the Envoy of the Chairmanship of the Nansen Initiative, points out that the initiative was not meant to replace official structures and processes such as the UNFCCC, "but rather complement it by framing messages and feeding into those processes" (Kälin Interview, 2016).

The particular issue on which the Nansen Initiative aimed to gain consensus was 'the needs of people displaced across international borders by natural disasters, including the effects of climate change' (Nansen Initiative, 2013: 1). This bears a striking resemblance to Principle IX of the Nansen Principles, which stated:

> [A] more coherent and consistent approach at the international level is needed to meet the protection needs of people displaced externally owing to sudden-onset disasters. States, working in conjunction with UNHCR and other relevant stakeholders could develop a guiding framework or instrument in this regard. (Norwegian Refugee Council, 2011: 5, Principle IX)

The argument that has been made for selecting this particular focus of cross-border disaster-induced displacement concerns an obvious gap in terms of normative standards, from hard law to very soft standards (Kälin Interview, 2016).

The focus on disasters also side-stepped a tricky conceptual issue with drawing causality between climate change and particular displacements of people, with this focus seen to reflect the multi-causal nature of displacement scenarios.

'Disaster by definition is about the effects of a natural hazard on a given society or community, so in that sense what we were trying to say by talking about "in the context of disasters" is to acknowledge that it is multi-causal, that there are lots of things that influence a movement.' (Nansen Initiative Interview, 2015)

The role of knowledge has been incredibly important for the Nansen Initiative. Although it already had a basis legitimising its existence in both the Cancun Adaptation Framework and the Nansen Principles, as well as the fact that it had been initiated by states, there was still a great deal of scepticism surrounding the issue. It is worth bearing in mind that calls for a deeper understanding of human mobility in the context of climate change feature in both paragraph 14(f) as well as Principle I of the Nansen Principles. Therefore, the first priority for the Nansen Initiative was to gather and consolidate knowledge on displacement and disasters:

'That part was really about consulting and saying to what extent is this an issue in your region, how are you responding, where do you see the gaps, what's working well, how do we understand this phenomenon? And then commissioning studies alongside of that, so that was really consolidating what's known.' (Nansen Initiative Interview, 2015)

The first step for the Nansen Initiative was to carry out ten sub-regional consultations, with one intergovernmental and one civil society consultation taking place in the following five regions: Pacific; Central America; Greater Horn of Africa; South-East Asia; and South Asia (Nansen Initiative, 2014a). Not only did these consultations allow for knowledge to be gathered from states and other actors in these sub-regions, but it also gave states ownership of the process through the opportunity to input to the knowledge informing the *Protection Agenda* that was the ultimate intended outcome of the process. Another important strand of knowledge was the Foresight report, which 'contributed very directly to the launch of the Nansen Initiative' (Foresight, 2011a: 22) by utilising its findings to inform a report entitled *The Nansen Initiative, UNHCR and the Foresight Report on Migration and Global Environmental Change*, which was then submitted to the Nansen Initiative (Williams and Black, 2012).

Due to the very basis of its work being concerned with the collation and creation of knowledge, the use of research and the authority ascribed to knowledge has been described as "extremely important" in allowing the Nansen Initiative to bring attention to the migration and climate change nexus (Kälin Interview, 2016). The use of commissioned research to complement and inform the consultations "was very instrumental and helped a lot to have very meaningful discussions, to get away from a kind of political bickering..." (Kälin Interview, 2016).

As the first intergovernmental process to address human mobility in the context of climate change, the Nansen Initiative has been described as "quite instrumental" (Kälin Interview, 2016) in putting the issue on the global agenda, particularly because of its tight focus on cross-border disaster-induced displacement. Indeed, the awareness created among states, through the involvement of state representatives in the initiative's sub-regional consultative processes, has been identified as being particularly important in progressing discussions on the issue and ensuring its enshrinement in the COP decision of the UNFCCC in Paris in December 2015 (UNHCR Interview 2, 2016; IOM Interview 4, 2016).

This use of knowledge to influence debates surrounding climate change and human mobility is therefore identified as perhaps the greatest impact of the Nansen Initiative, overshadowing even the stated intention of agreeing a Protection Agenda (although this was also achieved).

> 'I think that's what the Nansen Initiative has achieved, to bring states together and to have a serious discussion on it, to have a discussion that was not just entirely political but very much informed by research, by facts.' (Kälin Interview, 2016)

Episode 6: *Where the Rain Falls* Global Policy Report – academia responds to the call for knowledge

Also working at the interface between knowledge and policy on the migration and climate change nexus is the United Nations University Institute for Environmental and Human Security (UNU-EHS) and in particular the Environmental Migration, Social Vulnerability and Adaptation Section that was headed at the time by Koko Warner. The section had already been involved in a large research project entitled Environmental Change and Forced Migration Scenarios (EACH-FOR), examining the links between environment and migration (Jäger et al, 2009). The results were published in 2009 and the project is frequently referenced as one of the most in-depth studies (at that time) into this relationship.

The UNU-EHS is an interesting entity in that it is primarily an academic institution concerned with knowledge creation, but at the same time it does so from a privileged position within the UN system, giving researchers unprecedented access to representatives of states, negotiators at international meetings such as the climate change negotiations, and policy makers. This hybrid role means that the UNU-EHS is classed as an international epistemic organisation (IEO), which can be understood as an institutionalised form of epistemic community. Social network analysis into policy making in relation to the migration and climate change nexus places this section, and particularly Koko Warner, at its centre, in a very powerful position in terms of influencing policy making, and also argues that Koko Warner and UNU-EHS were instrumental in the emergence of Cancun's paragraph 14(f) (Pilath, 2016). Furthermore:

> UNU-EHS's 'UN label', mission, and mandate put it in a unique position, particularly in comparison with other research institutions involved in the issue of environmental migration, as it distinguishes UNU-EHS as an interface between science and politics at the UN level. (Pilath, 2016: 221)

In a move that further consolidated its position as a source of authoritative knowledge on the migration and climate change nexus, UNU-EHS completed another large research project in 2012 together with CARE International (CARE International and UNU-EHS, 2012). *Where the Rain Falls* explores 'the interrelationships among rainfall variability, food and livelihood security, and human mobility in a diverse set of research sites in eight countries in Asia, Africa and Latin America' (Warner et al, 2012: 14). The Global Policy Report for the project was released in November 2012 (Warner et al, 2012) and was followed by academic publication of the results in 2014 (Warner and Afifi, 2014a).

The project was launched in 2011 and represents the first concerted post-Cancun effort from the research community to produce original research with the stated intention of

> … [enhancing] the capacity of governments, civil society and the private sector to better understand and effectively address the relationship between changing weather patterns, food security and human mobility in some of the world's most vulnerable countries and communities. (CARE International and UNU-EHS, 2012)

The need to inform policy-making processes was therefore the raison d'être for the study, with the Global Policy Report arguing that the research carried out by the initiative is *needed* in order for decisions on these issues to be made:

> [I]n order to make informed decisions about adaptation planning, development, and transition to a more climate-resilient future, policymakers and development actors need a better understanding of the linkages among changes in the climate, household livelihood and food security profiles, and migration decisions. (Warner et al, 2012: 14)

Given the involvement of UNU-EHS and Koko Warner in the creation of paragraph 14(f), which is based on a call for greater understanding of the relationships between climate change and human mobility, the effort of the Environmental Migration, Social Vulnerability and Adaptation Section to address this call is not particularly surprising.

The report makes a series of recommendations for policy makers and practitioners, aimed at UNFCCC parties, global food and nutrition and sustainable development policy makers, developed and developing country governments, non-governmental organisations (NGOs), multilateral institutions and UN agencies (Warner et al, 2012: 22–3). It also uses strong wording; for example, there is no sense that there is any choice about whether or not the recommendations are adopted. In fact, the key points are presented not as recommendations but as 'reflections for policymakers and practitioners', and the verb used to describe the need to carry out these actions is 'must' (Warner et al, 2012: 22). The strength of these imperatives, and the research used to back them up, reinforces the report's authority.

In terms of content, the study links to both the Cancun Adaptation Framework through its focus on adaptation and to one of the narratives introduced by the Foresight report in terms of migration as an adaptation strategy. The alignment of these findings is no coincidence, with UNU-EHS having 'consulted with many of the leaders of the [Foresight] Project while building its research questions and methodologies for the "Where the Rain Falls" project' (Foresight, 2011a: 3). The report also looks forward, linking to forthcoming UNFCCC processes by emphasising the importance for parties to the UNFCCC to consider the emerging area of loss and damage (Warner et al, 2012: 22), which had previously not been connected to human mobility in the context of climate change negotiations.

Episode 7: COP18 of the UNFCCC in Doha – human mobility as an aspect of loss and damage

In the COP decision of the COP18 of the UNFCCC in 2012 in Doha (hereafter the Doha decision), human mobility was acknowledged in a second text agreed at the global level. The decision acknowledged work being undertaken to advance 'the understanding of and expertise on loss and damage', one aspect of which is 'how impacts of climate change are affecting patterns of migration, displacement and human mobility' (UNFCCC, 2013: 3/CP.18 7(a)(vi)). Notably, although once again being mentioned in a UNFCCC document, the wording anchored in the Doha decision differs from the frequently referenced tripartite formulation of Cancun paragraph 14(f).

Also notable is the placement of the migration issue. Until the Doha COP, migration had largely been considered in terms of adaptation, having entered the Cancun Adaptation Framework as an activity related to adaptation. However, in the Doha decision, the issue was included as an aspect of loss and damage. As well as including human mobility as an aspect of loss and damage for the first time, the Doha decision sets out the path for continued work on loss and damage under the UNFCCC, agreeing that institutional arrangements to address loss and damage would be established (UNFCCC, 2013: 3/CP.18, 9). This mandate led to the G–77 states and China proposing an international mechanism on loss and damage at the following COP19 in Warsaw in 2013 and to controversial discussions where the same block lobbied for this mechanism to be established as a separate mechanism (constituting a third pillar of the UNFCCC). Meanwhile, another block, consisting of developed states, was lobbying for loss and damage to remain under adaptation and continue to be housed under the Cancun Adaptation Framework (McNamara, 2014). A compromise was reached and the Warsaw International Mechanism for Loss and Damage associated with Climate Change Impacts (WIM) was established, but housed under the Cancun Adaptation Framework. The core components of the mechanism were to enhance 'knowledge and understanding of comprehensive risk management approaches to address loss and damage associated with the adverse effects of climate change, including slow onset impacts', promote 'dialogue, coordination, coherence and synergies amongst relevant stakeholders', and enhance 'action and support, including finance, technology and capacity-building, to address loss and damage associated with the adverse effects of climate change' (UNFCCC, 2014: 2/CP.19, 5 (a),(b),(c)).

It is therefore the subsequent creation of the WIM in 2013 that gives the reference to migration, displacement and human mobility in the Doha decision its importance. This reference justifies the consideration of migration as a loss and damage issue, and, with the decision in Warsaw, establishes a mechanism for work in this area. Therefore, a new arena within climate change negotiations is created where migration can be considered, in addition to adaptation where the climate change and migration nexus is already anchored thanks to the Cancun Adaptation Framework.

Aside from opening up a new forum within which to advance 1human mobility concerns, the inclusion of loss and damage in the migration and climate change nexus is of discursive significance. To understand it, we need to return to the emergence of the narrative of loss and damage in the context of climate change negotiations more broadly. At the outset, climate change negotiations were focused around mitigation efforts, which 'seemed to be logical and straightforward: there was a clear identification of the problem (increased greenhouse gas (GHG) emissions resulting in a changing climate) and solution (mitigate emissions)' (McNamara, 2014: 242). However, emerging scientific research in the mid-2000s (including the reports of the Intergovernmental Panel on Climate Change; see IPCC, 2007) indicated that existing mitigation efforts would not be sufficient to prevent negative impacts, and, combined with the amount of warming already locked in due to previous emissions, made a convincing argument for adaptation.

Loss and damage takes this logic a step further, arguing that neither mitigation nor adaptation efforts will be sufficient to prevent the adverse impacts of climate change. Essentially, 'it argues that existing policy mechanisms are not enough to extend limits to adaptation, to prevent private and collective loses and damages, or to ensure human welfare in the face of climate change' (Wrathall et al, 2015: 277). Discussions surrounding loss and damage have therefore centred on assisting people affected by climate change, the possible creation of insurance mechanisms and, most controversially, the issue of compensation.

Inserting migration, displacement and human mobility back into this argument, the narrative is that 'migration as adaptation' will not be the only kind of mobility taking place in the context of climate change. Displacement and planned relocation are both types of mobility that are inevitable (given the failures surrounding mitigation and the limits of adaptation) and that these kinds of movements (which are fundamentally different from the more-or-less voluntary 'migration as adaptation') require different responses.

Episode 8: Advisory Group on Climate Change and Human Mobility – cooperation and consensus as a tactic to influence climate change negotiations

The Advisory Group on Climate Change and Human Mobility (hereafter the Advisory Group) is an informal group composed of UNHCR,

IOM, UNU-EHS, the United Nations Development Programme, the International Labour Organization (ILO), the Norwegian Refugee Council/Internal Displacement Monitoring Centre, Sciences Po-CERI and Refugees International, and was founded in 2013 in the run-up to COP19 in Warsaw as a vehicle for engaging with climate change negotiations (UNHCR, 2014: 18). The organisations forming this group 'consider that close cooperation in framing and communicating issues surrounding human mobility in response to climate change is the most effective way to inform policy-making' (Advisory Group on Climate Change and Human Mobility, 2014a: 14).

Although the group first appeared under this name and in this particular formation in 2013, many of the organisations involved have been cooperating on advocacy work within the UNFCCC process since shortly after the issue made its way on to the UNFCCC agenda. Indeed, in the lead-up to COP15 of the UNFCCC in 2009, various combinations of these organisations along with the Representative of the Secretary General on the Human Rights of Internally Displaced Persons made submissions to the UNFCCC (IOM et al, 2009; UNHCR, et al, 2009a, 2009b, 2009c). This was also the case in 2012 and 2013 (UNHCR et al, 2012, 2013), with both of these submissions subsequently being listed as Advisory Group publications (IOM, 2016b), although the group was not working under this banner at this point.

The combination of actors involved in the group is significant, with all of the heavyweights already involved in promoting the migration and climate change nexus represented, in addition to some relatively new faces. UNHCR has been the focal point for the group, and is listed as the contact in Advisory Group documents (Advisory Group on Climate Change and Human Mobility, 2014a, 2015a, 2015b). This is perhaps surprising, given that UNHCR did not receive the nod from states to undertake this area of work. However, since 2011, someone working on climate change has been situated within the organisation[2] and has continued to attend climate change negotiations. A link was also created with the 2011 Nansen Conference by the presence in the group of the Norwegian Refugee Council, which organised the conference and was involved in the preparation of the Nansen Principles (Hall, 2013: 101). The inclusion of IOM is also important, with its work on climate change increasing around this time, and, crucially, UNU-EHS is a member of the group. The strong position of UNU-EHS, including the volume of research expertise it has developed and its strong links with the UNFCCC process, makes it a formidable partner.

The Advisory Group has focused on influencing policy making, in particular the climate change negotiations taking place under the auspices of the UNFCCC, producing recommendations for COP20 in Lima in 2014 (Advisory Group on Climate Change and Human Mobility, 2014a), as well as for National Adaptation Plans (NAPs) (Advisory Group on Climate Change and Human Mobility, 2014d) and the Nairobi Work Programme (Advisory Group on Climate Change and Human Mobility, 2014b, 2014e). It was also involved in drawing up the draft work programme of the WIM (Advisory Group on Climate Change and Human Mobility, 2014c). Over the course of 2015, in the lead-up to COP21 in Paris, the Advisory Group also submitted documents informing preparatory as well as final negotiations, and commented on the drafts of the Paris Agreement (Advisory Group on Climate Change and Human Mobility, 2015c, 2015a, 2015b, respectively).

Despite the complexity of the migration and climate change nexus, the lack of agreed narratives on the issue, the use of different terminology by different actors, and the different mandates (and therefore foci) of the members of the Advisory Group, a common position has been reached in these advocacy documents. The ability of the group to arrive at coordinated messages and undertake collaborative advocacy work has been partially attributed to the informal nature of the group and the personalities involved (UNHCR Interview 1, 2015). The group is 'composed of technical experts from various organizations that are committed to the climate change and mobility issue and are not too keen to raise their organization flag but would rather see that sending a coordinated message is more relevant and effective' (UNHCR Personal Communication, 2015). These personal relationships between the core group members (many of whom are based in Geneva) have been important for agreeing issues such as common terminology and messaging. During COP21 in Paris, group members also held joint side events (IOM, 2015e) and press conferences (UNHCR, 2015), and met frequently to continue to coordinate their work (UNHCR Interview 2, 2016).

The group aims to produce documents that are accessible to state parties and negotiators, which affects the terminology and messaging used: "The messaging in our group tends to be … cautiously progressive, so we push the boundaries but we are talking to nation states so … it has a very purposeful vocabulary" (Warner Interview, 2015). In its terminology you see one of the most deliberate usages of the Cancun tripartite distinction between types of human mobility, with the group stating that 'human mobility *is* an umbrella term that encompasses displacement of populations, migration and planned relocation' (Advisory Group on Climate Change and Human Mobility, 2015a: 2, emphasis added). In the context of climate negotiations, it is perhaps not surprising that wording already agreed within this context would be given emphasis. However, the portrayal of this understanding of mobility as a matter of fact (for example, the wording does not read 'human mobility is understood as', or include any hint that complete consensus might not exist), has the effect of naturalising the phrase, more so than already the case given the weight attributed to paragraph 14(f).

The power of this group of actors working under the banner of the Advisory Group is extraordinary. The establishment of a common position by a group containing what are often identified as the key human mobility actors shrinks the space for alternative narratives emerging. The group becomes the gatekeeper of knowledge on human mobility in climate negotiations, with alternative conceptions that do not become part of its common position likely to be sidelined in the advocacy space. Legitimacy as an authority on questions concerning human mobility, and therefore prioritisation of the group's narratives, is also conferred on the group, and its members, by state negotiators who turn to the group for information on human mobility. Group members have reported being approached by negotiators for briefings on the issue and for technical assistance regarding human mobility in the context of climate change (IOM Interview 4, 2016; UNHCR Interview 2, 2016).

A further interesting characteristic of the group is its appropriation of the 'Advisory Group' label. The group sees itself as existing to inform policy making and, indeed, has concentrated its activities around informing UNFCCC negotiations. However, the group has not been established by the UNFCC or any of the mechanisms working under the UNFCCC. Instead, it is a coalition of different advocacy actors working together to carry out advocacy work in a coordinated manner. Giving this entity, essentially concerned with lobbying negotiators, the label of 'Advisory Group' gives the impression of an official function and legitimacy, again adding to the power of the group to prescribe which knowledge acquires truth status.

Episode 9: Fifth Assessment Report of the IPCC – hegemonic closure from climate science on human mobility as a societal impact of climate change

The publication of the Fifth Assessment Report of the Intergovernmental Panel on Climate Change (IPCC) in 2014 is the next big juncture in the development of the migration and climate change nexus. The report states:

> Climate change over the 21st century is projected to increase displacement of people (medium evidence, high agreement).

> Displacement risk increases when populations that lack the resources for planned migration experience higher exposure to extreme weather events, in both rural and urban areas, particularly in developing countries with low income. Expanding opportunities for mobility can reduce vulnerability for such populations. Changes in migration patterns can be responses to both extreme weather events and longer-term climate variability and change, and migration can also be an effective adaptation strategy. (IPCC, 2014: 73)

These few sentences have removed much of the contention concerning the question of whether human mobility will be one of the societal impacts of climate change and is frequently reproduced as 'evidence' of this link, often providing the justification for work taking place into this phenomenon. For example, IOM argues:

> [I]t is widely recognized that human mobility, in both its forced and voluntary forms, is increasingly impacted by environmental and climatic factors and that migration in turn also impacts the environment. The Fifth Assessment Report of the Intergovernmental Panel on Climate Change (IPCC) highlights the importance and complexity of human mobility in the context of climate change. (IOM 2014d: ix)

UNHCR also draws on the IPCC, quoting the passage from the assessment report that makes the link between climate change and human mobility, under the heading of 'Climate change as a driver of human mobility' (UNHCR, 2014: 13), in such a self-explanatory manner that there is no further discussion of the evidence behind it. The Advisory Group also draws on this evidence, emphasising the recent addition of this issue in the 2014 IPCC report: 'the last Intergovernmental Panel on Climate Change (IPCC) report includes, for the first time, a chapter addressing human security, including aspects pertaining to migration and mobility' (Advisory Group on Climate Change and Human Mobility, 2014a).

The Nansen Initiative also accedes to the authority of the IPCC in its definition of climate change, defining it as 'any change in climate over time, whether due to natural variability or as a result of human activity, according to the Intergovernmental Panel on Climate Change (IPCC)' (Nansen Initiative, 2014a). This scientific authority of the IPCC is cited not only by policy makers, but also by the research community, with social scientists frequently unquestioningly using the IPCC as a proxy for explaining the climate science behind the migration and climate change nexus.

The IPCC is organised such that it does not undertake any new research into climate science or monitor climate data, but rather has the role of reviewing and synthesising existing scientific research in order to document state-of-the-art research and produce a summary report that is accessible to policy makers who do not necessarily have a background in climate science or even climate policy. Critiques levelled at the IPCC claim that by only drawing on existing research, it merely reproduces the geopolitical landscapes of scientific research (Chaturvedi and Doyle, 2015: chapter 2).

The IPCC is an intergovernmental body established in 1988, with membership open to member states of the UN and the World Meteorological Organisation (WMO). It is not a purely scientific body and 'from its very beginning the IPCC has acted as a hybrid or "boundary" organisation, operating as it does across the worlds of science, public discourse and policy' (Hulme, 2009: 96). Due to its organisational structure as an intergovernmental organisation, 'governments participate in the review process and the plenary Sessions, where main decisions about the IPCC work programme are taken and reports are accepted, adopted and approved' (IPCC, no date). As an intergovernmental body, the IPCC is subject to political decision making, and the fact that reports are 'accepted, adopted and approved' by states makes such documents highly political in nature. Despite this, the IPCC emphasises the 'scientific' nature of its work:

> Because of its scientific and intergovernmental nature, the IPCC embodies a unique opportunity to provide rigorous and balanced scientific information to decision makers. By endorsing the IPCC reports, governments acknowledge the authority of their scientific content. The work of the organization is therefore policy-relevant and yet policy-neutral, never policy-prescriptive. (IPCC, no date)

By labelling the particular (actually highly political) knowledge it produces as 'policy-neutral' and emphasising such knowledge as 'rigorous', 'balanced' and 'scientific', the IPCC confers authority on its reports, and conveys the impression that this knowledge is comprehensive, rather than partial.

Within discussions surrounding the migration and climate change nexus, the claims made by the IPCC have become naturalised to the point that a hegemonic closure has been reached – the power of the IPCC to confer 'truth' status on knowledge means that human mobility is now accepted as one of the effects of climate change. The way that the

IPCC works in terms of drawing purely on existing research also means that a self-perpetuating relationship exists between the IPCC and the academic community conducting research on the nature of the migration and climate change nexus. The increased publication of the results of these studies in academic journals makes the inclusion of the issue in the IPCC report more likely, while the inclusion of the issue in the IPCC report is also used as legitimation for work to be carried out in the first place.

Episode 10: 2015 – a year of global agreements

The year 2015 deserves to be identified as a juncture in the emergence of the migration and climate change nexus in its own right. It has been described as a "massive international confab" (OHCHR Interview, 2018) because of the multitude of international policy-making processes and subsequent increased advocacy efforts taking place during that year. The post-2015 development agenda has been used to refer to the Sustainable Development Goals (SDGs) agreed in 2015 (United Nations General Assembly, 2015), but with 2015 also marking the culmination of the Sendai Framework for Disaster Risk Reduction (Sendai Framework for Disaster Risk Reduction, 2015) and the Paris Agreement (UNFCCC, 2016a), the post-2015 label often also bundles these processes together.

The junctures that have already been identified have to been seen in the context of flowing into these international processes, which have been on the radar of the international community for a number of years. The Millennium Development Goals expired in 2015, building the pressure for a successor. The Hyogo Framework, the precursor to the Sendai Framework for Disaster Risk Reduction, also expired in 2015. The outlier was the climate change negotiations, with the Kyoto Framework having already expired and COP15 in Copenhagen in 2009 having been anticipated as the successor agreement. However, no agreement was reached at COP15 and negotiations continued over the coming years, with COP21 in Paris crystallising itself as the new opportunity to create a successor to Kyoto.

Particular challenges (and indeed opportunities) arose from the convergence of these policy processes in 2015. The pressure to create holistic agreements that complemented each other without duplicating work, or in the worst case conflicting with each other, was great. At the same time, the danger of policy silos emerging, without interaction between people concentrating on different processes, was ever present. Finally, a danger of fatigue with so many international processes being conducted in parallel (bearing in mind that preparations and pre-negotiations for the final meetings where agreements are actually made are long and complex) was great, and resources among those engaging in these policy-making processes were spread thinly.

Episode 11: IOM creates a migration, environment and climate change division – manoeuvring for position as a leader on the migration and climate change nexus

Although IOM has worked on the migration and climate change nexus since the early 1990s (for a timeline, see IOM, 2014d: 17) and became widely cited in discussions on migration and climate change when it published a working definition of the term 'environmental migrants' in 2007 (IOM, 2007), it was really in 2015 with the creation of a division working specifically on migration, environment and climate change (IOM, 2014c: 2) that the organisation seemed to be manoeuvring into a position as a key actor in this area in its own right. This shift is so important because it alters the internal structure of the organisation, and serves as "recognition" of the importance of this issue and a strategy to "bring this topic on the forefront" (IOM Interview 2, 2015). This has led to one staff member describing IOM as "really *the* organisation focused on migration that works on migration, environment and climate change" (IOM Interview 2, 2015).

This shift builds on the momentum of an acceleration in work in this area by the organisation since 2010/11 and the anchoring of human mobility in the Cancun Adaptation Framework. In 2014, the IOM published a series of documents emphasising its work in this area, including a survey on environmental migration (IOM, 2014a) and a report detailing its programmatic activities on environmental migration (IOM, 2014f). A key document is the extremely weighty *IOM Outlook on Migration, Environment and Climate Change*, which outlines different aspects of the nexus in a series of briefing documents and emphasises the (potential) role for IOM throughout (IOM, 2014d).

These publications have served a dual purpose, publicising IOM and its work on migration, environment and climate change to an external audience, as well as promoting the topic internally within the organisation. During the period that this acceleration in work on the migration and climate change nexus was taking place in IOM, there was a feeling that some members of staff within the organisation were "still not feeling completely comfortable [about working] on climate issues" (IOM Interview 2, 2015). This was because of the complexity of the topic, so work was undertaken internally to raise awareness of the issue, by producing guidance notes and glossaries and providing training in regional offices and national divisions to help staff understand the terminology (IOM Interview 2, 2015).

The involvement of IOM in the migration and climate change nexus also extends to knowledge creation. In 2013, the organisation launched the *Migration, Environment and Climate Change: Evidence for Policy* (MECLEP) programme, a policy-oriented research project that 'aims to benefit policymakers and practitioners in the six target countries and to contribute globally to policymaking on migration, environment and climate change, especially climate-related adaptation strategies and planning' (IOM, 2014f: 2).

This project was a big step towards establishing IOM not simply as a communicator of existing knowledge from the research community on migration and climate change, but in the role of creating this knowledge.

IOM has also been increasingly active in its outreach and advocacy efforts in relation to the migration and climate change nexus. It has established an online portal that is billed as a *Knowledge Platform on People on the Move in a Changing Climate*, gathering together work on migration, environment and climate change (IOM, 2016c), and produces a monthly newsletter available via email subscription (for example, IOM, 2015a). This is a concerted effort to raise the profile of IOM's work on migration and climate change. Another characteristic of IOM publications on the migration and climate change nexus is that they frequently self-reference the organisation, drawing attention to its expertise, the long history the organisation has with working on this issue, and the practical, on-the-ground activities it undertakes in this area. For example, a short briefing titled *IOM Perspectives on Migration, Environment and Climate Change* includes discussion under the following headings and sub-headings: 'IOM response to environmental migration: What do we do?'; 'What are IOM's objectives in managing environmental migration?'; 'IOM's work encompasses operational, policy and research dimensions'; and 'What are the impacts of IOM's operational activities?' (IOM, 2014e: 3).

The positioning of the organisation as a major player in this area has been, in part at least, strategic. "We also have to position the organisation in a way that we can apply for adaptation funding, and green funding, and climate funding" (IOM Interview 2, 2015). This strategic thinking includes internal moves such as prioritising the issue within the organisation, creating an active presence for the organisation in discussions on the issue, producing research and publications on the issue, as well as emphasising the operational work carried out by IOM on the ground in relation to migration, environment and climate change.

This story is very different from that of UNHCR in 2011 during the 60th anniversary of the 1951 Refugee Convention, when it was clear that states were unwilling to back the organisation's deeper engagement with the issue, with an alternative tack being taken by some states in founding the Nansen Initiative in order to build consensus at the intergovernmental level. However, "for IOM's side, it was quite clear that the states are always keen on the migration, environment and climate change subject" (IOM Interview 2, 2015). This is highlighted by states selecting the topic for discussion during IOM meetings (in 2014 the Standing Committee on Programmes and Finance discussed the issue; IOM, 2014d: 12) and for a high-level panel discussion during the 105th session of the IOM council in 2014 (IOM, 2014c). This is taken by IOM as evidence that states "are ready to talk about it, and want to do more and to see more" (IOM Interview 2, 2015).

The shifting role of IOM into a more central actor in the context of the migration and climate change nexus is relevant, as there are key ways in which the discourse adopted by IOM in discussing this issue differs from that of other actors. First, the organisation's focus is not purely on displacement scenarios, but on migration more broadly, which, according to the IOM, is taken to include both forced and voluntary forms of movement (IOM, 2014d: 6). This makes articulation of the 'migration as adaptation' narrative easier, as movement is not considered by the organisation as an inherently forced, or negative, phenomenon. However, it does go against the emerging consensus that sees human mobility as the dominant way in which to talk about people moving in the context of climate change. This is particularly visible in IOM's use of the terms 'environmental migration' and 'environmental migrant', which are not widely used by other organisations.

IOM also appears to have adopted the phrase 'migration, environment and climate change' to describe the area of work. The use of only one word to describe human mobility categories is unusual compared with other organisations that are at pains to emphasise different types of human mobility that are taken to be present in the climate change context. The separation of environment and climate change is also unusual, with other contexts either focusing on climate change or on disasters that do not have the same attribution issues. The IPCC report also legitimises a climate change focus (and is used by IOM for this purpose, for example IOM, 2014d: ix), but the organisation nevertheless retains the reference to 'environment' more broadly.

The final discursive influence that may stem from a more central role for IOM is the introduction of a migration management discourse in relation to climate change (Nash, 2016). The migration management discourse centres on the claim that migration that is managed effectively can have positive effects (in a so-called 'triple-win' scenario where migrants, as well as both sending and receiving communities benefit). For the migration and climate change nexus, this narrative is often coupled with the 'migration as adaptation' narrative in order to argue that migration can be a form of adaptation when managed properly. This can then lead to the argument that one appropriate response to the migration and climate change nexus would be to actively facilitate migration, with one of the positive effects related to this being a decrease in forced migration movements, which are more harmful for all of the actors involved. In more general terms (not specifically related to the migration and climate change nexus), this is a discourse for which IOM is known and has been heavily criticised (Georgi, 2010).

Episode 12: Sendai Framework for Disaster Risk Reduction – a policy home for work on disaster displacement

The Sendai Framework for Disaster Risk Reduction (hereafter the Sendai Framework) that was agreed by states in March 2015 contains multiple references to climate change playing a role in exacerbating disasters and being an 'underlying disaster risk driver' (Sendai Framework for Disaster Risk Reduction, 2015: 4, 6). The forthcoming climate change negotiations were also mentioned explicitly, with interaction with the SDGs process and climate change negotiations presenting 'a unique opportunity to enhance coherence across policy institutions' (Sendai Framework for Disaster Risk Reduction, 2015: 11) and emphasis being placed on the importance of working together with institutions or intergovernmental processes focussing on climate change (Sendai Framework for Disaster Risk Reduction, 2015: 28(b), 47(d), 48(c), 48(e)).

The Sendai Framework also contains references to both displacement and migration. Migrants are identified as relevant stakeholders (Sendai Framework for Disaster Risk Reduction, 2015: 7) with whom local authorities should engage in disaster risk management (Sendai Framework for Disaster Risk Reduction, 2015: 27(h)). A further reference to migrants relates to the potential positive outcomes of migration: 'migrants contribute to the resilience of communities and societies and their knowledge, skills and capacities can be useful in the design and implementation of disaster risk reduction' (Sendai Framework for Disaster Risk Reduction, 2015: 36(a)(vi)). The inclusion of this paragraph has been praised by an IOM staff member as follows:

> [D]espite the political sensitivities that are often associated with human mobility issues, it clearly recognizes that moving can be a well-being and resilience option- and articulates the idea in quite some detail, for such a high-level document. (Guadagno, 2015)

The Sendai Framework also includes provisions relating to displacement, calling on measures for temporary shelters for people displaced by disasters (Sendai Framework for Disaster Risk Reduction, 2015: 33(j)), 'ensuring rapid and effective response to disasters and related displacement' (Sendai Framework for Disaster Risk Reduction, 2015: 33(h)) and promoting transboundary cooperation, with one of the outcomes being increased resilience to reduce disaster risk and thus also displacement risk (Sendai Framework for Disaster Risk Reduction, 2015: 28(d)). The nature of the provisions relating to displacement, emphasising the need to react to or prevent displacement, highlights an understanding of displacement as a negative, forced phenomenon. However, the provisions on migration, especially paragraph 36(a)(vi), are based on a (potentially) positive phenomenon. This highlights an understanding of mobility dynamics and terminology compatible with the dominant terminology also circulating in the discourses on the migration and climate change nexus.

The inclusion of both migration and displacement in so many provisions of the Sendai Framework has been hailed as a policy success, especially as it addresses a gap that was identified in the preceding Hyogo Framework, which had only referred to displacement in a very limited manner (UNISDR, 2005: 4 (ii)(i)). This may be down to the contentious nature of discussions surrounding human mobility, with displacement being one of the 'remaining contentious issues' that caused negotiations in Sendai to overrun (Kälin, 2015b).

The focus on disasters has led to a different constellation of advocacy organisations, with an absence in Sendai of particular personalities otherwise present at climate change negotiations. A key absence was UNU-EHS, which seems to have concentrated its efforts around the UNFCCC process. Other absentees were representatives from UNHCR and IOM who were key members of the Advisory Group involved in the climate change negotiations; in their place at Sendai were representatives from other divisions within these organisations (UNHCR Interview 1, 2015; IOM Interview 3, 2015). These organisations were therefore both represented, but their presence was not directly joined up with the climate change work.

The main actor present from the group working closely on the migration and climate change nexus was the Nansen Initiative.

This is not surprising, given the mandate of the initiative to look at cross-border disaster displacement. The initiative used the results from its consultations to bring knowledge to the process and push for the inclusion of displacement in the framework, for example by feeding information into the discussion during the preparatory stages in the run-up to the Senai conference (Nansen Initiative, 2014b). During the Sendai conference itself, the Nansen Initiative also held a side event featuring governmental speakers, emphasising its relationship with states (Nansen Initiative, 2015e).

During the Sendai Framework negotiations, the Nansen Initiative collaborated informally with IOM (IOM Interview 3, 2015) and other organisations. The intergovernmental nature of the Nansen Initiative is important to bear in mind here. While it "[fed its] outcomes into" various policy processes (Nansen Initiative Interview, 2015) the initiative actually works for states and cannot lobby as an organisation in its own right. However, this means that the Nansen Initiative can influence processes through its member states, which it did in Sendai (Nansen Initiative Interview, 2015). States affiliated with the Nansen Initiative, 'together with the International Organization for Migration and UNHCR, worked to introduce a series of draft texts related to displacement, migration, and relocation' (Kälin, 2015b). Walter Kälin credits negotiators from Bangladesh, Norway, the Philippines and Switzerland, the two founding states of the Nansen Initiative and a further two members of its steering committee, with their work in 'fighting hard and ultimately succeeding to get important language on human mobility into the Framework' (Kälin, 2015b).

Perhaps the most interesting aspect of the Sendai Framework for Disaster Risk Reduction for the emergence of the migration and climate change nexus is the way in which its agreement has been used retrospectively by advocacy organisations. The framework now features alongside the Cancun and Doha decisions as examples of international agreements justifying work in this area, emphasising the relevance of the phenomenon, and for the first time being used to back calls for a holistic approach to the migration and climate change nexus that includes different policy silos.

Episode 13: Sustainable Development Goals – overlooked, but perhaps relevant after all

Similarly to the Sendai Framework, the SDGs that were agreed by the international community in September 2015 have mainly been drawn on retrospectively by actors concentrating on the migration and climate change nexus in order to emphasise the importance and relevance of their work. However, in the process that led up to the SDGs being agreed, there was a notable absence of advocacy work on the migration and climate change nexus from actors that were not engaged with the process.

The SDGs are undoubtedly relevant for the politics of the migration and climate change nexus. Goal 13 of the SDGs is to 'take urgent action to combat climate change and its impacts' (United Nations General Assembly, 2015: Goal 13). The preamble to the document outlining the SDGs includes a reference to climate change, and the introduction describes climate change as 'one of the greatest challenges of our time' (United Nations General Assembly, 2015: paragraph 14). The document, again similarly to the Sendai Framework, also creates links to the UNFCCC process, acknowledging it as the primary international intergovernmental forum working on climate change (United Nations General Assembly, 2015: paragraph 31) and underscoring the importance of 'an ambitious and universal climate agreement' being agreed in Paris at COP21 (United Nations General Assembly, 2015: paragraph 32).

Human mobility is less solidly represented in the document. While the introduction recognises the 'positive contribution of migrants' (United Nations General Assembly, 2015: paragraph 29), the threat that the forced displacement of people poses to development progress (United Nations General Assembly, 2015: paragraph 14) and the intention to 'cooperate internationally to ensure safe, orderly and regular migration involving full respect for human rights and the humane treatment of migrants regardless of migration status, of refugees and of displaced persons' (United Nations General Assembly, 2015: paragraph 29), there is no overarching goal specifically related to human mobility. A sub-goal under Goal 10, reducing inequality within and among countries, does, however, state the intention to 'facilitate orderly, safe, regular and responsible migration and mobility of people, including through the implementation of planned and well-managed migration policies' (United Nations General Assembly 2015: Goal 10.7).

Therefore, similarly to Sendai, the two sides of the migration and climate change nexus are not explicitly linked in the SDGs but the presence of both in the same international agreement, and the negative impacts both climate change and forced migration are identified as having on sustainable development, means that arguing the relevance of the SDGs for the nexus is not a big logical leap.

However, since the focus of the SDGs was squarely on sustainable development and not primarily concerned with either side of the migration and climate change nexus, the absence of this issue is not a surprise. As a weighty and contentious document in its own right, any fight to include the migration and climate change nexus explicitly in the SDGs would likely have been unsuccessful. Particularly given the context of growing pressure and controversies surrounding migration and refugee flows more generally in 2015 with growing attention being paid to the so-called 'migration crisis' or 'refugee crisis' in Europe, the issue of human mobility was becoming even more prickly for discussions on the global stage.

Despite a lack of engagement from the Advisory Group on Climate Change and Human Mobility with the SDG process, the SDGs have been highlighted retrospectively in documents concerning the UNFCCC process (Advisory Group on Climate Change and Human Mobility, 2015a: 8). This has turned what was being treated almost as a non-event by the advocacy community surrounding the migration and climate change nexus prior to the agreement of the goals into a key international policy process, with great relevance for the nexus and a normative power that makes it worth referencing in advocacy documents. For example, the first page of an Advisory Group document making recommendations for the Paris Agreement highlights a number of decisions that align with its own recommendations: this list includes the Cancun Adaptation Framework, the IPCC Fifth Assessment Report, the Sendai Framework and the Protection Agenda of the Nansen Initiative as well as the SDGs. Here, the Advisory Group recommendations are described as being 'in line with Paragraph 14 and the outcome document of the Sustainable Development Goals of the 2030 agenda' (Advisory Group on Climate Change and Human Mobility, 2015c: 1). Therefore, the package deal of the different policy processes that have culminated in 2015 is taken to be an important combination for legitimising future work. According to one staff member from IOM,

> '[T]his builds up at policy level, also the fact that the SDGs recognise migrants and the fact that the DRR in Sendai recognised migrants, so we have now three key policy processes that were the key policy processes in 2015 to draw agendas for the next ten, 15 years that all, from our perspectives, have recognised special needs and strengths of migrants.' (IOM Interview 4, 2016)

Episode 14: Launch of the Nansen Initiative Protection Agenda – consensus on cross-border disaster displacement endorsed by 114 states

In October 2015, the Nansen Initiative process stemming from the pledges made by the governments of Norway and Switzerland during the 2011

UNHCR Ministerial Meeting to commemorate the 60th anniversary of the 1951 Refugee Convention culminated in 114 state delegations endorsing the *Agenda for the Protection of Cross-Border Displaced Persons in the Context of Disasters and Climate Change* (hereafter the Protection Agenda) (Nansen Initiative, 2015d). The very title of the Protection Agenda is interesting. Drawing on the gap in international norms identified in the Nansen Principles (Norwegian Refugee Council, 2011: 5, Principle IX) related to the cross-border displacement of people in the context of the disasters, this was the initial mandate set for the Nansen Initiative. However, in the title of its final report (timed for release shortly before COP21 of the UNFCCC where a new climate change agreement was to be negotiated), displacement in the context of disasters was joined by 'climate change'.

In the press release announcing the endorsement of the Protection Agenda, Walter Kälin emphasises the challenge surrounding the initial mandate, but also takes the consensus that the initiative has created around this type of displacement to signal a willingness by states to engage with emerging displacement challenges more broadly.

> Disaster displacement represents one of the biggest humanitarian challenges of the 21st century. Yesterday's overwhelming endorsement of the Protection Agenda shows that States are ready to work together to tackle current and future displacement challenges. The Agenda provides States and other stakeholders with an innovative and forward-looking framework for action. (Nansen Initiative, 2015d)

Walter Kälin also draws on the knowledge gathered during the Nansen Initiative's lifespan and the subsequent consensus that has been created to link forward to Paris:

> Let's not leave books on bookshelves. It is time to act and turn theory into action to address cross-border disaster-displacement. We have a historic opportunity to use the endorsed Protection Agenda as a guide and ensure that the issue is included in the Paris agreement. We cannot miss it. (Nansen Initiative, 2015d)

In its briefing document for the Paris negotiations, the Advisory Group also refers explicitly to the Nansen Initiative, dedicating a page to highlighting the Protection Agenda in a very short briefing document (Advisory Group on Climate Change and Human Mobility, 2015a:

6). The initiative is described as being 'complementary' to work being undertaken within the UNFCCC on human mobility and, in order to highlight this, the document also stresses the links between the Advisory Group and the Nansen Initiative: 'All members of the Advisory Group contributed to the Nansen Initiative and are feeding its findings and recommendations into work under the UNFCCC' (Advisory Group on Climate Change and Human Mobility, 2015a: 6).

Despite the displacement focus of the Nansen Initiative, it is clear that the initiative has been influenced by broader discussions that have been taking place surrounding the migration and climate change nexus, particularly the different types of mobility that are involved, with the Protection Agenda also engaging with different kinds of mobility following the tripartite differentiation anchored in Cancun. Disaster displacement is treated as a negative, forced phenomenon that 'creates humanitarian challenges, affects human rights, undermines development and may in some situations affect security' (Nansen Initiative, 2015a: 6) to which one solution is managing disaster risk and building resilience to prevent displacement, which could allow people to 'withstand the impacts of sudden-onset natural hazards and impacts of climate change' (Nansen Initiative, 2015a: 8).

This is a fairly predictable narrative, given the mandate of the initiative, but the Protection Agenda also engages with migration, employing the narrative used elsewhere in relation to the migration and climate change nexus:

> [M]anaged properly, migration has the potential to be an adequate measure to cope with the effects of climate change, other environmental degradation and natural hazards. Circular or temporary migration can create new livelihood opportunities, support economic development, and build resilience to future hazards by allowing migrants to send back remittances and return home with newly acquired knowledge, technology and skills. (Nansen Initiative, 2015a: 9)

This narrative came out of the consultations undertaken by the Nansen Initiative that

> '… from the beginning on made it clear that this [the mandate of the Nansen Initiative] would be too narrow and that unlike in situations of persecution or a foreign conflict, in disaster, climate change scenarios, you have much better possibilities to … avoid, avert, prevent displacement'. (Kälin Interview, 2016)

It is therefore a product of these consultations that planned relocation, conceived as 'a last resort' (Nansen Initiative, 2015a: 9), also became a type of mobility that the Nansen Initiative engaged with.

Finally, in terms of mobility dynamics outside of the tight mandate of the Nansen Initiative, the Protection Agenda engages (briefly) with the issue of internally displaced persons (IDPs). In the opening passages, the Protection Agenda recognises that 'most disaster displaced persons remain within their own country' (Nansen Initiative, 2015a: 6). However, the Guiding Principles on Internal Displacement are identified as a mechanism that already exist in order to protect IDPs, hence the existence of a normative gap surrounding cross-border displacement in this context specifically. IDPs are identified as people who, should they be sufficiently protected, could be prevented from becoming displaced across borders in the context of disasters (Nansen Initiative, 2015a: 9).

The Nansen Initiative generally, especially given the successful endorsement of its Protection Agenda by more than 100 states, wields a great deal of authority. The links that it has to members of the Advisory Group means that it is also well connected to the central, coordinated, advocacy effort aimed at the UNFCCC. Therefore, despite being restricted in terms of its ability to carry out concerted advocacy efforts due to its status as an intergovernmental initiative rather than an organisation in its own right, the Nansen Initiative has been able to feed into and influence this advocacy work. The key links between the Nansen Initiative, and both UNHCR and IOM, became visible during the Nansen Initiative's Global Consultation Conference in October 2015, where keynote statements were given by both Volker Türk, UNHCR's Assistant High Commissioner for Protection, and William Lacy Swing, IOM's Director General (Nansen Initiative, 2015c: chapter 6). Despite these close links, the initiative's intergovernmental make-up is also pivotal to its success. The ownership of states over the process, having fed into the knowledge creation process leading up to the Protection Agenda, is high, as is their exposure to the topics and narratives through participation in this process.

Perhaps the greatest contribution of the Nansen Initiative is therefore the knowledge it has collected, combined with an awareness of the issues concerned and the authority with which it conveys this knowledge. This has changed the nature of engagement with the migration and climate change nexus in other contexts (such as in engaging with state negotiators in the forum of climate negotiations), with more informed discussions being possible (IOM Interview 4, 2016). In this way, the Nansen Initiative has played an important role in feeding into the momentum behind the inclusion of human mobility in the Paris Agreement.

Episode 15: COP21 of the UNFCCC in Paris (December 2015) – returning full circle, ushering in another new era for the migration and climate change nexus

COP21 of the UNFCCC, which took place in Paris in December 2015, has been hailed by many as a turning point in climate change politics, because it marks the occasion when international climate change negotiations successfully culminated in a new climate change agreement to replace the expired Kyoto Protocol. Human mobility has not disappeared from the negotiation table since Cancun and has been a constant presence in draft texts and pre-negotiations leading up to the Paris conference.

Human mobility concerns survived the negotiations and, although they are not explicitly included in the core text of the Paris Agreement, they feature in the COP decision, which establishes

> … a task force to complement, draw upon the work of and involve, as appropriate, existing bodies and expert groups under the Convention including the Adaptation Committee and the Least Developed Countries Expert Group, as well as relevant organizations and expert bodies outside the Convention, to develop recommendations for integrated approaches to avert, minimize and address displacement related to the adverse impacts of climate change. (UNFCCC, 2016a: 49)

The absence of human mobility from the core text has not been viewed as problematic by those carrying out advocacy on the issue, "because there is a reference in the agreement to the WIM and then in the decisions this is detailed" and anyway, "now when people refer to the Paris Agreement … they refer to Agreement and Decisions, so it's not such a big deal" (UNHCR Interview 2, 2016). The issue of human mobility is therefore perceived as being part of the Paris Agreement (for example, an article published in the New York Times shortly after the end of the negotiations leads with the heading 'Paris Accord Considers Climate Change as a Factor in Mass Migration' (Chan, 2015)).

The creation of this task force represents a compromise position. In the lead-up to the conference, the proposal in the negotiating text relating to human mobility was for a 'climate change displacement coordination facility', which was situated under considerations related to loss and damage. According to the text, the coordination facility should have been in place to 'a. Establish measures for emergency relief; b. Assist in providing organized migration and planned relocation; c. Establish procedures for coordinating compensation measures' (ADP, 2015h: 37(a)(b)(c), 2015a: 76).

This proposal is very specific, going far beyond the vague commitment contained in the Cancun Adaptation Framework for Parties to undertake 'measures to enhance understanding, coordination and cooperation with regard to climate change induced displacement, migration and planned relocation' (UNFCCC, 2010: paragraph 14(f)), yet is sufficiently vague that the precise implications of creating such a facility are largely unknown and would have required large amounts of technical work to establish mandates.

The mood before the conference was generally that this proposal was not likely to be retained in this form. According to Koko Warner:

> 'My guess is that this facility is too specific ... it might be too specific to be in the core tiny tight legal binding agreement, but it's okay, it's often we overshoot in order to get what we really want. And so you might see a COP decision, you may see a COP decision with some text mandating that the Executive Committee of the Warsaw International Mechanism include the facility....' (Warner Interview, 2015)

Indeed, at the end of the day this is exactly what happened, with the task force on displacement being housed under WIM. Therefore, the previous junctures of the Doha decision and the establishment of WIM under the Cancun Adaptation Framework increase in relevance for the migration and climate change nexus with this text.

Interestingly, a very similar proposal had already been made in 2014 in a submission to WIM by the Advisory Group:

> The Advisory Group on Climate Change and Human Mobility suggests that the Excom's [Executive Committee's] workplan contributes to the articulation of the Warsaw International Mechanism by *establishing a suitable group (expert group, task force, forum) in order to advise the Warsaw International Mechanism regarding the impacts on, needs of, and solutions for populations vulnerable to climate change including those affected by climate change-related human mobility.* Such a body should include relevant climate change and human mobility experts including from governments, UN organizations, operational organizations, non-governmental organizations and research institutions. (Advisory Group on Climate Change and Human Mobility, 2014c: 1, emphasis in original)

Whether this proposal by the Advisory Group influenced the outcome of the Paris conference is impossible to tell. However, the proposal is so strikingly similar to the actual task force that was established in the decision document in Paris that a link between this text and the final COP21 decision in Paris cannot be ruled out.

Two particular aspects of this text can be identified as relevant for the future development of the migration and climate change nexus. First, the issue is housed under loss and damage, rather than adaptation. This is despite the fact that there was a concerted lobbying effort arguing that human mobility concerns should be contained throughout the text, with strong emphasis being placed on adaptation (Advisory Group on Climate Change and Human Mobility, 2015a, 2015b, 2015c). In retrospect, advocacy groups read the Paris Agreement and COP decision as allowing for considerations of human mobility under both the areas of adaptation and loss and damage, despite it being located under loss and damage in the decision:

> 'It brings back the adaptation dimension, it's about recommendations to prevent displacement so that's what we needed. So, I mean, we are not really picky about the fact that it's not in the adaptation article.' (UNHCR Interview 2, 2016)

It is also argued that human mobility considerations are not excluded from being considered under discussions surrounding adaptation, with the adaptation article in the Paris Agreement referring to the protection of people, resilience, livelihoods, opportunities and so on (UNHCR Interview 2, 2016), opening up possibilities for action related to human mobility. Given the anchoring of human mobility in the Cancun Adaptation Framework, which is not superseded by the Paris Agreement, this avenue is still seen as being very much open.

The second aspect to pull out from the wording on human mobility in the COP decision from Paris is that only displacement is explicitly referred to in the text. Given the emphasis on the tripartite differentiation under the umbrella term that has been dominant since Cancun, this is perhaps surprising. However, given the anchoring of the issue under loss and damage this makes sense. It has also been argued that this represents a deeper understanding of mobility on behalf of negotiators and state Parties (UNHCR Interview 2, 2016). It has widely been argued that the inclusion of all of these terms in the Cancun Adaptation Framework actually highlights a lack of understanding about what all of the terms refer to, leading to them all being contained in the framework (UNHCR Interview 1, 2015). However, now "they have a better idea", understanding that "migration, planned relocation is more prevention" of displacement, so just by including "preventing displacement" in the text, "they know they refer to everything now" (UNHCR Interview 2, 2016).

The focus on displacement can also be attributed in part to the Nansen Initiative, which had displacement as its focus but used the overall narrative of preventing displacement to introduce the other types of mobility (migration and planned relocation) included in this tripartite distinction. The increased prevalence of discussions concerning (forced) mobility generally throughout 2015 can perhaps also be pointed to as a factor leading to more awareness of the issue and the coexistence of different types of human mobility.

In the lead-up to the Paris negotiations, the nature of discussions surrounding human mobility is reported to have changed: there has been "an upgrade, upscale of how people are interested" in the issue (IOM Interview 4, 2016). A 'shift' is reported to have taken place and instead of fighting to have negotiators attend meetings on human mobility, state negotiators are approaching advocacy actors for in-depth analyses of displacement and migration in negotiating text and answers to specific questions, as well as engaging in prolonged dialogues about the issue at regular intervals (IOM Interview 4, 2016). This is undoubtedly related to the targeted and coordinated work of the Advisory Group and its regular presence at all of the COP meetings, to continued awareness raising from researchers, and to the Nansen Initiative's efforts to promote this issue.

3

A Spotlight on Negotiating Mobility in Paris: Ushering in Another New Era for the Migration and Climate Change Nexus

While much of the world was still preoccupied with scenes of people arriving at Europe's external borders in 2015 and the search for solutions to the crisis of migration that these scenes were widely taken to represent, in a setting that could not contrast more with the rawness of life and refuge being depicted in the viral images beaming their way around the world, negotiators from around the globe gathered in Paris for the 21st Conference of the Parties (COP21) of the United Nations Framework Convention on Climate Change (UNFCCC). The bureaucratic, meticulous and technical world of climate change negotiations was, however, being explicitly connected to these emotional images, amid warnings that climate change would be the 'Syria refugee crisis times 100' (Toles, 2015). The prominence of the topic of the large-scale displacement of people thus reportedly added 'an ominous, politically sensitive undercurrent in the talks and side events' in Paris (Chan, 2015). In a COP that was already being seen as highly relevant for the policy community on migration and climate change due to the large coordinated advocacy effort leading up to it, events playing out beyond the walls of the conference arguably brought even more relevance to this policy juncture.

Leading into the COP21, human mobility was already anchored in two UNFCCC texts agreed at high level.[3] The first mention is within the Cancun Adaptation Framework, where 'migration, displacement and planned relocation' (UNFCCC, 2010: paragraph 14(f)) features as an aspect of adaptation where more knowledge and understanding is required. The second mention of human mobility is in the Doha decision, which acknowledged work being undertaken to advance understanding of loss and damage, one aspect of which is 'how impacts of climate change are affecting patterns of migration, displacement and human mobility' (UNFCCC, 2013: 3/CP.18 7(a)(vi)). Therefore, the Paris decision adds to these two references, this time establishing

> … a task force to complement, draw upon the work of and involve, as appropriate, existing bodies and expert groups under the Convention including the Adaptation Committee and the Least Developed Countries Expert Group, as well as relevant organizations and expert bodies outside the Convention, to develop recommendations for integrated approaches to avert, minimize and address displacement related to the adverse impacts of climate change. (UNFCCC, 2016a: 49)

Proposals for governing human mobility in the lead-up to COP21

Before COP21, it was anticipated from many quarters that human mobility would feature in any global climate agreement adopted in Paris. This was partly due to the references to human mobility contained in the documents from Cancun and Doha, as well as the importance that was being placed on the issue for certain negotiating blocks. The continued presence of human mobility in the various versions of the negotiating text throughout the build-up to the conference supported the view that human mobility would at least feature in the negotiations, if not in the final agreement.

In a non-paper published in July 2014 summarising Parties' views and proposals for a climate change agreement, the migration and climate change nexus is not explicitly mentioned (ADP, 2014b). However, in a follow-up submission by Nepal on behalf of the least developed countries (LDCs) group, a proposal for an 'international climate change displacement coordination support mechanism' was included under the heading of loss and damage (Nepal, 2014: 4). This proposal then made its way into the following non-paper that was published in November 2014 incorporating Parties' submissions (ADP, 2014a). Leading into the conference itself, the final negotiating text still contained this proposal, including text on a 'climate change displacement coordination facility' situated under considerations related to loss and damage. In wording very similar to that of Nepal's 2014 submission,[4] the purpose of the coordination facility should have been to 'a. Establish measures for emergency relief; b. Assist in providing organized migration and planned relocation; c. Establish procedures for coordinating compensation measures' (ADP, 2015h: 37(a)(b)(c), 2015a: 76). However, this draft was still very much open to change; the draft decision and 'cluttered 31 page draft text' featured 'little consensus on any of the core elements of the Paris Agreement, and no overall sense of direction' (Savaresi, 2016: 17).

The proposal for the displacement coordination facility was very specific, going far beyond the vague commitment contained in the Cancun Adaptation Framework for Parties to undertake 'measures to enhance understanding, coordination and cooperation with regard to climate change induced displacement, migration and planned relocation' (UNFCCC, 2010: paragraph 14(f)), yet is sufficiently vague that the precise implications of creating such a facility are largely unknown and would have required large amounts of technical work to establish mandates. The mood before the conference was generally that this proposal was not likely to be retained in this form. According to Koko Warner, in a prediction uncannily similar to the actual Paris outcome,

> 'My guess is that this facility is too specific … it might be too specific to be in the core tiny tight legal binding agreement, but it's okay, it's often we overshoot in order to get what we really want. And so you might see a COP decision, you may see a COP decision with some text mandating that the Executive Committee of the Warsaw International Mechanism include the facility….' (Warner Interview, 2015)

During COP21

A series of draft texts were released over the course of the Paris negotiations (ADP, 2015b, 2015c, 2015e, 2015f, 2015g), which ran from 30 November until 12 December 2015. Until 10 December, the proposals related to human mobility that had been included in the pre-COP21 drafts were largely unchanged and a displacement coordination facility was still contained within the text. Progress was slow, and at the end of the first week the 48-page negotiating text still contained 'more than 900 square brackets' of text still under discussion (Savaresi, 2016: 19).

Between the final draft text that was issued on 10 December and the Paris Agreement of 12 December, two major changes to the text on human mobility took place. First, explicit wording concerning human mobility in the core legally binding Paris Agreement was removed. Second, the mention of human mobility contained within the COP decision (the broader text agreed at COP21) changed. In the draft text of 10 December, which was included under loss and damage, the proposal for a climate change displacement coordination facility disappeared and the focus was much more general, relating to knowledge generation and improved cooperation in work on climate change displacement (ADP, 2015g: 51(b)). This is a clear departure from the displacement coordination facility that had been proposed in previous versions of the text and is more in line with previous inclusions of human mobility in the UNFCCC. The final decision adopted takes up a middle position, establishing a task force to develop recommendations for averting, minimising and addressing displacement related to the adverse impacts of climate change (UNFCCC, 2016a: 49).

Table 2 charts the issue of human mobility throughout the different draft negotiating texts that were released, from the final negotiating text going into the negotiations, through to the final agreement itself and including the various working drafts that were released during the negotiations in Paris. In addition to charting the different wording used, the table highlights whether the text was contained in the agreement or the COP decision and under which issue area the text was included.

Leading into COP21, two distinct alternatives of wording were present in the negotiating text. First, a paragraph included in the draft COP decision mirrored the wording of the Cancun Agreement, calling on Parties 'to enhance understanding, coordination and cooperation with regard to displacement, migration and planned relocation in the context of climate change' (ADP, 2015d: 59). Option two involved the establishment of a climate change displacement coordination facility, which was to be tasked with assisting in developing arrangements for emergency relief and assisting 'in providing organized migration and planned relocation' (ADP, 2015d: 56). In this draft, the proposal for a climate change displacement coordination facility is also contained within the proposed text for the Paris Agreement, where the purpose of the facility is to 'help coordinate efforts to address the displacement of people as a result of the extreme impacts of climate change' (ADP 2015d: Article 5).

These two mutually exclusive alternatives are not just interesting from the perspective of migration, but betray a controversy in the loss and damage discussion more generally, which was a feature of the Paris COP (Dimitrov, 2016: 4). Option one contains a weaker version of work on loss and damage, more reminiscent of the pre-2015 status quo on loss and damage and written in more formal UNFCCC language, for example in opening by recalling previous decisions on loss and damage. The remainder

Table 2: Human mobility in COP21 documents

Date	Document	Issue area	Wording
23 Oct	Draft decision option 1	Loss and damage	'displacement, migration and planned relocation in the context of climate change'
23 Oct	Draft decision option 2	Loss and damage	'climate change displacement'/ 'organized migration and planned relocation'
23 Oct	Draft agreement	Loss and damage	'climate change displacement'/ 'displacement of people'
3 Dec	Draft decision	Loss and damage	'displacement, migration and planned relocation in the context of climate change'/'climate change displacement'/'organized migration and planned relocation'
3 Dec	Draft agreement	Loss and damage	'climate change displacement'/ 'displacement of people'
4 Dec	Draft decision	Loss and damage	'climate change displacement'/ 'organized migration and planned relocation'
4 Dec	Draft agreement	Loss and damage/ adaptation	'climate change displacement'/ 'climate change induced displacement, migration and planned relocation'
5 Dec	Draft decision	Loss and damage	'climate change displacement'/ 'organized migration and planned relocation'
5 Dec	Draft agreement	Loss and damage/ adaptation	'climate change displacement'/ 'climate change induced displacement, migration and planned relocation'
9 Dec	Draft decision	Loss and damage	'climate change displacement'/ 'organized migration and planned relocation'
9 Dec	Draft agreement	Loss and damage/ adaptation	'climate change displacement'/ 'climate change induced displacement, migration and planned relocation'
10 Dec	Draft decision	Loss and damage	'[…climate change induced displacement, migration and planned relocation]…[climate change displacement]'
10 Dec	Draft agreement	Loss and damage	'climate change induced displacement, migration and planned relocation'
12 Dec	Final COP decision	Loss and damage	'displacement related to the adverse impacts of climate change'

of the option one text 'invites all Parties to reduce the risk of and address loss and damage associated with the adverse effects of climate change' (ADP, 2015d: 54), as well as encouraging the strengthening of early warning mechanisms and risk management, deciding the continuation of the work of the WIM, requesting the Executive Committee of the WIM to develop guidance on comprehensive climate risk management and to establish a clearing house for risk transfer in addition to the article that includes migration (ADP, 2015d: 54–9). Option two, while also including the development of early warning systems and risk management, as well as guidelines on climate risk management and a clearing house for risk transfer, diverges from option one in including the climate change displacement coordination facility that goes far beyond the status quo of work on climate change migration. It also goes further than option one in establishing a 'financial technical panel' to be housed under the WIM (ADP, 2015d: 55). The proposal for a climate change displacement coordination facility is therefore introduced in the text as part of a package of far-reaching measures that would have moved the area of work on loss and damage far beyond the status quo. This placed negotiations on human mobility within one of the most controversial areas of the negotiations.

Both proposals were also contained in the first draft text released during COP21 (ADP, 2015b: 65), but subtle changes were made in the draft released on 4 December, where the Cancun wording was subsumed into the proposal for the displacement coordination facility to be contained within the Paris Agreement:

> A climate change displacement coordinated facility shall be established under the [Warsaw International Mechanism] [CMA] to help coordinate efforts to address climate change induced displacement, migration and planned relocation. (ADP, 2015c: Article 5.3)

In the bracketed sections of text, which indicate elements still up for debate, the facility is proposed as being under either the WIM, where work on human mobility was already located, or under the new Conference of the Parties serving as the meeting of the Parties to the Paris Agreement (CMA). Inclusion under the CMA would have elevated human mobility from a technical body working on loss and damage to a higher level, although this is likely to have been very controversial. The option for the COP decision text that had previously mirrored the wording of the Cancun Agreement had at this stage been removed, and the second option for a displacement coordination facility was the only remaining option (ADP, 2015c: 57). These proposals remained stable throughout the following two drafts, released on 5 and 9 December (ADP, 2015e, 2015f).

The deletion of the Cancun wording was then reversed in the draft text released on 10 December. Two options for the article of the Paris Agreement text relating to human mobility were included. The first option omitted human mobility entirely, while the second contained 'climate change induced displacement, migration and planned relocation' in a list of aspects of loss and damage associated with the adverse effects of climate change (ADP, 2015g: Article 5.2(f)). This wording had also returned to the proposed text for the COP decision, in a bracketed section of text as an alternative to 'climate change displacement':

> To [enhance understanding, coordination and cooperation with regard to climate change induced displacement, migration and planned relocation] [initiate a process of identifying arrangements, modalities and procedures to convene and promote work on climate change displacement]. (ADP, 2015g: 51(b))

Between 10 December and the Paris Agreement being released on 12 December, the text underwent further drastic changes. The text of the COP decision (which in the final text is the only explicit reference to human mobility) now established a task force (rather than a coordination facility) to work 'to avert, minimize and address displacement related to the adverse impacts of climate change' (UNFCCC, 2016a: 49).

The article of the Paris Agreement within which 'climate change induced displacement, migration and planned relocation' (ADP, 2015g: Article 5) had previously been contained remained in the final text, although this phrase (and with it the only explicit mention of human mobility within the core agreement) was removed from the text, being replaced with 'resilience of communities, livelihoods and ecosystems' as 'areas of cooperation and facilitation to enhance understanding, action and support' under loss and damage (UNFCCC, 2016a: Article 8.4(h)). Aside from the removal of the explicit reference to human mobility, the wording of this article has also been turned around, no longer listing aspects of loss and damage associated with the adverse effects of climate change in a negative manner, but instead looking to more positively list areas of cooperation.

Similarly to the Cancun Adaptation Framework and the previous draft of 10 December, the focus again seems to be on knowledge generation, something much softer than the displacement coordination facility, which suggested an active mandate, perhaps even working directly with mobile people. However, the step that is new is that a specific entity is established with the sole purpose of working on the migration and climate change nexus.

What's in a word? The importance of human mobility terminology in UNFCCC negotiations

Charting the use of different mobility terminology is not just of purely semantic interest, but gives an indication of the direction of negotiations and of the level of understanding of human mobility held by negotiators. Wording can also later influence what concrete measures can be taken and by whom, in an area of work dominated by mandates and questions of who has ownership of different areas. Here, the use of mobility terminology that does not match the tripartite distinction set out in Cancun is particularly interesting, considering it is the wording most commonly adopted by scholars and advocacy actors working specifically on this issue, with human mobility being utilised as an umbrella term, under which three distinct categories of mobility can be filed.

Although a nuanced view of human mobility is apparently contained within the Cancun formulation, which differentiates between different types of movement, the terminology is neither defined nor explained: the "UNFCCC Convention, it's still a bit unclear because you have migration, forced displacement and planned relocation. It doesn't really say ... what is what!" (IOM Interview 2, 2015). It has therefore been argued that the Cancun wording does not necessarily reflect a deep knowledge of human mobility and the corresponding terminology on the part of state delegations. The terminology was still 'widely misinterpreted' (UNHCR Personal Communication, 2015) and concerns have been raised that the differentiated terminology in paragraph 14(f) has actually been included because of a lack of understanding of the different terms on the part of states (UNHCR Interview 1, 2015) rather than the deeper understanding of mobility dynamics frequently touted.

The realisation that states did not necessarily have a deep understanding of the terminology being used in this area despite its nuanced portrayal in the Cancun Adaptation Framework has influenced the work of actors carrying out advocacy work in the context of the UNFCCC and the way they present the issues. 'Since Paragraph 14(f) is a basis for our work on human mobility and climate change it is essential for us to clarify what is meant by displacement, migration and planned relocation in all our submissions' (UNHCR Personal Communication, 2015). This has the result that "in our new submissions ... we are very explicit, so instead of saying 'to avoid displacement in the context of climate change' we say 'to avoid forced displacement, forced internal and cross-border displacement, in the context of climate change'"(UNHCR Interview 1, 2015).

However, there is a perception that now, given the exposure that delegations have had to the issue in the years between Cancun and Paris, and the concerted efforts of advocacy actors, "they have a better idea", understanding that "migration, planned relocation is more prevention" of displacement, so just by including "preventing displacement" in the text, "they know they refer to everything now" (UNHCR Interview 2, 2016).

Aside from a potentially better understanding of mobility terminology on behalf of state actors and negotiators, the Paris negotiations highlight the malleability of terminology related to migration; rather like a set of nesting dolls, terms can be opened up to reveal further terms nestled within them. For example, while 'human mobility' is the favoured umbrella term of advocacy actors (under which 'displacement, migration and planned relocation', the types of mobility identified in Cancun, can be filed), displacement has also functioned as an overarching term. When framed as an issue that needs to be prevented, displacement has been linked to migration and planned relocation, with the latter two functioning as potential mobilities that can be encouraged in order to achieve this goal. To put it simply, no matter which of these terms becomes the headline or whether some of the terms are not explicitly mentioned, advocacy actors have been able to successfully relate them to the other terms in their arsenal. Furthermore, as they do so they consistently refer back to the Cancun formulation.

Explaining change so late in the day

That the proposal for a displacement coordination facility did not survive the negotiations and enter the core Paris Agreement is no great surprise. In fact, what is perhaps more surprising is that it stayed within the negotiating text for such a long time, given how contentious the issue of human mobility frequently is for states. For certain constituencies, in particular some developing countries, human mobility is an issue of great importance, which they were "pushing very hard on", turning the issue into "a bit of a bargaining chip" (UNHCR Interview 2, 2016).

This also explains the option that entered the text on 4, 5 and 9 December for the wording on human mobility to be included under considerations on adaptation. Because some states (mostly industrialised countries) were apprehensive of the displacement coordination facility and the implications for financing that this wording could have led to, the proposal to include the text under adaptation was included as an alternative. However, it is also important to note that the alternative proposal was not simply a means to remove human mobility from the text altogether, underscoring the argument that the debate on human mobility has changed from *if* the issue is relevant to *how* best to include it.

The most drastic changes to be made to the references to human mobility within the negotiating text were made between the last draft text released on 10 December and the actual agreement on 12 December. This is the point where human mobility disappeared from the core agreement and the displacement coordination facility was reworded into a weaker, but equally ill-defined, 'task force' housed under the WIM. The rather last-minute nature of this decision was not accidental, with the issue of human mobility reportedly being saved until the end of the discussions due to its contentious nature.

> '[W]e realised that states didn't have the opportunity to discuss the displacement issue in the first week, [then in the] second week we were like, okay, they are really keeping that issue for the very end of the negotiations. It's because it was one of the most sensitive issues and all the very sensitive issues were kept until the very end.' (UNHCR Interview 2, 2016)

So during the first week of negotiations, which were held at the technical level, no progress was made on the issue of human mobility, with some delegations reportedly having been given instructions not to move on the issue until the high-level discussions the following week, due to the perception that making the first step towards giving in too early may have resulted in the issue being completely removed from the agreement. The negotiating text was then given over to the French Chairmanship to smooth and shorten the text. It was within high-level negotiations between 10 and 12 December that the issue of human mobility was finally broached. Unfortunately, these negotiations are held behind closed doors, meaning that it is extremely difficult to gain insights into how particular passages of text survive, what leads to particular passages being edited, or who is behind specific paragraphs. What is clear is that the migration and climate change nexus was still controversial enough to be saved for the culmination of discussions, but equally the phenomenon has become legitimate enough to survive these controversies not just in a reformulation of previous decisions, but with a decision that creates an entity mandated to carry out further work on the issue.

Since the negotiations where the migration and climate change nexus was finally broached were held behind closed doors, and the proposal for a task force was not contained in any of the negotiating texts leading into the Paris conference, it is extremely difficult to know where this proposal, and the wording for the article of the Paris decision establishing the task force, came from. However, in a 2014 submission on the work plan of the WIM, the Advisory Group on Climate Change and Human Mobility (hereafter the Advisory Group) made a recommendation that bears a striking similarity to the final text of the decision from Paris:

> The Advisory Group on Climate Change and Human Mobility suggests that the Excom's workplan contributes to the articulation of the Warsaw International Mechanism by *establishing a suitable group (expert group, task force, forum) in order to advise the Warsaw International Mechanism regarding the impacts on, needs of, and solutions for populations vulnerable to climate change including those affected by climate-related human mobility.* Such a body should include relevant climate change and human mobility experts including from governments, UN organizations, operational organizations, non-governmental organizations and research institutions. (Advisory Group on Climate Change and Human Mobility, 2014c: 1, emphasis in original)

While a definitive link cannot be made between this excerpt of text and the final decision made in Paris, it is possible that this recommendation influenced the proposal for a task force that was then ultimately adopted in Paris. Given the strong similarity, it is unlikely that there is absolutely no relation. The strong similarity also emphasises the centrality of the Advisory Group as an advocacy actor on the migration and climate change nexus, with decisions made within the UNFCCC resembling recommendations from the group. Even if a direct link cannot be made between the recommendations and final decisions, the Advisory Group's discourse is being reproduced.

Although still contentious as an issue and for this reason kept until the end of the negotiations in Paris, a shift was reported at COP21 in terms of how discussions related to the migration and climate change nexus were carried out. For advocacy actors, the agenda-setting work of the previous years had been completed and discussions in the setting of international climate change negotiations had mainly circled around *how* to include human mobility as opposed to *if* it should be included at all (UNHCR Interview 2, 2016; IOM Interview 4, 2016).

Caught up in contention: wider debates surrounding loss and damage

In order to understand the particular controversy of human mobility in the climate change negotiations, it is necessary to step back slightly to consider where the issue is situated within the climate change negotiations. This involves turning in particular to the politics of loss and damage and where it sits in relation to adaptation. As Figure 1 illustrates, policy making on the migration and climate change nexus within the UNFCCC cannot be separated from developments related to loss and damage, a UNFCCC work stream where migration has occupied a dominant position (Mayer, 2016a). This also highlights the importance of digging beyond the high-level agreements made at the COPs of the UNFCCC, to the work that takes place between these meetings by a variety of entities constituted under the UNFCCC. While, prior to the Paris Agreement, the migration and climate change nexus has only been linked to loss and damage once in a high-level document, the decision of the Doha COP18 (UNFCCC, 2013: 3/CP.18 7(a)(vi)), there are other institutional developments in loss and damage that are highly relevant. For example, 'migration, displacement and human mobility' also features in the WIM work programme (SBSTA and SBI, 2014: Annex II, Action Area 6), with the establishment of the mechanism stemming from a mandate from COP19 in Warsaw, which in turn referred to the Doha decision in setting out the issues to be included in the work programme (UNFCCC, 2014: 2/CP.19, paragraph 9). This work plan was then further endorsed by the final COP before the Paris negotiations, in Lima in 2014 (SBSTA and SBI, 2014).

Therefore, it is not simply the Doha and Paris decisions that link the migration and climate change nexus to loss and damage; rather, this link is institutionally much deeper. Loss and damage has been broadly defined (not without contention) by the UNFCCC Secretariat in a literature review as 'the actual and/or potential manifestation of impacts associated with climate change in developing countries that negatively affect human and natural systems' (UNFCCC, 2012: paragraph 2). However, an official definition does not exist and therefore space for different interpretations of the concept of loss and damage, and contestation between different competing terms, is created, even in the highly technical and bureaucratic forum of the UNFCCC. Swenja Surminski and Ana Lopez identify two dominant dimensions that are at play when framing the concept of loss and damage: 'the technical concept, which looks at tools and processes to assess and manage risks, and the political dimension, where boundaries to climate adaptation, compensation and equity play a role' (Surminski and Lopez, 2015: 269).

Figure 1: Human mobility and loss and damage at the UNFCCC: from Cancun to Paris

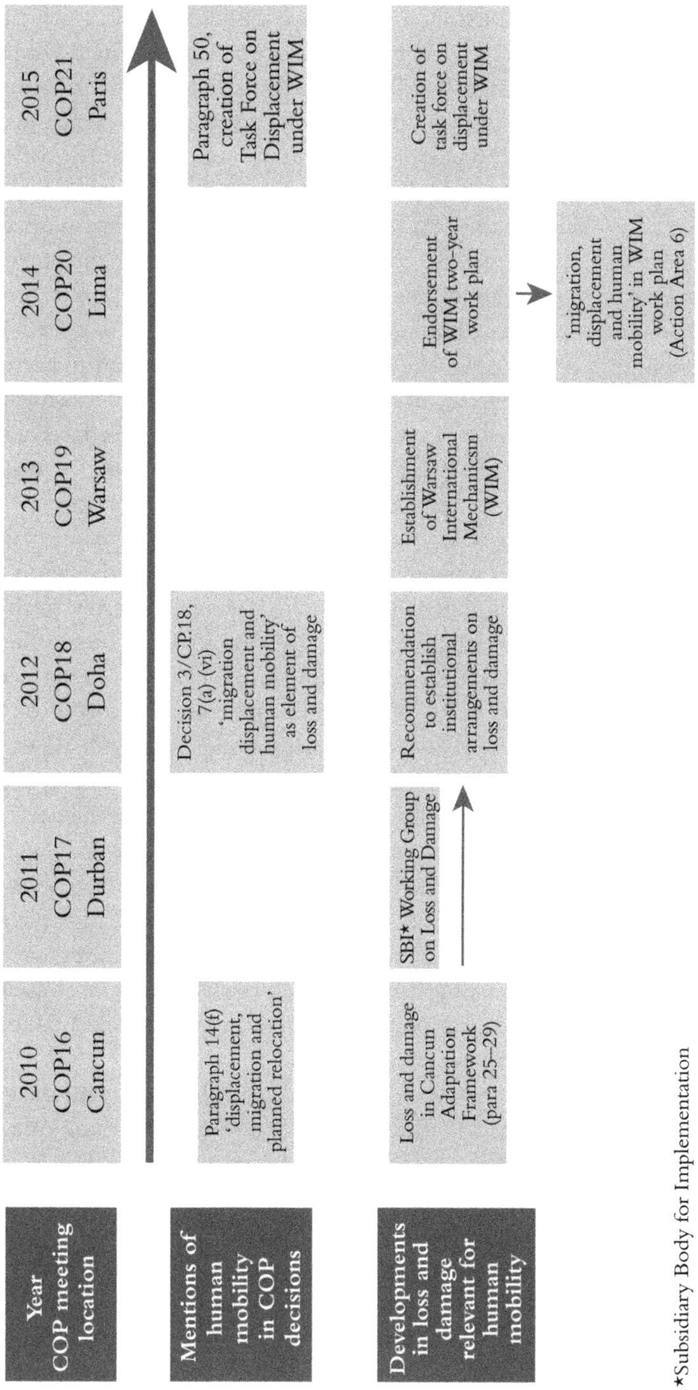

Year COP meeting location	2010 COP16 Cancun	2011 COP17 Durban	2012 COP18 Doha	2013 COP19 Warsaw	2014 COP20 Lima	2015 COP21 Paris
Mentions of human mobility in COP decisions	Paragraph 14(f) 'displacement, migration and planned relocation'		Decision 3/CP.18, 7(a) (vi) 'migration displacement and human mobility' as element of loss and damage			Paragraph 50, creation of Task Force on Displacement under WIM
Developments in loss and damage relevant for human mobility	Loss and damage in Cancun Adaptation Framework (para 25–29)	SBI* Working Group on Loss and Damage	Recommendation to establish institutional arrangements on loss and damage	Establishment of Warsaw International Mechanism (WIM)	Endorsement of WIM two-year work plan	Creation of task force on displacement under WIM

'migration, displacement and human mobility' in WIM work plan (Action Area 6)

*Subsidiary Body for Implementation

Both of these dimensions have had important effects on how the migration and climate change nexus can be conceptualised. When loss and damage is treated as a political issue, migration has frequently been used as a warning flare, an issue that signals in human terms the gravity of the losses and damages that are accompanying and will increasingly accompany climate change. The conceptualisation of migration in the context of climate change as part of loss and damage necessitates an extension of previous discourses beyond the way that migration fits together with climate change mitigation and adaptation. One of the most dominant narratives on migration and climate change is that (forced) migration is something to be prevented through mitigation of climate change. When adaptation is brought into play, the central narrative is based on an understanding that climate change mitigation will not be completely successful and that people will have to adapt to new situations caused by the effects of climate change; here the narrative that migration may be a useful adaptation strategy becomes a discursive possibility. However, the concept of loss and damage, understood here most plainly as 'the impacts of climate change that are not avoided through mitigation and adaptation efforts' (Roberts and Pelling, 2018: 4), takes this narrative one step further; it is no longer only mitigation but also adaptation that will be insufficient to prevent adverse impacts associated with climate change. For the migration and climate change nexus, this implies the consideration of unwanted movements that are non-preventable (or in any case have not been prevented), forced in nature, and caused by the negative effects of climate change. It is here that the migration and climate change nexus connects with the political discourse around loss and damage that has 'heightened discussions on historical responsibility, liability and compensation and as such is highly political' (Roberts and Pelling, 2018: 5). Therefore, at least in this political discursive framing, the loss and damage conversation opens up space for responsibility, liability and compensation to be considered in relation to unwanted but non-preventable human mobility taking place in the context of climate change.

This discussion is, however, light years apart from the technical concept of loss and damage identified by Swenja Surminski and Ana Lopez (Surminski and Lopez, 2015), which is bureaucratic, technical and tied into the complex layers of previous UNFCCC decisions. At this point, it has to be remembered that discussions around loss and damage have been, and continue to be, anything but straightforward. The main point of contention surrounds the placement and purpose of the issue of loss and damage within the convention, a difference in opinion that was already present during the period between the Bali Action Plan (2007), when loss and damage entered the text of the UNFCCC (UNFCCC, 2008), and the

Doha decision (2012) that established a mechanism on loss and damage that was later to become the WIM (2013). In Warsaw, G-77 countries and China argued for the inclusion of loss and damage as a third pillar of the UNFCCC, joining mitigation and adaptation. However, most developed states were reluctant to allow this, as they feared it would lead to extremely difficult debates surrounding compensation, which they were keen to avoid given the potentially astronomical costs that could be involved, especially given the principle of historical responsibility (McNamara, 2014). Therefore, the loss and damage mechanism established in Warsaw was situated under the Cancun Adaptation Framework, to limit the interpretation of loss and damage possible.

As a result, although discursively often treated as such, loss and damage does not constitute a third pillar of climate policy in the UNFCCC but is instead subsumed under adaptation. The consequence of this for the migration and climate change nexus is that despite the situation of the issue within the WIM in the Paris decision, the situation of the WIM (and therefore this whole stream of work) under the Cancun Adaptation Framework (UNFCCC, 2014: 2/CP.19, paragraph 1) means that the issue cannot be entirely disconnected from adaptation. However, with the Paris Agreement's inclusion of loss and damage, the area of work has been established 'as a permanent feature of the global climate regime, which should open up space for, encourage and legitimate research on loss and damage' (Roberts and Pelling, 2018: 4). Article 8 of the Paris Agreement, on loss and damage, 'has tiptoed around' the most 'complex and contentious' issues on loss and damage (Savaresi, 2016: 24), recognises 'the importance of averting, minimizing and addressing loss and damage associated with the adverse effects of climate change, including extreme weather events and slow onset events, and the role of sustainable development in reducing the risk of loss and damage' (UNFCCC, 2016a: Article 8.1), and reiterates the institutional position of the WIM, which 'may be enhanced and strengthened' if Parties so decide (UNFCCC, 2016a: Article 8.2). Article 8 also sets out areas to be considered under loss and damage as follows:

> ... areas of cooperation and facilitation to enhance understanding, action and support may include:
> (a) Early warning systems;
> (b) Emergency preparedness;
> (c) Slow onset events;
> (d) Events that may involve irreversible and permanent loss and damage;
> (e) Comprehensive risk assessment and management;

(f) Risk insurance facilities, climate risk pooling and other insurance solutions;

(g) Non-economic losses;

(h) Resilience of communities, livelihoods and ecosystems. (UNFCCC, 2016a: Article 8.3)

These articles are of great importance for the sedimentation of loss and damage as an area of work in the UNFCCC. Furthermore, although not constituting a definition of loss and damage, Article 8 of the Paris Agreement provides a stable reference point of different elements that are considered as part of a loss and damage agenda.

The second axis of contention concerns the connected issues of compensation and liability. Already in the discussions that took place between Bali and Warsaw, 'any association or mention of compensation or liability for such loss and damage was a cause for discomfort for industrialized countries' (Warner and Zakieldeen, 2011: 3). In the constitution of the WIM, this discomfort won out and there is no mechanism for allocating responsibility, and therefore no mechanism for triggering compensatory action, included in the WIM. This holds the mechanism, and therefore the actual practical considerations being made in regard to loss and damage within the institutional set-up of the UNFCCC, at the mercy of voluntary donor contributions rather than any compensatory action based on attribution and historical responsibility.

For this reason, it is important to distinguish between the politics of loss and damage in a broader sense, where debates regarding compensation and historical responsibility are lively, and discussions on loss and damage playing out within the strict parameters of the WIM. This position is emphasised in the Paris Agreement, with the COP decision containing a caveat by which the Parties agree that 'Article 8 of the Agreement [the provisions on loss and damage] does not involve or provide a basis for any liability or compensation' (UNFCCC, 2016a: 51). Again, to return to the migration and climate change nexus, this has a knock-on effect. The situation of the nexus within the issue area of loss and damage (specifically the WIM) closes down the potential for technical discussions, recommendations and solutions to revolve around liability and compensation. This is at odds with the political discourse on loss and damage and the way that forced migration in particular is considered within it. Moreover, it not only restricts the potential for the outputs of the WIM on migration and climate change, but also limits the discourse as a whole. The UNFCCC is a strong, normative influence that has wide-reaching consequences on how climate change is conceptualised and acted on beyond the remit of international negotiations. Therefore, the restriction of UNFCCC-related outputs on migration in the context of climate change to exclude liability and compensation, a restriction that is largely invisible from the outside without tracing the contentious story of loss and damage and the institutional history of the UNFCCC, may have knock-on effects on policy making taking place in other fora as well as on the discourse more broadly.

The provisions on human mobility, and the Paris Agreement as a whole situated in relation to previous decisions of the UNFCCC, therefore orient human mobility in somewhat of a middle ground between adaptation and loss and damage. Discursively, the issue has moved beyond adaptation, encompassing recognition that mitigation and adaptation efforts will not be sufficient to prevent losses and damages in relation to mobility impacts of climate change. However, the discourse has not progressed in such a manner as to open up space to consider either allocating liability or providing compensation for those who, in the context of their climate change-related mobility, experience losses or damages. Indeed, many of the discussions that were taking place in the context of adaptation (such as the potential of migration as an adaptation strategy) have been slightly reframed and transported to loss and damage without changing substantively.

Ushering in another new era for the migration and climate change nexus

COP21 can be described as ushering in a new era for the migration and climate change nexus (Nash, 2018b). First, it marks the institutionalisation of the issue on the back of a direct decision made at a COP (in this case to establish a task force on the issue). This is not just simpler to follow than the circuitous series of decisions that have led to previous work on the issue (for example, the chain of decisions that led to the WIM work plan including Activity Area 6), but also gives a greater degree of visibility and legitimacy to this work and makes it much more difficult to remove it from future agendas.

Second, COP21 marks a shift in discussions surrounding the migration and climate change nexus within the UNFCCC context. Discussions surrounding human mobility have revolved around *how* to include human mobility in the negotiations and in agreed texts, rather than *if* they should be discussed by the UNFCCC at all. While the nexus remained contentious during the Paris negotiations, it held its place in the decision document and even during the negotiations any counter-proposals that were made were based around relocating the nexus within the text (from loss and damage to adaptation) rather than removing it altogether. This shows that the issue has become firmly fixed on the agenda, with its status as one of the societal impacts of climate change gradually moving beyond question.

Third, changes have taken place in the advocacy effort that has grown up around the migration and climate change nexus. The advocacy actors that have been working on the nexus have established a regular presence in UNFCCC fora, have become more coordinated, and have used their combined legitimacy in order to create one set of very dominant narratives on the migration and climate change nexus. The narratives that have been promoted by these advocacy actors have, at least in the context of the UNFCCC where it is very difficult to be heard if not a 'legitimate' voice, moved in the direction of hegemonic closure.

Fourth, the post-Paris era of policy making on the migration and climate change nexus is supported by a much greater weight of knowledge, coming from academia directly (supported by initiatives such as the COST Action Network), through research projects conducted collaboratively by academia and advocacy actors (such as the International Organization for Migration's *Migration, Environment and Climate Change: Evidence for Policy* project) and initiatives such as the Nansen Initiative and its widely supported Protection Agenda. The purpose of the task force included in the Paris decision to make recommendations furthermore functions as a starting gun for the process of officially drawing this weight of knowledge directly into UNFCC policy making.

While it is easy to be swept up in the feeling of progress resulting from the increased recognition of the migration and climate change nexus and the creation of a formalised entity as a focus for the work of the UNFCCC, a note of caution is necessary. Although among advocacy actors the UNFCCC has become unquestioningly accepted as the main stage on which policy making on the nexus is playing out, this assumption deserves to be called into question. The juggernaut of progress towards ever-greater inclusion of the migration and climate change nexus within the UNFCCC apparatus should therefore not be understood as self-explanatory. One point of caution is related to the accessibility of policy making; if the UNFCCC remains the main stage on which policy making on the migration and climate change nexus plays out, the small group of actors that possesses legitimacy within the UNFCCC context becomes extremely powerful because of its access to negotiators and official fora.

On a more fundamental level, greater take-up of the nexus by the UNFCCC is generally seen as a 'positive' step towards recognition of the migration and climate change nexus, making the policy 'successes' of inclusion of human mobility within the framework largely naturalised as such. On the other hand, it cannot be taken as given that the governance of mobile persons should be undertaken by an entity concerned with climate change, a standpoint that was argued in a lively manner in the run-up to COP21 (Bettini, 2015). This is a view that has also been put forward by advocacy actors coming from a migration background:

> 'I don't think that UNFCCC is the place to do policy on migration ... but it's important that us stakeholders on migration policy are able to have dialogue with UNFCCC and within the climate negotiations on migration.' (IOM Interview 4, 2016)

Despite the limits this perspective places on engagement with the UNFCCC, the climate negotiations have until now been the main site for negotiating mobility in relation to climate change and, unless the naturalisation of this forum as a suitable site for considering this issue is questioned and other perspectives and sites are introduced into more open discussions, it is quite possible that the governance of the migration and climate change nexus will remain firmly anchored in the territory of the UNFCCC.

Benoît Mayer, who has also questioned the WIM as the best forum for carrying out governance on migration, has identified one potential role for the work on loss and damage in relation to migration governance, namely 'to unveil many shortcomings in global migration governance, and it could play an important role in raising awareness of the need for more genuine international cooperation for the protection of the human rights of all' (Mayer, 2016a: 23).

One conceivable role for the continued policy making that is taking place in the context of the UNFCCC is therefore to highlight weaknesses in other areas, in particular migration governance, and inform debates taking place here. This being said, it would also be unwise to view migration governance as an unproblematic alternative stage for policy making.

4

From Paris to Katowice: Moving from Agenda Setting to Recommendations

This chapter continues the overview and analysis of the second chapter. The story is picked up at the close of the United Nations Framework Convention on Climate Change (UNFCCC) Paris negotiations, which, in the form of the decision of 21st Conference of the Parties (COP21), created a specific entity to work on the issue of migration and climate change and thus marked the beginning of a new era of policy making in this area (Nash, 2018b). This analysis covers the time period from 2015 until the end of 2018, when this entity – the Task Force on Displacement – presented its recommendations. Despite events from the UNFCCC both setting the scene for and closing this chapter, a marked difference from the first 15 episodes detailed in Chapter 2 is that the UNFCCC is much less the focus of policy making, with other policy fora also becoming important and actors that are new to the area creating new spaces for discussion.

Episode 16: Platform on Disaster Displacement – the Nansen Initiative mark two

After the launch of the Nansen Initiative's Protection Agenda in October 2015, there was a short break before the launch of the Platform on Disaster Displacement (PDD), the successor to the Nansen Initiative. The PDD was launched at the World Humanitarian Summit in Istanbul in May 2016 and, similarly to the Nansen Initiative, has an architecture that is built up around strong state participation. This is particularly highlighted by the fact that the Chair and Vice-Chair of the PDD are states that perform these functions for a term of 1.5 years before the roles are taken up by other members of the PDD's Steering Group of states. The Chair role was held first by Germany, with Bangladesh performing the role of Vice-Chair. In January 2018, Bangladesh moved into the role of Chair, with France becoming Vice-Chair. In June 2019, France moved into the Chair position, with Fiji taking on the Vice-Chair role. Further members of the Steering Group are Australia, Brazil, Canada, Costa Rica, the EU, Kenya, Madagascar, Maldives, Mexico, Morocco, Norway, Philippines, Senegal and Switzerland (PDD, 2017). It is interesting to note that Norway and Switzerland, the two states that were behind the pledges that established the Nansen Initiative in 2012, both continue to be involved, although have not yet taken on a leadership role. Due to its state-led structure, the PDD cannot be described as an 'organisation' in its own right, something that brings both limitations and strengths: "it is at the end of the day a state-led process and that gives of course quite a few limitations on what we can say and what we can do in certain circumstances, for example advocacy, but it gives us an enormous opportunity to influence policy processes" as well as to support these processes via member states (PDD Interview, 2018).

The PDD also relies heavily on the resources generated by the Nansen Initiative, in particular the Protection Agenda. Indeed, the establishment of the PDD is directly related to this agenda, with the PDD having been set up with the express purpose to 'follow up on the Nansen Initiative and support states in implementing the Protection Agenda' (PDD, 2017: 2). However, in a break from the architecture of the Nansen Initiative, the PDD is not temporally limited, suggesting a planned longevity for the PDD that was never envisaged for the Nansen Initiative and a sense of legitimacy for the area of work that justifies this move. This suggests that the Nansen Initiative has been successful in staking out this area of work and raising enough interest among states to support its continuation in a less temporary format.

The PDD is also broader than the Nansen Initiative, which focused on producing the Protection Agenda: "the Nansen Initiative had ... an objective around generating consensus, identifying what could be the principles and the practices to address these gaps and then the Nansen Initiative then formulates recommendations on how these gaps can be filled" – recommendations that were set out in the Protection Agenda (PDD Interview, 2018). In that sense, the Nansen Initiative was principally a pure policy process that "developed policy recommendations whereas the moment the Platform on Disaster Displacement is launched, it is actually tasked to support implementation of these policy recommendations" (PDD Interview, 2018).

The PDD has four strategic priorities: addressing 'knowledge and data gaps'; enhancing 'the use of identified effective practices' and 'strengthening cooperation among relevant actors to prevent, when possible, to reduce and to address cross-border displacement at the national, regional and international levels'; promoting 'policy coherence and mainstreaming of human mobility challenges in, and across, relevant policy and action areas'; and promoting 'policy and normative development in gap areas' (PDD, 2017: 1). These strategic priorities rest on two seemingly conflicting assumptions. First, the fact that knowledge and data gaps are identified suggests that there is still knowledge to be gathered on disaster displacement and that this is necessary for action to prevent, reduce and address it. Second, however, the strategic priorities suggest that sufficient evidence exists for effective practices to have been identified and that these can be drawn on in practice, as well as being used for policy and normative development.

Another striking element in the PDD's strategic priorities is the wording of the second priority, '… to prevent, when possible, to reduce and to address cross-border displacement …' (PDD, 2017: 2). This is reminiscent of the wording from the COP decision from Paris in 2015 that established the Task Force on Displacement, which was tasked with developing recommendations for approaches 'to avert, minimize and address displacement related to the adverse impacts of climate change' (UNFCCC, 2016a: 49). On the one hand, this is an example of intertextuality, with particular phrasings appearing in different settings within a discourse. On the other hand, this phrasing could also have been a strategic decision. The PDD was constituted after COP21, and therefore following this decision, but before the constitution of the Task Force to which this language refers. It is therefore highly possible that the PDD was aligning its strategic priorities to fit with the remit of the Task Force that was known to be forthcoming.

What is most striking about this alignment of the PDD with the central task of the Task Force on Displacement is that the PDD is not only concerned with displacement in the context of climate change, but also focuses on (cross-border) displacement that occurs in the context of disasters. This is the same focus that was staked out by the Nansen Initiative and is thus not surprising. However, the PDD prominently links its particular focus with climate change; for example in identifying the legal gap that justified its existence, it argues that 'people who are forced to cross a border in the context of a disaster *and the effects of climate change* have limited protection when they arrive in another country' (PDD, 2017: 1, emphasis added). Therefore, while maintaining distance from phrases such as 'climate displacement' by not drawing direct links between climate change and displacement, but rather through the proxy of disasters, the PDD distances itself from problematic discussions regarding attribution and the difficultly of drawing causal links between climate change and particular instances of human mobility. At the same time, the PDD has made the links between its work and human mobility in the context of climate change explicit enough to be able to move in this community.

Episode 17: Technical Meeting on Migration, Displacement and Human Mobility – pre-empting the Task Force

In July 2016, the International Organization for Migration (IOM) organised a Technical Meeting on Migration, Displacement and Human Mobility in Morocco with support from the Ministry of Foreign Affairs and International Development of the French Republic. The involvement of both the French and Moroccan governments linked the meeting to the Paris COP21 as well as to the COP22 that was due to take place in Marrakech in 2016. Although sitting outside the UNFCCC process, the meeting was closely linked to the work of the Executive Committee of the Warsaw International Mechanism for Loss and Damage associated with Climate Change Impacts (WIM). This meeting was therefore embedded in work that was already being carried out by the WIM based on the Warsaw and Lima COP mandates and at the same time looked forward to the imminent creation of the Task Force on Displacement.

Before the creation of the Task Force, the WIM was already carrying out work on migration under Activity Area 6 of its two-year work plan. The particular purpose of this action area was to 'enhance the understanding of and expertise on how the impacts of climate change are affecting patterns of migration, displacement and human mobility; and the application of such understanding and expertise' (SBSTA and SBI, 2014: Annex II, Action Area 6). The first activity set out for this particular area of work was to 'invite relevant organizations and experts to provide scientific information on projected migration and displacement based on projected climate and non-climate related impacts in vulnerable populations' (SBSTA and SBI, 2014: Annex II, Action Area 6, Activity a (AA6a)).

This activity was completed in May 2016 when stakeholders were invited to make submissions (United Nations Climate Change Secretariat, 2016), with a total of 69 inputs subsequently received from 15 organisations and 16 independent experts (UNFCCC, 2016b: 7). At a meeting of the Executive Committee in April 2016 (by this point 19 submissions from stakeholders had been received), the co-chairs proposed 'to organize a workshop/technical meeting with the interested respondents to the invitation under activity (a) of this Action Area, with the aim of synthesizing relevant information' (WIM, 2016: 4), which was realised by the Technical Meeting. Therefore, although organised by IOM, this Technical Meeting can also be seen as part of the work of the WIM.

The Technical Meeting also officially served the purpose of fulfilling Activity (b) specified in the work plan under Action Area 6, which was to 'invite United Nations organizations, expert bodies and relevant initiatives to collaborate with the Executive Committee to distil relevant information, lessons learned and good practices from their activities' (SBSTA and SBI, 2014: Annex II, Action Area 6, Activity b (AA6b)).

The meeting was designed

> ... to bring together the members of the Excom [Executive Committee], national policymakers and practitioners, interested respondents to the invitation under activity (a) of AA (6) [of the work programme of the Executive Committee], and relevant experts from different horizons with the aim of synthesising relevant information and make it available widely in line with the expected results of this Action Area. (IOM, 2016f: ii)

Knowledge gathered during work on these two activities was also being lined up to feed into the yet to be constituted Task Force on Displacement, with the Executive Committee also expecting the Technical Meeting in July 2016 to provide 'a set of initial inputs/recommendations to support the work of the task force on displacement' (UNFCCC, 2016b: 11).

The output of the meeting was a series of three synthesis documents of relevant information, good practices and lessons learned that were organised according to the three purposes of the WIM: enhancing knowledge and understanding (IOM et al, 2016); strengthening dialogue, coordination (PDD and UNHCR, 2016), and coherence and synergies; and enhancing action and support (IOM, 2016e). An additional document set out recommendations, including those on actions that could be taken by the Executive Committee in its future work (IOM, 2016d). The recommendations ranged from improving data sets and synchronising methodologies, to promoting multi-sectoral work across policy silos, enhancing the role of the Executive Committee, and ensuring that programming is inclusive and prioritises capacity building.

From this brief sketch, it is clear that the recommendations are not specific actionable points that are directed at a particular implementing agency, but are rather a wish list of sorts for the entire community working on human mobility in the context of climate change, ranging from knowledge production, through policy development, to concrete implementation. These recommendations also provide insights into the very epistemic community that is being imagined here, with recommendations being made that fit well with the expertise of many of the organisations already present and highly influential in the area of work. Furthermore, the recommendations specifically draw the Executive Committee deeper into the community, not just as a receiver of the knowledge that external organisations may be providing, but as playing a 'catalytic role' that should be further enhanced (IOM, 2016d: 7).

Episode 18: New York Declaration for Refugees and Migrants – a high-level reaction to perceived crisis

In September 2016, the New York Declaration for Refugees and Migrants was agreed at a high-level United Nations Summit (UN General Assembly, 2016). The Declaration was a response to large-scale movements of people travelling towards Europe during the so-called 'refugee crisis' or 'migration crisis' that included large numbers of people fleeing the war in Syria. However, the Declaration is broadly oriented, acknowledging various types of movement, as illustrated by its opening paragraph, which also recognises climate change as a reason for movement:

> Since earliest times, humanity has been on the move. Some people move in search of new economic opportunities and horizons. Others move to escape armed conflict, poverty, food insecurity, persecution, terrorism, or human rights violations and abuses. Still others do so in response to the adverse effects of climate change, natural disasters (some of which may be linked to climate change), or other environmental factors. Many move, indeed, for a combination of these reasons. (UN General Assembly, 2016: 1)

The Declaration lays out sets of separate commitments for refugees and for migrants, as well as the process for achieving a Global Compact for Refugees (UN General Assembly, 2016: Annex 1) and a Global Compact for Safe, Orderly and Regular Migration (hereafter Global Compact for Migration) (UN General Assembly, 2016: Annex 2). While the Global Compact for Refugees was to be developed by the United Nations

High Commissioner for Refugees (UNHCR), the Global Compact for Migration was to be achieved through a process of intergovernmental negotiations. The process of intergovernmental negotiations therefore suggested a more dynamic process with opportunities to influence the text of the second Global Compact. For organisations working to promote human mobility in the context of climate change in policy frameworks, this process combined with the hook already provided by the inclusion of climate change in the introduction of the New York Declaration to create an opportunity to engage with policy making on human mobility and bring climate change into discussions. This is a shift from the majority of previous work, which has been concerned with bringing human mobility concerns into policy making on climate change in the forum of the UNFCCC. However, it builds on the perspective of advocacy actors who are working with the dual aim of mainstreaming migration into other areas of policy making and inserting climate change into policymaking on migration:

> '[We work on] mainstreaming migration into … all these policy areas, very often at the international level, international processes, but also at the national offices, or at regional level, for the regional consultative processes, also. Then we do the opposite. We do integrating … climate, environment factors into our migration work.' (IOM Interview 2, 2015)

Episode 19: COP22 of the UNFCCC in Marrakech – the relevance of a non-event

Despite the attention that had been given to human mobility at the Technical Meeting in Casablanca in July 2016, in terms of human mobility the 2016 Marrakech COP22 of the UNFCCC was very much a non-event. The text of the Marrakech decisions did mention human mobility, however, encouraging Parties 'to incorporate or continue to incorporate the consideration of extreme events and slow onset events, non-economic losses, displacement, migration and human mobility, and comprehensive risk management into relevant planning and action…' (UNFCCC, 2017: 3/CP.22, 9) as part of a decision on the WIM. This decision did not alter the work being carried out on human mobility in the context of climate change within the UNFCCC: the anchoring within the work area of loss and damage solidified in Paris remained, and no new tasks were allocated.

There are most likely two main reasons for this lack of movement on the issue of human mobility. First, the Task Force on Displacement initiated in the COP decision from Paris had not yet been convened and further action was therefore already highly likely to be delayed until after the Task Force had completed its mandate and produced findings. Second, COP22 was very much concerned with the implementation of the Paris Agreement, which had been ratified by enough Parties in record time so that it had already entered into force by the time of COP22. In itself, the Paris Agreement did not contain all of the technical information necessary for its implementation and thus further work on the so-called *guidebook* for implementing the Agreement took priority. COP22 was therefore referred to as 'the implementation conference' (Trent, 2016).

In terms of the content of decisions, COP22 was a non-event for human mobility. However, this does not mean that the topic was entirely excluded from COP22, with side events on human mobility taking place throughout the meeting. Indeed, in one of the strongest showings of interest in the topic at any COP, a total of 20 side events centred on human mobility were identified by IOM as taking place throughout the conference (IOM, 2016a). The conference was therefore not only about implementation of the Paris Agreement; for the community of advocacy actors working around human mobility, the focus had also turned to implementation. The 'main goal' of people working on the policy level was therefore

> '… to evaluate states' frame of mind in terms of having this issue on the agenda. Are they ready to work on it? I think they are. I think the Paris Agreement actually put the issue of climate migration so high up on the agenda that now it's not even about discussing whether it is a good idea or not to do something about it but it's become almost compulsory to do something about it.' (IOM Interview 5, 2016)

The second goal identified by advocacy actors at COP22 was to "gather ideas about how you concretely implement programmes" (IOM Interview 5, 2016), therefore building on the perceived acceptance of the policy area and moving towards actions. The non-event of Marrakech was therefore uncontroversial but nevertheless important: despite an absence of decisions being made on the topic, human mobility was represented in the conference space, the position of human mobility on the COP agendas was solidified, and regardless of the content up for negotiation, continued attention was given to the topic. Furthermore, concurrent to the focus on implementation of the Paris Agreement taking place in the UNFCCC more generally, advocacy actors working on human mobility started looking towards implementation and focusing on the potential for concrete programmes related to human mobility in the context of climate change.

Episode 20: Constituting the Task Force on Displacement – a gathering of familiar faces

For human mobility, the most direct impact of COP21 and the Paris Agreement was the constitution of a Task Force on Displacement, although by COP22, a year after the Paris Agreement and the accompanying decisions, the Task Force was still nowhere to be seen. However, first moves towards the Task Force had already been made, with draft Terms of Reference being published in the context of the September 2016 meeting of the WIM Executive Committee (Executive Committee of the WIM, 2016) and being adopted into final Terms of Reference by the Executive Committee's following meeting in March 2017 (Executive Committee of the WIM, 2017).

The terms of reference did not contain any particular surprises, with the mandate of the Task Force being drawn directly from the Paris decision wording and being set out in the Terms of Reference as follows:

> The mandate of the task force, in line with 1/CP.21, paragraph 49, is to complement, draw upon the work of and involve, as appropriate, existing bodies and expert groups under the Convention including the Adaptation Committee and the Least Developed Countries Expert Group, as well as relevant organizations and expert bodies outside the Convention, to develop recommendations for integrated approaches to avert, minimize and address displacement related to the adverse impacts of climate change. (Executive Committee of the WIM, 2017)

The Terms of Reference also set out the composition of the Task Force, establishing the criteria by which members are to be selected. The Task Force is to be made up of a maximum of 14 members, with up to four members being drawn from the Executive Committee of the WIM (two of which are to be co-facilitators of the Task Force), with a balance of Annex 1 and Non-Annex 1 Parties to the UNFCCC[5] being represented. In addition, up to eight technical experts reflecting regional diversity, as well as one representative from the Adaptation Committee and one member of the Least Developed Countries (LDCs) Expert Group are to be included on the Task Force (Executive Committee of the WIM, 2017: vi). Specific criteria are also set out for how the technical expert members 'could be drawn':

a. Representatives from UNFCCC NGO [non-governmental organisation] constituency groups, with no constituency having more than one representative;
b. Representatives from intergovernmental organizations (IGO) [*sic*], that have been admitted by the COP to the UNFCCC process;
c. Any other institution agreed for inclusion by the Excom. (Executive Committee of the WIM, 2017: vi(14))

This constellation is striking in that it is entirely made up of groups that are already insiders to the UNFCCC process, with the only route for outsiders to the process to be admitted being a decision by the WIM Executive Committee. Although unsurprising given the institutional setting of the UNFCCC, a highly bureaucratic elite forum, this has significant consequences for knowledge within the Task Force, which will only ever be able to represent this partial position. Perspectives that are not represented within the UNFCCC bubble are likely to be excluded, with existing dominant voices continuing to reinforce their dominance in the discourse.

The first meeting of the Task Force took place in May 2017, with representatives of the PDD, IOM, International Federation of the Red Cross, United Nations Development Programme, International Labour Organization and the Advisory Group on Climate Change and Human Mobility (hereafter Advisory Group) attending, in addition to four members of the WIM Executive Committee and two representatives of UNFCCC constituencies. UNHCR was also represented remotely (Task Force on Displacement, 2017a: 1). Further underlining the elite nature of the Task Force, the first meeting of the Task Force was closed to observers, as per UNFCCC protocol relating to technical groups (Personal Communication, 2017).

At this first meeting, the work plan for May 2017 until December 2018 was agreed (Task Force on Displacement, 2017b). Twelve activities were set out, five of which were mapping exercises of existing policies and frameworks, activities and tools. A further three activities were concerned with providing overviews and analysis of existing data. The final activities were knowledge synthesis, preparation of summaries of outputs and the organisation of a stakeholder meeting and a second Task Force meeting to finalise its recommendations (Task Force on

Displacement, 2017b). The occasion for the final delivery of the recommendations was set out in the Terms of Reference as COP24, which was due to take place in December 2018 in Poland (Executive Committee of the WIM, 2017: ix).

A further striking aspect of the work plan was that the leads for all Task Force activities were divided between IOM, the Advisory Group, UNHCR and PDD (Task Force on Displacement, 2017b). Since IOM and UNHCR are themselves members of the Advisory Group, which in turn works extremely closely with the PDD, this concentrates responsibility for delivery of the Task Force recommendations in the hands of an elite few.

Episode 21: Finalisation of the MECLEP project – the culmination of the biggest research project to date

March 2017 saw the culmination of potentially the biggest research project that has been carried out to date, which had been running since January 2014. The project, Migration, Environment and Climate Change: Evidence for Policy (MECLEP), was funded by the European Union and implemented by IOM through a consortium of six university research partners (IOM, 2017). The stated aim of the project was:

> … to contribute to the global knowledge base on the relationship between migration and environmental and change [sic]. More specifically, it aimed to formulate policy options on how migration, including displacement and planned relocation, can benefit adaptation strategies to environmental and climate change. (IOM, 2017)

The comparative methodology of the project, which compared findings across the six research sites of the Dominican Republic, Haiti, Kenya, the Republic of Mauritius, Papua New Guinea and Viet Nam, was important for the goal of the research project to contribute to the global research base (and presumably move it forward). The comparison of findings from geographically and climatically diverse states imbued the research conclusions with a generalisability that is not present in smaller research projects. The sheer size of the research project was also an important marker of prestige.

The legitimacy of the project was also enhanced by the number of academic institutions involved as research partners. In addition to the research skills and capacities that these institutions doubtlessly brought to the project, the academic credentials of the institutions represented provided the research outputs with greater standing than would be associated with research conducted solely under the banner of IOM. Set against the background of IOM's self-branding as one of the biggest players in the area of human mobility in the context of climate change, the successful completion of such a prestigious research project is another feather in IOM's cap when it comes to expertise on human mobility and climate change.

The in-depth collaboration between IOM and the six university research partners is not only important for IOM, but for the field of climate change and human mobility in general, further solidifying the already close relationship between research and policy communities, intertwining the expertise of the two groups and producing knowledge products, such as the final project report, that cannot be easily assigned as either purely scientific publications on the one hand, or as policy documents on the other (Melde et al, 2017). Furthermore, it is likely that MECLEP will continue to reverberate around policy communities, with IOM deeply involved in processes such as the UNFCCC Task Force on Displacement and therefore highly likely to submit the findings of this report as evidence in policy fora and heavily promote it to a range of stakeholders.

Episode 22: OHCHR and human rights – a human rights heavyweight enters the fray

Following a series of resolutions on human rights and climate change that had become somewhat of a tradition of the Human Rights Council of the UN General Assembly (Human Rights Council, 2008, 2009, 2011, 2014, 2015, 2016), in 2017 the Human Rights Council resolution on human rights and climate change concentrated on the links between human rights, climate change and human mobility (Human Rights Council, 2017b). This was a significant development in terms of the international policy-making discourse on climate change and human mobility, as until this point the human rights perspective and the UN human rights apparatus had been conspicuous by their absence (Nash, 2018a). It is also interesting to note that two of the three core sponsors of the resolution (Bangladesh, the Philippines and Viet Nam) are also members of the PDD's Steering Group, making a link between the two state-led actors.

The Human Rights Council's interest in climate change and human mobility gave the Office of the High Commissioner for Human Rights (OHCHR), the UN human rights agency, the green light to work on this area. Indeed, it was the Human Rights Council resolution and its membership of the Steering Group that provided "two different things driving [OHCHR] to engage more on the issues of climate change, migration and human rights" (OHCHR Interview, 2018).

In its *Key Messages on Human Rights, Climate Change and Migration*, OHCHR emphasises the existing duties of states and the international community via various international human rights declarations and covenants, and links these to obligations to 'address the human mobility challenges created by climate change' (OHCHR, no date: 1) and in particular to existing 'affirmative obligations to take preventative and remedial actions to uphold the rights of migrants and address violations and abuse at all states of migration' (OHCHR, no date: 1).

Rather than proposing new legal routes within the human rights architecture such as a new treaty on the rights of people moving in the context of climate change, OHCHR uses a human rights perspective to join up disparate areas of work on human mobility in the context of climate change. According to one OHCHR employee:

> 'I think that we've pretty consistently tried to view these issues as linked and ... relative to the mandates of the High Commissioner, as figuring out how to mainstream human rights in these different contexts, sort of human rights policy coherence.' (OHCHR Interview, 2018)

This is not particularly surprising, given one of the central activities of the agency, which is leading 'efforts to integrate a human rights approach within all work carried out by United Nations agencies' (OHCHR, 1996–2018).

This effort to mainstream human rights by introducing a human rights perspective across all areas of work is highlighted in repeated references to both the New York Declaration for Refugees and Migrants and the process to develop the Global Compacts, as well as the work of the WIM and the Task Force on Displacement (OHCHR, no date: 1), which OHCHR has been engaging with (OHCHR, 2017b).

As mandated by the 2017 Human Rights Council resolution, in September 2017 OHCHR organised an 'intersessional panel discussion prior to the commencement of phase II of the intergovernmental process leading to the global compact on safe, orderly and regular migration, with the theme "Human rights, climate change, migrants and persons displaced across international borders"' (Human Rights Council, 2017b: 9). The objectives of the discussion were identified as follows:

- *To enhance understanding* of the relationship between the adverse impacts of climate change, human rights and international migration;
- *To identify challenges* in the promotion, protection and fulfilment of the human rights of migrants in the context of the adverse impacts of climate change;
- *To identify opportunities* for States, civil society and other relevant stakeholders to facilitate the protection and fulfilment of the human rights of migrants in the context of the adverse impacts of climate change;
- *To highlight the need* for international cooperation and assistance in responding to the challenges posed by climate change and migration, particularly for those most vulnerable to the adverse impacts of climate change;
- *To contribute to* relevant processes that address migration in the context of climate change, including the stocktaking efforts for the global compact on safe, orderly and regular migration and the work of the Task Force on Displacement under the United Nations Framework Convention on Climate Change (UNFCCC). (Human Rights Council, 2017c, emphasis in original)

After the intersessional meeting, a summary report was presented to the Human Rights Council and fed into both the Global Compact on Safe, Orderly and Regular Migration and the work of the WIM and its Task Force on Displacement (Human Rights Council, 2017d).

The second output linked to the 2017 human rights and climate change resolution is a report conducted by OHCHR, responding to the following passage of the resolution:

Also requests the Office of the High Commissioner to undertake research on addressing human rights protection gaps in the context of migration and displacement of persons across international borders resulting from the sudden-onset and slow-onset adverse effects of climate change and the necessary means of implementation of adaptation and mitigation plans of developing countries to bridge the protection gaps and submit a report on the research to the Human Rights Council at its thirty-eighth session. (Human Rights Council, 2017a: 12)

The formulation of this request is particularly interesting because of the parallels that can be drawn with the formulation of the Nansen Initiative back in 2012, which was also concerned with cross-border movements because of the protection gaps that were perceived as existing in this area (Nansen Initiative, 2013). Speculatively, this might in part be down to the state-led nature of both the Nansen Initiative and OHCHR, with concerns related to cross-border movements being easier to broach in these contexts than internal movements, which are often perceived as the preserve of states and where international action could be seen as encroaching on state sovereignty.

Where the OHCHR report departs from the mandate of the Nansen Initiative is in its inclusion of slow-onset events in addition to the sudden-onset disasters included in the Nansen Initiative, as well as the consideration of migration in addition to displacement. This may well be a lesson learned through the work of the Nansen Initiative, which, despite the narrow focus in its mandate, frequently drew forms of mobility other than displacement into its analysis and considered the interlinkages between them.

The link to the Nansen Initiative is further emphasised in the form of cooperation with its successor, the PDD, with OHCHR sitting on the PDD's Advisory Committee. Together with the PDD, OHCHR co-commissioned a report on the slow-onset effects of climate change and the effects on the human rights protection of cross-border migrants (Human Rights Council, 2018). An expert meeting had also been convened on the topic the day before the 2017 intersessional meeting (OHCHR, 2017a). The scene setting for the report is interesting, as the slow-onset effects of climate change are perceived as the new great unknown, taking the place of cross-border disaster displacement, which had been framed in a very similar manner:

> Global data indicates that the number of people displaced by sudden onset climate and weather-related disasters, such as storms and cyclones averaged 22.5 million persons per year since 2008. But such a figure does not account for those who move due to the slow onset effects of climate change, processes like sea level rise, salinization, drought, and desertification. (Human Rights Council, 2018: 2)

Given the scale of the statistics given for the 'known' problem, the potential of an equally great 'unknown' is sobering. In identifying the protection gaps in cross-border mobility, this problem is set out even more broadly:

The mobility – and immobility – associated with slow onset effects is a global phenomenon that will test the limits of international law and cooperation. Current international law is able to meet some of these challenges and falls short in other areas, leaving gaps in rights protection for persons who cross borders in this context. (Human Rights Council, 2018: 6)

Here, the inclusion of immobility broadens the statement out to effectively encompass the entire population, drawing both the mobile *and* the immobile into the discussion.

Episode 23: Stakeholder meeting of the Task Force on Displacement – re-weighting climate change and human mobility expertise

In May 2018, IOM and PDD co-convened a stakeholder meeting of the Task Force on Displacement, to discuss recommendations for integrated approaches to avert, minimise and address displacement related to the adverse impacts of climate change. The meeting was a chance for invited stakeholders who were not members of the Task Force (and thus unable to access the regular closed-door Task Force meetings) to provide input to the work of the Task Force and gain insights into the work that had been taking place. The dual purpose was reflected in the central goals of the meeting, which were 'to take stock on all areas of the TFD's [Task Force on Displacement's] work and on the implementation of its workplan' and 'to synthesize findings and to assist the drafting of recommendations by the TFD for integrated approaches to avert, minimise and address displacement related to the adverse impacts of climate change' (PDD, 2018).

The wording of this second aim mirrors the wording from the Paris COP decision and the Terms of Reference of the Task Force on Displacement that mandate the Task Force to deliver recommendations on 'integrated approaches to avert, minimise and address displacement related to the adverse impacts of climate change' (Executive Committee of the WIM, 2017: 5). The wording also serves to make the link between the meeting and the official work of the Task Force indisputable despite the meeting being hosted by Task Force members rather than the UNFCCC. Positioned within the rigid mandate-bound architecture of the UNFCCC, this is important for ensuring the legitimacy of the meeting within UNFCCC processes.

However, the hosting of the meeting by Task Force members rather than the UNFCCC and the meeting's geographical location near to Geneva, the centre for work by Task Force members and UN work on human mobility but not a traditional location for the work of the UNFCCC, also sends a decisive sign, shifting the balance in the weighting given to climate change expertise and human mobility expertise respectively. As a result, the stakeholder meeting became a more "horizontal meeting" (PDD Interview, 2018) than other formal UNFCCC meetings, providing a forum more conducive to discussion between Parties and non-Parties. The meeting therefore had symbolic significance in addition to being an opportunity to conduct substantive work on the tasks listed in the Task Force's work plan. The expertise of the organising agencies, as well as the extent of their networks, is emphasised in an IOM press release about the meeting:

> IOM, the UN Migration Agency, and the Platform on Disaster Displacement (PDD) are jointly hosting the stakeholder meeting on behalf of the UNFCCC Task Force on Displacement in Bogis Bossey, Switzerland. More than 60 experts from governments, regional organizations, civil society and international organizations in the field of migration and climate change are in attendance. (IOM, 2018b)

The designation of the attendant stakeholders as 'experts' emphasises the role of knowledge as a currency in policy making on climate change and human mobility. However, this knowledge is still to be understood as situated knowledge, with the processes of the hosting organisations inviting experts to attend the meeting putting them in a gatekeeping position, enabling them to grant people or organisations access to the meeting and thus make decisions (whether explicit or implicit) about which knowledges are admitted to the process and can feed into the recommendations.

Episode 24: Global Compact for Safe, Orderly and Regular Migration – another tool in the advocacy arsenal

In contrast to the New York Declaration for Refugees and Migrants, the final draft of the Global Compact for Migration agreed by states in July 2018 contains substantial references to climate change. The document is broken down into 23 objectives, under which a number of actions are listed. Under Objective 2, 'Minimize the adverse drivers and structural factors that compel people to leave their country of origin', is a sub-section on 'Natural disasters, the adverse effects of climate change, and environmental degradation' (Global Compact for Migration, 2018: Objective 2). Two of the following actions explicitly mention climate change:

(h) Strengthen joint analysis and sharing of information to better map, understand, predict and address migration movements, such as those that may result from sudden-onset and slow-onset natural disasters, the adverse effects of climate change, environmental degradation, as well as other precarious situations, while ensuring the effective respect, protection and fulfilment of the human rights of all migrants.

(i) Develop adaptation and resilience strategies to sudden-onset and slow-onset natural disasters, the adverse effects of climate change, and environmental degradation, such as desertification, land degradation, drought and sea level rise, taking into account the potential implications on migration, while recognizing that adaptation in the country of origin is a priority. (Global Compact for Migration, 2018: Objective 2(h (i))

Two particular aspects of these paragraphs are striking in the context of the longer genealogy of policy making on migration and climate change. First, the prominence of the paragraphs is notable, being included very early in the text and being given a separate sub-heading (this is the only place in the Global Compact where that occurs). When we compare the Global Compact with the Paris Agreement, where the paragraph on migration was included fairly late in the COP21 decision and not in the core legal text, this becomes even more striking. Moreover, climate change is much more prominent in the Global Compact than in the New York Declaration that initiated it. In the New York Declaration, climate change is only mentioned in the preamble to the text, while in the Global Compact a significant portion of the text is concerned with climate change. Second, the use of the phrase 'adverse drivers' in the objective itself is reminiscent of the 'adverse effects of climate change' wording of the UNFCCC, an interesting marker of intertextuality between the climate change and migration regimes.

Three further actions under Objective 2 fail to mention climate change explicitly, but concentrate on disasters, with relevant actions including the integration of 'displacement considerations into disaster preparedness strategies' (Global Compact for Migration, 2018: Objective 2(j)), the harmonisation of mechanisms at the regional and sub-regional levels to 'address the vulnerabilities of persons affected by sudden-onset and slow-onset natural disasters' through sustainable, rights-respecting humanitarian assistance (Global Compact for Migration, 2018: Objective 2(k)) and the development of 'coherent approaches to address the challenges of migration movements in the context of sudden-onset and slow-onset natural disasters' (Global Compact for Migration, 2018: Objective 2(l)).

The explicit inclusion of both sudden-onset and slow-onset disasters in these paragraphs suggests that disasters connected to the adverse impacts of climate change may also be considered as part of these action points. However, the use of the phrase 'natural disasters' jars with terminology used by the disaster (and disaster displacement) community. The avoidance of 'natural disaster' terminology is explained in one of the key documents of the Nansen Initiative as follows:

> While hazards are a force of nature, disasters are not natural. Disasters occur when a community, society or country is not sufficiently prepared to cope with the impacts of a hazard. In this sense 'natural' disasters have multiple causes, many of which are human made. (Nansen Initiative, 2015b: 12)

This poses the question of whether disasters that occur in the context of climate change, and are definitely not 'natural' given the anthropogenic actions that have caused climate change, can still be considered under this action.

Elsewhere in the second objective, references are made to investment in 'climate change mitigation and adaptation' programmes (Global Compact for Migration, 2018: Objective 2(b)) and, in an indication of awareness of policy processes that have been taking place in other areas, an aim to

> Promote the implementation of the 2030 Agenda for Sustainable Development, including the Sustainable Development Goals and the Addis Ababa Action Agenda, and the commitment to reach the furthest behind first, as well as the Paris Agreement and the Sendai Framework for Disaster Risk Reduction 2015–2030. (Global Compact for Migration, 2018: Objective 2(a))

This paragraph includes references to all of the other key policy processes that have been targets for advocacy actors working on migration and climate change, as well as the global agreements from 2015 that are frequently cited to legitimise work on migration and climate change. A final acknowledgement of a relevant process is citation of the Nansen Initiative's Protection Agenda as relevant recommendations from state-led consultative processes that could be used to address migration movements in the context of disasters (Global Compact for Migration, 2018: Objective 2(l)). Given the state-led process that led to the Protection Agenda and the continued participation of states in the PDD, this was not an unlikely reference. However, it is also important as it highlights the continued influence of the Nansen Initiative on this area of policy making.

Unsurprisingly, the Global Compact has been welcomed by actors working on migration and climate change, with IOM describing the document as 'an exciting and important achievement for the governance and management of international environmental migration, both now and in the future' (IOM, 2018a). The positivity is, however, tempered with realisation of the challenges of implementation:

> Yet the challenges of translating global policy into national and regional practices should not be underestimated. Environmental migration remains a relatively newly emerged topic, with little stocktaking and evaluation of the effectiveness of existing practices, especially those experiences that pertain to the most innovative commitments outlined in the GCM [Global Compact for Migration]. What is certain is that achieving the ambitious commitments set out in the Global Compact will be contingent on robust political will, adequate funding resources and successful development of pioneering coalitions of actors. (IOM, 2018a)

Despite the challenges, the Global Compact has already taken up a central role in the arsenal of advocacy actors, strategically refocusing and orienting themselves in relation to the new global agreement:

> '[T]he policy landscape has changed now in the sense that we have a new Global Compact for Migration ... that's going to be the big or new kid on the block or the game in town in terms of migration; ... it is the overall policy framework for human mobility or how states are going to deal with human mobility and international migration for the foreseeable future

and that means that we need to really position PDD in relation to the Global Compact for Migration so that is going to be a strategic decision, what does that mean for PDD to support implementation of the Global Compact for Migration?' (PDD Interview, 2018)

Episode 25: Finalisation of the Task Force on Displacement – making recommendations within the lines

The Terms of Reference of the Task Force on Displacement set COP24 of the UNFCCC in December 2018 as the occasion for the delivery of its recommendations, to be presented by the WIM Executive Committee (Executive Committee of the WIM, 2017). The Task Force therefore presented the Executive Committee with a report of its work in September 2018, inviting it to

> ... consider the information contained in the report, in particular the recommendations contained in Chapter III below, with a view to forward them for consideration by the Conference of the Parties serving as the meeting of the Parties to the Paris Agreement (CMA), as appropriate. (Task Force on Displacement, 2018: 7)

This invitation highlights the fact that the Task Force cannot unilaterally take its recommendations to the COP and that a filter exists in the form of the Executive Committee, although in practice, given the presence of Executive Committee members on the Task Force, this filter has been in place since the Task Force was established.

Showing awareness of the larger global policy agenda, including but also going beyond the UNFCCC, the Task Force sets its work against the following relevant international processes that it took into account when making its recommendations:

(a) The Paris Agreement;
(b) Decisions 1/CP.16, 3/CP.18, 2/CP.19 and 1/CP.21;
(c) The 2016 New York Declaration for Refugees and Migrants of the UN General Assembly;
(d) The intergovernmentally negotiated and agreed outcome of the Global Compact for Safe, Orderly and Regular

Migration (13 July 2018) and, in particular, commitments under Objective 2, 5 and 23;

(e) The final text of the proposed Global Compact on Refugees;

(f) The Resolution on Human Rights and Climate Change, of the Human Rights Council;

(g) The IPCC 5th Assessment Report;

(h) The Guiding Principles on Internal Displacement;

(i) The Sendai Framework for Disaster Risk Reduction 2015–2030;

(j) The Sustainable Development Goals of the 2030 Agenda for Sustainable Development;

(k) The Agenda for the Protection of Cross-Border Displaced Persons in the context of Disasters and Climate Change (Nansen Initiative Protection Agenda). (Task Force on Displacement, 2018: 4)

This is important because it creates a coherent policy agenda out of the puzzle pieces from different policy processes that all clustered around the 2015 flurry of international policy-making activity.

The recommendations contained in the report are broad, and are levelled at the Executive Committee itself, UNFCCC bodies, state Parties to the UNFCCC and other UN agencies and stakeholders (Task Force on Displacement, 2018: 26–37). As is to be expected from a highly technical UNFCCC entity, the recommendations of the Task Force are highly technical, and include proposals for extending the Task Force (Task Force on Displacement, 2018: 26); providing information on intended financial support (Task Force on Displacement, 2018: 27); creating synergies with other areas of the WIM work plan, including civil society, experts and affected communities, to compile existing knowledge and develop new knowledge in gap areas (Task Force on Displacement, 2018: 28(a)(b)(c)); and supporting developing countries in integrating displacement concerns into their National Adaptation Plans (NAPs) and Nationally Determined Contributions (NDCs) to the UNFCCC, mapping displacement risks, and providing technical support (Task Force on Displacement, 2018: 28(d)(e)(f)). There are also recommendations relating to general coordination, coherence and collaboration across the UNFCCC (Task Force on Displacement, 2018: 29), more concrete actions to help countries to develop risk assessments and data collection standards, and the mobilisation of financial resources for developing countries (Task Force on Displacement, 2018: 30, 31). The Task Force calls on the Adaptation Committee and the LDCs Expert

Group in particular to support developing country Parties (Task Force on Displacement, 2018: 32).

The recommendations to Parties largely relate to integrating displacement into current work or into work commitments in other fora, such as adopting and implementing national and sub-national legislation, policies and strategies, enhancing research, data collection and risk analysis, strengthening preparedness and early warning systems, integrating human mobility into NDCs and NAPs, protecting and assisting internally displaced persons, and facilitating 'orderly, safe, regular, and responsible migration and mobility of people' (Task Force on Displacement, 2018: 33(a)(b)(c)(d)(e)(f)). There are also recommendations for UN agencies and other stakeholders to continue to support efforts in finance, technology and capacity building, transboundary cooperation, in the development of good practice in the areas of risk, support and assistance to affected people, and in the application of legal and normative frameworks (Task Force on Displacement, 2018: 34(a)(b)(c)). Relevant organisations are also requested to provide the WIM Executive Committee with information arising from future work and to engage with bodies under the UNFCCC (Task Force on Displacement, 2018: 35, 36). Finally, the UN Secretary General is asked to consider steps for greater coherence in the UN system (Task Force on Displacement, 2018: 37).

The recommendations were well received by the WIM Executive Committee, and all made their way into its draft report for presentation at COP24 (Executive Committee of the WIM, 2018). On one hand, this reflects the expertise of the Task Force members in making suitable recommendations. On the other hand, it reflects the ability of Task Force members to stick to both the spoken and unspoken rules of the UNFCCC, only making recommendations that are possible within the highly regimented policy process within which they are operating. The only striking difference between the two documents is additional caveats along the lines of 'as appropriate and consistent with their mandates and work plans' inserted into the Executive Committee document (Executive Committee of the WIM, 2018; compare Task Force on Displacement, 2018: 30), in phrasing that is typical of the UNFCCC. The Executive Committee report was then passed without any major upsets by COP24 in Katowice (UNFCCC, 2019: 10/CP.24).

Perhaps of most direct interest for the analysis of policy making is the recommendation, prominently placed in the Executive Committee report, that the Task Force be continued (Executive Committee of the WIM, 2018: 1), to help guide the work of the Executive Committee in an advisory role as part of its five-year rolling work plan. This is important as it further concretises work on migration in the context of climate negotiations and, particularly if the Task Force receives an open-ended mandate, thus becomes part of the furniture of the WIM.

PART II

Deconstructing Policy Making on Migration and Climate Change

5

The Process of Naming: Deconstructing Terminology Used to Conceptualise the Migration and Climate Change Nexus

The second part of this book gets down to the nitty gritty of deconstructing the policy-making discourse on migration and climate change in 'an attempt to renew an acquaintance with the strangeness of the present against all the attempts to erase it under the necessary dialectic of reason in history' (Dean, 2010: 56). It takes the ideas and concepts shown by the episodes documented in Part I of this book to be beyond question, and holds them up to the light to examine their component parts, their links to other discourses and some of their productive effects.

It is in these chapters of the book that the analysis moves away from the chronologically structured analysis of episodes of policy making to analyse the construction of the 'phenomenon'[6] of the migration and climate change nexus and the people whose lives are being affected by it. This is closer to the classical domain of genealogy, which is concerned with identifying and deconstructing shifts, dislocations, contradictions and silences. This chapter therefore marks a shift in tone of the analysis, moving from the detailed documentation of episodes of policy making to deconstruction. The importance of the chapters in this part of the book is twofold. First, they highlight that it is not just particular events, decision documents or policy agreements that are relevant for the analysis of policy making on migration and climate change, but the ideas that are created and transported by them. Second, these chapters are a vital element of the critical approach that this book takes, distinguishing it from more instrumental approaches to policy making. The construction of migration in the context of climate change as a problem that requires policy solutions is not a given, but rather a process of construction to be interrogated.

On the surface, this chapter is concerned with language; what language is used to label the phenomenon of the migration and climate change nexus, and the quirks and discontinuities of this language use. However, this analysis also has a deeper level whereby, following one of the core ideas of discourse analysis, language is not a neutral tool by which to simply express pre-existing thoughts or ideas. Rather, discourse is both constituted by and *constitutive of* reality. Set against this premise, the analysis conducted here goes beyond a linguistic analysis (for instance simply charting, in terms of phonics, what terms are being used) to consider the ideational component (the meanings attributed to phonic components) that is central to an analysis of meaning making. Furthermore, the pairing of ideational components to phonics is not stable (Saussure, 1960), meaning that a core consideration of the analysis is discursive struggles that are playing out around migration and climate change.

Somewhat counterintuitively, the phenomenon of the migration and climate change nexus that is analysed in this chapter is both a nodal point in the discourse on migration and climate change and is essentially contested (White, 2011: chapter 1) in that a plethora of terms exist, with multiple meanings sometimes being attached to the same term or, conversely, multiple terms sometimes sharing the same meaning. In essence, despite the huge level of contestation that exists surrounding what the phenomenon actually is and how we should talk about it, the phenomenon is a vital central point for the discourse, which is built up around its (perceived) existence.

Therefore, while on the surface this chapter is concerned with language, it is actually also about performativity, 'that reiterative power of discourse to produce the phenomenon that it regulates and constrains' (Butler, 1993: xxi). Tangled up in the (re)production of language and visuals that adhere to institutional conventions for communication and the constitutive effects this has, is the role of the speaker in the discourse. Despite being the subject of this discourse, (potentially) mobile people are rarely heard in the discourse, especially in the realm of international policy making. The speakers are instead advocacy actors. It is their voices that are present in the discourse that is setting the boundaries of how it is possible to think about and understand migration and climate change.

Struggles to define the 'phenomenon' of the migration and climate change nexus

The nodal point of the phenomenon of the migration and climate change nexus is key to the discussions in this book, for without it the policy-making discourse on migration and climate change would not be possible. The construction of the phenomenon in such a way that is has become accepted as existing, valid and fixed in some way has allowed for the discourse to be reproduced and for policy-making endeavours to be undertaken. However, there is still a great deal of contention surrounding what the phenomenon is, with it meaning different things to different people. The result is that there is no single clear term that is attached to this phenomenon, with a plethora of language sharing the same discursive space. Equally, the different terms carry different nuances of meaning, which are also shifting as the discourse develops, or depending on who employs the term. This chapter analyses three different discursive constructions that are all prominent in international policy making, before turning to four additional concepts that are also occupying the discursive space.

Human mobility as an umbrella term, containing 'displacement, migration and planned relocation'

This particular tripartite formulation of 'displacement, migration and planned relocation' has become increasingly dominant since its inclusion in the Cancun Adaptation Framework, with human mobility being added to the construction to function as an umbrella term encompassing all of the different types of mobility listed. This particular usage of the terminology has been visualised by the Advisory Group on Climate Change and Human Mobility (hereafter Advisory Group), which suggests a clear and unproblematic distinction between the different terms (see Table 3).

Table 3: Advisory Group key concepts

Human mobility		
Displacement	**Migration**	**Planned relocation**
Situations where people are forced to leave their homes or places of habitual residence	Movements that are predominantly voluntary	An organised relocation, ordinarily instigated, supervised and carried out by the state with the consent or on the request of the community

Source: Adapted from Advisory Group on Climate Change and Human Mobility (2014a: 3)

In the documents analysed in order to write this book, this categorisation is never explicitly questioned, and the phrase 'climate change-induced displacement, migration and planned relocation' is overwhelmingly portrayed as representing a nuanced understanding of the 'phenomenon'. The explanations of this terminology given in advocacy documents are overwhelmingly neutral, conveying a feeling that this terminology is correct and uncontroversial: for example, '"human mobility" *is* an umbrella term that encompasses displacement of populations, migration and planned relocation' (Advisory Group on Climate Change and Human Mobility, 2015a: 2, emphasis added). This conceptualisation is not unique to the Advisory Group. For example, the Nansen Initiative has also used a strikingly similar explanation of the terms:

> ... displacement (understood as the primarily forced movement of persons), migration (understood as the primarily voluntary movement of persons) and planned relocation (understood as planned process of settling persons or groups of persons to a new location), are referred to in this agenda in generic terms as '*human mobility*'. (Nansen Initiative, 2015c: 29, emphasis in original)

Although by presenting the constituent terms as 'understood' in a particular way, here it is also implicitly suggested that other understandings are possible.

After a brief hiatus in the United Nations Framework Convention on Climate Change (UNFCCC), where work on loss and damage used a different formulation of 'migration, displacement and human mobility' (UNFCCC, 2013: 3/CP.18 7(a)(vi)), the Cancun terminology worked its way into the most recent work of the Warsaw International Mechanism for Loss and Damage associated with Climate Change Impacts (WIM), with the Task Force on Displacement using the phrase 'human mobility (including migration, displacement and planned relocation)' (Task Force on Displacement, 2018: 29). The wording was included in exactly this form in the WIM Executive Committee's report for the 24th Conference of the Parties (COP24) (Executive Committee of the WIM, 2018: 1(o)).

This tripartite distinction in types of mobility is woven throughout the whole of policy making on migration and climate change, anchored in its inclusion in the Cancun Adaptation Framework, which represented the beginning of a new era of policy making on migration and climate change. Documents prepared for the purpose of advocacy frequently frame the terminology in this context; for example describing terminology as 'in line with the terminology suggested by paragraph 14(f) of the Cancun Climate Change Adaptation Framework' (Nansen Initiative,

2015c: 29) or advocacy work as 'anchored in decisions of UNFCCC Parties to enhance understanding and action in the area of climate change induced displacement, migration and planned relocation (Paragraph 14(f) of the Cancun Decision 1/CP.16 and Doha decision 3/CP.18 paragraph 7 (a) (vi))' (Advisory Group on Climate Change and Human Mobility, 2015a: 2).

This terminology can draw a great deal of legitimacy from being anchored in the Cancun Adaptation Framework, an agreed instrument of the UNFCCC, and is as such particularly frequently reproduced in documents that are directed at influencing negotiations taking place within the context of the UNFCCC (for example, UNHCR, 2011d: 3; IOM, 2014g: 1, 2015d: 3; Nansen Initiative, 2014a). However, beyond this targeted reproduction, the categorisation outlined in paragraph 14(f) of the Cancun Adaptation Framework is also becoming an accepted system into which to file types of mobility taking place in relation to climate change. The subsequent popularity of this delineation of terminology in academic publications also makes visible the uptake of elements of the policy-making discourse by academia.

When used in this tripartite formulation, the three separate terms contained under the umbrella term of human mobility have relatively fixed meanings, roughly adhering to the definitions set out by the Advisory Group in Table 3. In a paper written in his capacity as Envoy of the Chairmanship of the Nansen Initiative, Walter Kälin set out the three terms as follows:

> *Displacement* refers to situations where people are forced or obliged to leave their homes or places of habitual residence, in particular as a result of or in order to avoid the effects of disasters triggered by natural hazards.
>
> *Migration* can be a positive measure to avoid or adjust to changing environmental conditions, for instance by strengthening the resilience of individuals and families through improved economic opportunities. However, if not properly supported, migration may further exacerbate the vulnerability and undermine the resilience of individuals and families by placing them in a more precarious situation than if they had stayed in their place of origin.
>
> The *planned relocation* of people within a country is a measure taken in different parts of the world to move people from areas where they would face a high risk of exposure to a serious natural hazard. However, because of the many negative effects associated with past relocation processes, planned relocation is

> generally considered a last resort after all other options have
> failed and community resilience has significantly eroded.
> (Kälin, 2015a: 2, emphasis in original)

What is striking about this tripartite distinction is that the terms are
not located along one scale, with one element differentiating all three.
The distinction between displacement and migration in this formulation
is based on the level of compulsion involved in movements, with
displacement being forced and migration predominantly voluntary,
to which Kälin adds a value judgement by arguing that migration can
be positive (implying that displacement is viewed as negative). When
this categorisation system is used, the degree of compulsion, whether
a movement is deemed to be forced or voluntary, is therefore of great
importance. This is despite the difficulty of actually distinguishing between
forced and voluntary movements. As set out in the document prepared in
advance of the Nansen Conference,

> The complexity of drawing a sharp distinction between
> 'voluntary' and 'forced' migration (displacement) spurred by
> environmental and development factors must be borne in
> mind. Motivation is a continuum, with 'voluntary' at one
> end of the spectrum, in a gradual transition to 'forced' at the
> other. (Norwegian Refugee Council, 2011: 18)

The importance of this criterion for differentiating between different
types of movement is therefore coupled with the difficulty of actually
pinpointing which of these categories movements can be allocated to.

In contrast to displacement and migration, planned relocation is
not defined by being located along this forced–voluntary continuum.
Although planned relocation is framed in this context overwhelmingly
as 'a last resort, only after other options have been reasonably exhausted'
(Nansen Initiative, 2015b: 38), generally as a 'measure of last resort'
(Beyani, 2011b: 17) or, through the lens of climate change adaptation, as
'a last adaptation resort' (Advisory Group on Climate Change and Human
Mobility, 2014b: 4), it is not clear to what degree this is anticipated
to be forced or voluntary. Rather, planned relocation is distinguished
from migration and displacement in that it applies to the community
level rather than the individual or the household, it is planned rather
than spontaneous movement, and there is a degree of involvement by
authorities (the state) in organising the movement.

The relative stability of the constituent terms when used in this
tripartite formulation is particularly interesting, given the relative fluidity

of these terms, especially migration, when used in isolation. However, in this formulation, it is also easier for meanings to retain some stability, as they are defined in being differentiated from each other and thus displacement and migration logically need to take on different distinct meanings. However, the coexistence of other meanings when used outside of this formulation points to hegemonic closure not having been achieved. Therefore, other meanings can be (and are) ever present. That other meanings are possible also suggests that other typologies of movement are a possibility.

Migration, environment and climate change, coupled with environmental migration

Although not describing the 'phenomenon' itself but rather the area of work surrounding the migration and climate change nexus, the set phrase 'migration, environment and climate change' was introduced by the International Organization for Migration (IOM), which has used the same wording to name the division within its structure that works on climate change. The phrase is utilised exclusively by IOM and has therefore emerged in documents published by the organisation since the issue area started to become an increasing internal policy priority.

The use not only of climate change but also of environment in the phrase highlights reluctance to enter arguments surrounding causality and the ability to attribute particular movements to climate change. However, the inclusion of climate change vocabulary at all marks a shift for IOM, because "at the beginning we were speaking of migration, environment and we were staying a bit away from climate change" but since Cancun "where there was migration in the climate negotiations in the Adaptation Framework, ... we have moved towards more and more inclusion of climate change language" (IOM Interview 2, 2015).

IOM's labelling of the 'phenomenon' of migration and climate change is not aligned with Cancun terminology; rather, the organisation uses the term 'environmental migration', which it claims 'can take on many forms: sometimes forced, sometimes voluntary, often somewhere often in a grey zone somewhere in between' (IOM, 2014d: 6). Therefore, while the IOM accepts the idea of the continuum described earlier, with displacement at one end (forced) and migration at the other (voluntary), it labels movement placed at any point along this continuum as migration.

The discursive struggle around the term migration is an interesting point of (quiet) contestation regarding the use of the Cancun terminology. In order to understand IOM's divergence from the Cancun formulation and the terminology that the organisation does use, it is important to understand the meaning that the organisation attaches to the term. IOM defines migration as follows:

> The movement of a person or a group of persons, either across an international border, or within a State. It is a population movement, encompassing any kind of movement of people, whatever its length, composition and causes; it includes migration of refugees, displaced persons, economic migrants, and persons moving for other purposes, including family reunification. (IOM, 2014d: 23)

Following this definition, a very different meaning is attached to the term migration than the one that has become fixed to migration in the context of the phrase 'displacement, migration and planned relocation'. Following IOM, migration does not refer solely to voluntary movements, but also encompasses forced movements that are separated out from the more voluntary forms of movement in the Cancun formulation as displacement. One interesting dynamic that IOM's particular use of the term 'migration' facilitates is for different perceptions of whether movements are positive or not to be allocated to the same term:

> IOM promotes the balanced message that, inherently, migration is not 'good' or 'bad'. Rather, the impacts of migration – when individuals and communities do not have any emergency plans or are not prepared – can, in some cases, increase the vulnerability of the individuals and communities. In other situations when migration allows for income diversification, for instance, it can constitute an adaptation strategy and contribute to building resilience. (IOM, 2014d: 6–7)

However, IOM's allocation of meaning cannot be viewed in isolation, as the different usages of the term interact. Elsewhere in the discourse on the migration and climate change nexus (which is in this case an anomaly to migration discourse more broadly), migration is often allocated a positive connotation. IOM's choice of terminology may therefore benefit from this more positive connotation despite its definition of the term being much broader and also encompassing more 'negative' movements.

Aside from the obvious deviation from a formulation of terminology that seems otherwise to be close to achieving hegemonic closure, one of the most interesting aspects of IOM's usage of the term 'migration' in relation to the migration and climate change nexus is that it is not consistent. Although IOM states in its most weighty report on the migration and climate change nexus that 'IOM considers migration in all its forms – forced, voluntary, circular, temporary, seasonal, permanent and return movements' (IOM, 2014d: 6), the next sentence states that 'we also acknowledge the increased use of "human mobility" within the international debates' (IOM, 2014d: 6).

It is perhaps not surprising that, having acknowledged this terminology, IOM draws on it in direct references to the UNFCCC processes and decisions. For example, paragraph 14(f) of the Cancun Adaptation Framework is acknowledged as bringing 'the notion of human mobility to international climate negotiations' (IOM, 2014b: 6). Another document states the following:

> Since the COP14 migration has gained visibility and support as one of the key areas of the human dimensions of climate change. Two decisions have recognized 'climate induced migration, displacement and planned relocation': Decision on adaptation adopted in Cancun 2010 (decision 1.CP/16 paragraph 14(f)) and Decision on loss and damage adopted in Doha in 2012 (decision 3.CP/18 paragraph 7 (a) (vi)). (IOM, 2015d: 3)

This excerpt is interesting, not just because the UNFCCC texts are misquoted,[7] but because of the primacy given to the term migration, despite IOM's acknowledgement of and indeed citation of Cancun's tripartite formulation. Although all of the types of mobility listed in the Cancun paragraph are included here, *migration* is the focus. Equally, the reordering of the elements of paragraph 14(f) in the quoted text places migration to the fore, putting emphasis on this particular term.

However, in advocacy work aimed directly at international climate change negotiations, IOM goes beyond acknowledging this terminology to actively employing it, with its Key Messages on Migration and Climate Change for COP21 being that 'climate change is a cause of human mobility', 'human mobility is an adaptation strategy to climate change' and 'climate change policy should consider human mobility' (IOM, 2015b). This move by IOM is therefore an appropriation of terminology other than its stated terms for talking about migration and climate change.

Even more interestingly, IOM is a member of the Advisory Group that so straightforwardly defines migration as 'movements that are predominantly voluntary' (Advisory Group on Climate Change and Human Mobility, 2014a: 3), which amounts to a contradiction in how meaning is allocated to the term 'migration' depending on whether IOM is operating as a standalone organisation or as part of a collaborative advocacy effort. Therefore, while IOM does not directly challenge the human mobility terminology from Cancun, the alternative meaning applied to migration in its work disturbs potential hegemonic closure around this term and the tripartite distinction under human mobility more broadly, indicating ongoing discursive struggle.

(Cross-border) disaster-induced displacement

Cross-border disaster-induced displacement is a phrase designed to refer to a sub-area of the phenomenon of the migration and climate change nexus and has come from the Nansen Initiative process. The Nansen Initiative emerged out of the Nansen Principles developed during the 60th anniversary year of the 1951 Refugee Convention and in particular the gap that was identified surrounding 'the protection needs of people displaced externally owing to sudden-onset disasters' (Norwegian Refugee Council, 2011: 5, Principle IX). Although this phrase does not refer to the majority of people encompassed by the broader terms circulating in relation to the migration and climate change nexus, it has nevertheless been identified as a valid area for inquiry due to the normative gap it is taken to represent.

Over the course of the Nansen Initiative, a slight change in terminology has taken place. At the beginning of the initiative, the purpose was stated as 'addressing the needs of people displaced across international borders by natural disasters, including the effects of climate change' (Nansen Initiative 2013: 1). Disasters have been defined by the Nansen Initiative (throughout the process) following a definition by the United Nations Office for Disaster Risk Reduction (UNISDR), whereby disaster refers to

> ... a serious disruption of the functioning of a community or a society involving widespread human, material, economic or environmental losses and impacts which exceeds the ability of the affected community or society to cope using its own resources. (UNISDR, cited in Nansen Initiative, 2013: 3, 2015a: 6)

Linked to this, the Nansen Initiative has also set out a definition for the term 'disaster displacement', which refers to

> ... situations where people are forced or obliged to leave their homes or places of habitual residence as a result of a

disaster or in order to avoid the impact of an immediate and foreseeable natural hazard. Such displacement results from the fact that affect persons are (i) exposed to (ii) a natural hazard in a situation where (iii) they are too vulnerable and lack the resilience to withstand the impacts of that hazard. It is the effects of natural hazards, including the adverse impacts of climate change, that may overwhelm the resilience or adaptive capacity of an affected community or society, thus leading to a disaster that potentially results in displacement. (Nansen Initiative, 2015a: 16)

One particular definitional issue where preliminary work by the initiative diverges from its eventual outcomes relates to 'natural disaster' terminology. In 2013, the kind of disaster considered by the Nansen Initiative was 'understood as one primarily caused by *natural hazards* even if human factors often exacerbate the impact of natural events' (Nansen Initiative, 2013: 3, emphasis in original). The document goes on to list examples of these disasters:

[T]he Nansen Initiative addresses natural disasters regardless of the cause, including geophysical hazards such as earthquakes, tsunamis or volcano eruptions, as well as climatic and atmospheric hazards like flooding, tornadoes, cyclones, and drought. (Nansen Initiative, 2013: 3)

Although in later documents, such as the Protection Agenda, the same definition of disaster is used, the term 'natural disaster' has been dropped. Now the Nansen Initiative refers to 'disruptions triggered by or linked to hydro-metrological and climatological natural hazards, including hazards linked to anthropogenic global warming, as well as geophysical hazards' (Nansen Initiative, 2015a: 16). The initiative also recognises that these hazards do not exist in isolation, arguing as follows:

[D]isaster displacement is multi-causal with climate change being an important, but not the only factor. Population growth, underdevelopment, weak governance, armed conflict, violence, as well as poor urban planning in rapidly expanding cities, are important factors in disaster displacement as they further weaken resilience and exacerbate the impacts of natural hazards, environmental degradation and climate change. (Nansen Initiative, 2015a: 6)

This evolution in terminology over the course of the initiative has been put down to criticisms that were levelled at the initiative by the disaster risk reduction community, which argued that disasters are not natural (but are rather influenced by a range of social, political and economic factors in addition to the natural hazard itself) and therefore this terminology is not correct (Nansen Initiative Interview, 2015). So although previously the initiative had referred to natural disasters "for ease of reference" and "even though we'd had it in a footnote, we stopped saying natural disasters and we talk about cross-border displacement in the context of disasters caused by natural hazards, including the adverse effects of climate change" (Nansen Initiative Interview, 2015). This particular phrasing emerged from trying "to really describe what we are talking about" and intentionally avoiding problematic terminology (Nansen Initiative Interview, 2015).

While there has been a change in the way the initiative talks about disaster, the focus on natural hazards that cause disasters was retained, partly because of the initiative's origins, rooted very much in the gap identified in the Nansen Principles. However, the decision to retain this conceptualisation of disasters was made purposely:

'I remember we had some short discussion about it when we started to conceptualise the initiative and one reason not to go into other kinds of disasters was the realisation that some of them really kind of create different challenges. I mean, the Ebola crisis is a disaster according to the definition the UN uses but that's certainly not the kind of disaster where you would promote migration as adaptation! So we just felt there are so many possibilities for disasters and they have very different characteristics and it really would be problematic to have too broad an approach and then get lost in differentiations and get lost in too much of complexities because already disasters caused by natural hazards are complex enough.' (Kälin Interview, 2016)

The Nansen Initiative has also developed a more detailed conceptualisation of the term displacement than is usually included when considered as part of the human mobility umbrella. This conceptualisation is illustrated in Table 4, where displacement is set out as being triggered by a hazard combined with exposure and vulnerability.

Given the focus of the initiative on displacement, it is not surprising that extra attention has been given to defining the term. What is notable here is that movement is not simply categorised as 'forced', but that this is broken down into different elements. The inclusion of a need to reduce

Table 4: The Nansen Initiative's definition of displacement

Displacement = hazard + exposure + vulnerability so, avoiding displacement means reducing:		
Hazard	→	Climate change migration
Exposure	→	Migration as adaptation Planned relocation
Vulnerability	→	Climate change adaptation Disaster risk reduction Resilience building

Source: Adapted from the Nansen Initiative (2015b: 12)

displacement and routes by which to do this in the definition backs up the conceptualisation of displacement as something negative and other types of mobility as preferential in relation.

The phenomenon considered by the Nansen Initiative has been limited to cross-border movements, despite the initiative itself recognising that 'most disaster displaced persons remain within their own country' (Nansen Initiative, 2015a: 1). The same document continues with the statement that 'however, some cross borders in order to reach safety and/ or protection and assistance in another country' (Nansen Initiative, 2015a: 6), which is the issue the initiative was designed to address. Despite this, the initiative has touched on forms of mobility other than cross-border movement (for example, see Nansen Initiative, 2015a: 9). According to Walter Kälin, this "came up through the consultations and it was actually not a problem to bring it in. It was rather a problem to keep it out because of what people felt" (Kälin Interview, 2016).

The terminology used by the Nansen Initiative is highly compatible with the 'human mobility: displacement, migration and planned relocation' set-up that has been so widely used since Cancun. Indeed, the initiative has been identified as building on the Cancun paragraph and uses a very similar conceptualisation of these terms to that of the Advisory Group: for example, 'Building upon paragraph 14(f), the Nansen Initiative uses human mobility to refer to three categories of movement (predominantly forced) displacement, (predominantly voluntary) migration, and (voluntary or forced) planned relocation' (Kälin, 2015a: 2).

The Nansen Initiative has been identified as also emerging as a result of Cancun paragraph 14(f) (as well as the events surrounding the 60th anniversary of the 1951 Refugee Convention (Nansen Initiative, 2013)), so this is hardly surprising. With the Nansen Initiative's successor organisation, the Platform on Disaster Displacement (PDD), continuing seamlessly from the Nansen Initiative, the terminology developed by the former is also being carried forward and is ever present in policy debates.

The field of discursivity

The phenomenon of the migration and climate change nexus, regardless of the way it is constructed, does not exist in a vacuum. Instead, discourses are inherently linked to elements outside of the strict boundaries of a particular discourse, and in turn to other interconnected discourses. The interactions with different discourses are important for allowing for contingency of meaning, which can change through these interactions. Embedded in an infinite number of discourses, a single discourse is as such only 'a partial limitation of a "surplus of meaning" which subverts it' (Laclau and Mouffe, 1985: 97) but which is 'the necessary terrain for the construction of every social practice' (Laclau and Mouffe, 1985: 98). Therefore, the field of discursivity within which the international policy-making discourse on migration and climate change operates should also be interrogated in order to provide more insights into the particular discourse itself. Given the 'infinitude' of the field of discursivity (Laclau and Mouffe, 1985: 100), it is impossible to completely consider every possible influence to the discourse. However, particular floating elements influencing the discourse are examined in this section and related back to the different formulations of the phenomenon of the migration and climate change nexus considered in the first half of this chapter.

The discourse of the UNFCCC: mitigation, adaptation, and loss and damage

The international policy-making discourse on migration and climate change has been particularly influenced by climate change discourse generally, and specifically the institutional context of the UNFCCC. This is perhaps predictable, given that the meetings of the UNFCCC are the main fora within which policy making on the nexus has continually been pursued. Three elements in particular are pulled out and analysed here: mitigation, adaptation, and loss and damage.

Mitigation is the founding premise of the UNFCC, referring to the realisation that human beings are causing dangerous climate change and the corresponding need to limit greenhouse gas emissions in order to prevent further climate change and the associated adverse effects. Mitigation is so central to the UNFCCC that it is the third Principle set out in Article 3 of the convention, which states that 'Parties should take precautionary measures to anticipate, prevent or minimize the causes of climate change and mitigate its adverse effects' (UNFCCC, 1992: 3.3). Mitigation (although not a word newly coined by the climate regime) has come to have a relatively fixed meaning when used in this context, with mitigation in discussions concerning climate change automatically being connected to actions to prevent climate change.

This meaning has frequently been mobilised in connection to the migration and climate change nexus, with the figure of the displaced person or the forced migrant in particular representing the 'human face' of climate change and invoked to add pressure to calls for increased mitigation efforts (for example, Environmental Justice Foundation, 2009). The concept of mitigation is therefore tied to a narrative of prevention, which is also prevalent in discourse on displacement. A key argument made in advocacy documents in the lead-up to the Paris negotiations was that the 'Paris Agreement and decisions represent a unique opportunity for Parties to the UNFCCC to prevent and reduce climate change-related displacement' (Advisory Group on Climate Change and Human Mobility, 2015a: 3).

On the one hand, displacement provides a raison d'être for climate change mitigation efforts. On the other hand, the term 'mitigation' has made its way into the discourse on the nexus in another way, being used with a similar basic meaning (averting or avoiding something unfavourable from happening) but referring to displacement scenarios rather than climate change as the variable to be averted. For example: 'Anticipatory planning such as national adaptation process is crucial to preventing or mitigating displacement, reducing vulnerability, and strengthening the resilience of communities' (Advisory Group on Climate Change and Human Mobility, 2014a: 5). This is a particularly interesting turn of phrase and is a definitive echo of climate politics in the international policy-making discourse on the migration and climate change nexus.

Adaptation is also featured in the UNFCCC, with commitments made to 'cooperate in preparing for adaptation to the impacts of climate change' (UNFCCC, 1992: 4(e)). Climate change adaptation gained further prominence in the UNFCCC in 2010, with the agreement of the Cancun Adaptation Framework (UNFCCC, 2010). Adaptation (again, a term appropriated by rather than coined by the climate regime) has come to mean adjusting to cope with climate change (particularly its adverse effects).

Adaptation is a concept that has been highly visible in the international policy-making discourse surrounding migration and climate change. Here the dominant understanding of adaptation outlined earlier has been appropriated to give legitimacy to migration, which has been identified as 'both a consequence of climate change as well as an important dimension of adaptation' (Advisory Group on Climate Change and Human Mobility, 2014d: 2); 'a "transformational" adaptation to environmental change'

(Foresight, 2011b: 10); 'a positive response to environmental stressors, for example, as a form of adaptation strategy in the face of climate change' (IOM, 2014d: 6); and 'a rational adaptation strategy to climate change processes' (UNHCR, 2011d: 2), leading to calls for it to be supported in policy. The emergence of this migration as adaptation narrative is important, as it embodies a shift in the discourse away from mobility being portrayed singularly in a negative light as well as a potentially positive reaction to the adverse effects of climate change. Here, this narrative of migration as adaptation can be linked back to the discussion of the level of compulsion as a differentiating factor between the concepts of displacement and migration, particularly in the context of Cancun paragraph 14(f). The separation of 'positive' mobilities (here, migration) from 'negative' mobilities (displacement) is a core part of this argument, which is made easier by the separation that is achieved by these two ideas of mobilities being labelled differently.

Within the discourse on migration and climate change, adaptation has a positive connotation because it is set against the displacement or forced migration narrative and the destructive effects on people's lives that are imagined in these scenarios. As it is used in this discourse, the concept of adaptation also appears to be a close cousin of resilience, with increasing resilience being the preferred way to conceptualise and frame potential adaptation strategies, including migration.

The final element to be considered here is much harder to pin down and has not reached the same degree of hegemonic closure within climate change politics as mitigation and adaptation, for which there is near consensus concerning the meaning attached to each. Loss and damage, on the other hand, is not featured in the UNFCCC's 1992 framework convention and entered the fray much later. Although the idea itself actually predates the UNFCCC, raised by Vanuatu in the early 1990s as a proposal for an insurance pool and compensation in relation to sea-level rise (McNamara, 2014; Roberts and Huq, 2015), loss and damage did not feature in any agreed text of the UNFCCC until the Bali Action Plan agreed at COP13 in 2007. It was then in Cancun in 2010 that loss and damage as an area of work was properly inaugurated (Wrathall et al, 2015), with recommendations on loss and damage being made at COP18 in Doha and ultimately leading to the creation of the WIM at COP19 a year later.

Throughout this time, the meaning of the phrase 'loss and damage' has been highly contested. When raised by Vanuatu in the 1990s, the issue of compensation (and therefore responsibility for climate change) was central to the notion of loss and damage, but the WIM does not include any mechanism for allocating responsibility or triggering compensatory action.

This is a position that is also made explicit in the COP decision from Paris, which states that loss and damage 'does not involve or provide a basis for any liability or compensation' (UNFCCC, 2016a: 51). The debate between these two different notions of loss and damage has not receded, and during the Paris negotiations the placement and meaning of loss and damage was one of the contentious issues up for debate (Dimitrov, 2016; Savaresi, 2016). It is therefore important to distinguish between the politics of loss and damage in a broader sense, where debates regarding compensation and historical responsibility are lively, and debates on loss and damage play out within the strict parameters of the WIM and the Paris Agreement.

Loss and damage has also become an important component of the discourse on migration and climate change, partly because of the placement of the issue under loss and damage in climate change negotiations. With the issue of migration and climate change being anchored in the WIM, it is the narrower meaning attached to loss and damage (rather than a meaning with links to responsibility and climate justice) that is most often mobilised in the international policy-making discourse.

Loss and damage also provides a compelling narrative, which argues that in mobility responses to the adverse effects of climate change both losses and damages will be involved and must be considered.

> Population movement is extremely relevant to the debate in various ways. Those forced to move will likely have to abandon various types of assets (economic assets such as land and houses, ecological and sociocultural assets such as community support networks, etc.). These movements may in turn incur loss and damage for the communities left behind (e.g. loss of human capital). Compensation for such losses will be a complex but important issue. (IOM, 2014d: 68–6)

This is particularly the case when mobility takes the form of displacement. As argued during the Paris climate change negotiations:

> [I]f people are forced to move then this is a loss, or a damage. If people are forced from their homes, into temporary accommodation or end up permanently displaced this is clearly a loss and a damage. (UKCCMC, 2015: 1)

Loss and damage therefore becomes (largely) connected to negative forms of mobility (although again migration as adaptation can be used as a counterpoint and a solution to prevent some of these losses and damages, not all of which are inevitable).

In the lead-up to the Paris negotiations, there were hints of tension between adaptation and loss and damage in advocacy work on migration and climate change, which was often at pains to emphasise the importance of both areas for migration:

> … this political momentum has emphasized, the Paris Agreement must address human mobility. In the current draft of the negotiations, the issue is addressed under Loss and Damage but it is also important to address this issue under adaptation. Preventing and minimizing displacement must be a priority. (UNHCR, 2015)

As this excerpt illustrates, the emphasis in advocacy documents remained largely on the nexus being included in the Paris Agreement as an element of adaptation, despite it already being included under loss and damage in the draft texts leading into the negotiations.

In drawing on the concept of loss and damage, particularly in its WIM form, a space is opened for a narrative on insurance and for practices and actors related to the insurance industry to enter the discourse on migration and climate change. This could lead to schemes to insure the livelihoods of communities (or indeed states) against the adverse effects of climate change with links being made to the mobility of these people.

Resilience and vulnerability

Billed as 'the new superhero in town!' (Dunn Cavelty et al, 2015) and as a replacement to the once-fashionable 'sustainability' (Zolli, 2012), the concept of resilience has also been making an appearance in relation to migration and climate change. It is the malleability of this concept that has made it so popular, transitioning from ecology (Holling, 1973) into social research, having also been widely used in psychology (see Olsson et al, 2015) and today being used in areas as diverse as security, development and environment. Although a variety of definitions exist, the concept is generally concerned with the ability of a system (be it an ecological or social system) to withstand or adapt to external shocks or disturbances.

People who are resilient exhibit a great deal of agency, and resilience has therefore been described as a 'loose antonym for vulnerability' (defined, in one interpretation in relation to environmental shocks or disturbances as 'the exposure of groups of people or individuals to stress as a result of the impacts of environmental change') (Adger, 2000: 348). However, vulnerability is more to resilience than simply an antonym; indeed, they have been identified as 'two sides of the same coin' (Dunn Cavelty et al, 2015: 7), as vulnerability is presupposed by the concept of resilience. Vulnerability can therefore actually be understood as the 'underlying ontology of resilience': 'To be able to become resilient, one must first accept that one is fundamentally vulnerable' (Evans and Reid, 2013: 84). Advocacy actors working in the migration and climate change nexus have also linked these two concepts, with IOM arguing that 'human mobility can be read as a barometer of both resilience and vulnerability' (IOM, 2014d: xi).

Various attempts have been made to sort resilience into different typologies. In one of the most comprehensive attempts, different kinds of resilience are differentiated along two axes: meaning and attributes. The first meaning refers to a system being able 'to cope with stress and "bounce back"', the second to a system being able to both '"bounce back" and "transform"'. Along the second axis, usages are identified as either being descriptive, 'implying that resilience is "neutral"', or prescriptive, 'implying that resilience is desirable and "good"' (Olsson et al, 2015: 2).

This variety of uses highlights the ambivalence of the term resilience in general (Boas and Rothe, 2016). In advocacy documents on the topic of the migration and climate change nexus, the meaning of the term is also ambivalent, referring to a mixture of 'bounce back' or 'bounce back and transform' resilience. However, the attributes of the term are predominantly prescriptive, so usages of this term are located in the right-hand quadrants of Table 5.

Figure 2 illustrates the ways in which some of these concepts are understood by IOM, with its infographic charting the potential changes in vulnerability over time, in scenarios of adaptation, coping and survival, respectively. The infographic reproduces the connotations that are attached to displacement and migration, with displacement leading to an increase in vulnerability, and migration potentially leading to vulnerability that increases even above a baseline level. However, the connotations of migration are also set out in a more nuanced way here, with migration that is not successful adaptation being described instead as a coping

Table 5: Typology of resilience

Meaning	Attributes	
	Descriptive – neutral	Prescriptive – good
Bounce back	Bounce back/neutral	Bounce back/prescriptive
Bounce back and transform	Bounce back and transform/neutral	Bounce back and transform/prescriptive

Source: Adapted from Olsson, Jerneck et al (2015: 2)

Figure 2: IOM infographic on vulnerability and resilience scenarios

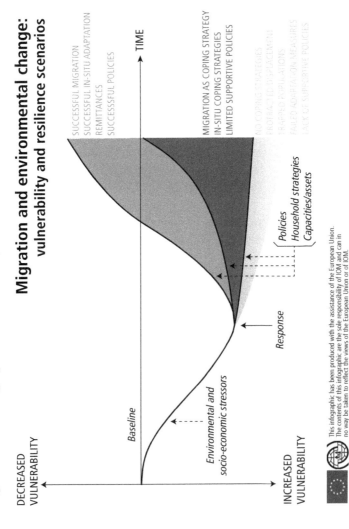

Migration and environmental change: vulnerability and resilience scenarios

DECREASED VULNERABILITY

INCREASED VULNERABILITY

TIME

Baseline

Environmental and socio-economic stressors

Response

Policies
Household strategies
Capacities/assets

SUCCESSFUL MIGRATION
SUCCESSFUL IN-SITU ADAPTATION
REMITTANCES
SUCCESSSFUL POLICIES

MIGRATION AS COPING STRATEGY
IN-SITU COPING STRATEGIES
LIMITED SUPPORTIVE POLICIES

NO COPING STRATEGIES
PROTRACTED DISPLACEMENT
TRAPPED POPULATIONS
FAILED ADAPTATION MEASURES
LACK OF SUPPORTIVE POLICIES

SUCCESSFUL ADAPTATION
Adjusting and improving skills and resources proactively to moderate harm or build on opportunities arising from climate change in the long term.

RESILIENCE
Ability to anticipate, absorb, accommodate, or recover from the effects of a hazardous event.

COPING
Using existing resources to ensure basic functioning of society in the short to medium term.

SURVIVAL
Staying alive in natural and man-made disasters i.e. flood, volcanic eruption but also slow-onset events.

VULNERABILITY
Propensity or predisposition to be adversely affected.

Definitions taken from MECLEP Glossary, adapted from IPCC Reports 2012 and 2014.
Graphic produced by Zoï Environment Network, © IOM 2015.

This infographic has been produced with the assistance of the European Union. The contents of this infographic are the sole responsibility of IOM and can in no way be taken to reflect the views of the European Union or of IOM.

Note: See https://environmentalmigration.iom.int/infographics
Source: IOM (2015c)

strategy that may lead to the recovery of a prior level of vulnerability but also potentially a more vulnerable position. This is a perspective that is mirrored in written contributions, where not all migration is portrayed as reducing vulnerability and thus acting as an adaptation strategy. Non-spontaneous, managed migration is identified as the optimal strategy in advocacy documents. IOM, for example, argues:

> ... that planned, safe, dignified and orderly migration is a viable adaptation strategy to cope with the adverse effects of environmental and climate change, foster development, increase resilience to disasters and reduce environmental pressure. (IOM, 2014d: ix)

Resilience, on the other hand, is associated with the highest decreases in vulnerability and triplicate success in migration, in-situ adaptation and policy, emphasising even more the positive nature of the concept.

The concept of resilience has also been used to argue for new ways of conducting adaptation:

> [W]hereas other notions of vulnerability focus on factors that might endanger the preservation of the status quo in the face of environmental change, resilience looks for ways to utilize this change in order to promote creative adaptation measures. (Methmann and Oels, 2014: 280)

One of the best-known examples of this narrative is the Foresight report:

> [M]easures that prevent harmful environmental changes, reduce their impact, and build resilience in communities will diminish the influence of environmental change on migration but are unlikely to fully prevent it. (Foresight, 2011b: 10)

This narrative is therefore based on a sense of inevitability in terms of both climate change (and thus the failure of climate change mitigation) and also in terms of migration. The Foresight report is perhaps also the most prominent example of the 'bounce back and transform' narrative in relation to the migration and climate change nexus:

> Policies to build long-term resilience are essential in the context of future global environmental change. Migration can represent a 'transformational adaptation' to environmental

change, and in many cases is an effective means to build long-term resilience. (Foresight, 2011b: 21)

The concept of resilience functions as a conjunction between different components of conceptualisations of the migration and climate change nexus. For example, in the human mobility umbrella term, resilience often plays an important enabling role in theorising a transition from negative mobilities (displacement) to positive mobilities (migration). As resilience is portrayed as being necessary in order to prevent displacement, and increased resilience is portrayed as arising from migration (among other strategies), resilience can provide a bridge between these two concepts. Resilience therefore plays a crucial role, as the resilience created by migration can prevent displacement from taking place. As argued by the Nansen Initiative:

> Disaster risk reduction activities such as infrastructure improvements, evacuation plans, relocating people at risk of displacement to safer areas, land reform, promoting voluntary migration as an adaptive measure to environmental degradation, and other measures to improve resilience are all potential actions to prevent displacement. (Nansen Initiative, 2014b: 4)

While in advocacy and policy work the concept of resilience has overwhelmingly positive connotations, in academic work some critical attention has been given to how resilience has cropped up in discourses on migration and climate change (Reid, 2012; Methmann and Oels, 2015), with three main critiques. The first critique centres around the depoliticising potential of a resilience narrative, drawing attention away from root causes that, in the case of climate change and human mobility, can lead to a dangerous diversion of attention away from climate change mitigation (Methmann and Oels, 2015). The second problem concerns the detraction of responsibility away from the international community (in particularly the industrialised states that are overwhelmingly responsible for climate change, and have enjoyed its benefits) on to the shoulders of individuals (predominantly the inhabitants of states that have barely contributed to climate change, but are feeling its effects). This shifting of responsibility has acquired a large normative question mark (Bettini et al, 2017). Finally, critiques have been levelled at the resilience narrative on climate change and migration because of its relationship to neoliberalism (Felli, 2013), placing people vulnerable to the effects of climate change at the mercy of markets rather than within support systems.

Disaster and risk

The concepts of disaster and risk are two further closely linked concepts from the field of discursivity that are highly visible and influential. As with most of the concepts discussed thus far, the definition of 'disaster' has not been straightforward, as the deliberations from the early stages of work of the Nansen Initiative highlighted. However, for the purposes of its work, the initiative has argued that 'the relevant distinction is not the character of the disaster, but rather whether it triggers displacement' (Nansen Initiative, 2015a: 16). Despite this statement, lines have been drawn around the kinds of disasters referred to in connection with the migration and climate change nexus, with this category tending to include those predicated by natural hazards (colloquially, and latterly formally in the Global Compact for Migration, referred to as 'natural disasters')[8] and being perceived as drivers of movement. A sub-set of this category of natural hazards is often mobilised, namely those hazards (often labelled 'extreme weather events') that will increase in magnitude and frequency with climate change.

As the self-created specialists on disaster–induced displacement (including climate change), the Nansen Initiative and its successor the PDD have become the most authoritative voice speaking to disasters in the context of the migration and climate change nexus. This legitimacy has grown as a result of the research and consultations undertaken by the initiative and drawn on as evidence to back up its position. A conceptualisation of the 'phenomenon' of the nexus anchored in disaster terminology has arguably opened up space for the nexus to be considered in the area of disaster risk reduction, with the Nansen Initiative in particular taking up the reins and spearheading the advocacy effort at the Sendai Conference (for example, see Nansen Initiative, 2014b). This opens up a stage other than the dominant climate change negotiations on which policy making can play out.

Although smattered throughout the discourse on the migration and climate change nexus, the concept of risk is used systematically in relation to disasters, with disaster risk reduction being one of the tools proposed for preventing displacement scenarios. The concept of risk is most frequently used to denote something along the lines of the 'combination of the probability of an event and its negative consequences' (UNISDR 2009), which, according to the Nansen Initiative, is 'determined by a combination of exposure to a natural hazard, the vulnerability of an individual or a community, and the nature of the hazard itself' (Nansen Initiative, 2015a: 17). What is particularly important in this concept (at least for this analysis) is not the particular composite parts of the concept, but rather the focus on 'likelihood' or 'potential'. Disaster risk therefore denotes the potentiality, but crucially *not* the inevitability of disasters, with disaster risk reduction in particular suggesting that practical steps can be taken to reduce this likelihood.

Turned on its head, risk has also been identified in relation to migration itself (rather than migration being a reaction to risk):

> [M]igration also carries specific risks, in particular for women and children. Migrants might be economically exploited, exposed to dangerous conditions at their place of work or home, face discrimination or become victims of violence or being trafficked. (Nansen Initiative, 2015a: 9)

However, this argument is very much at the margins of the discourse; in line with the dominant conceptions of migration outlined in the previous section, migration is generally viewed in a positive light in the context of the migration and climate change nexus. This narrative of risks connected to migration might be most compatible with IOM's definition of migration and the grey area of migration as a coping strategy illustrated in Figure 2 as having ambivalent impacts on vulnerability.

A clear link exists between risk (and indeed disaster risk reduction) and the concepts of resilience and vulnerability. Resilience building can be employed as a tool of disaster risk reduction and those populations who employ (or are subjected to) disaster risk reduction measures are hoped to become less vulnerable and more resilient in the face of climate change. While tied to the positively connoted resilience, the disaster concept is also tied closely to prevention, which has the more negative connotation of stopping something negative from taking place. This therefore means both preventing displacement or, in situations where displacement is not preventable, carrying out protection activities.

A consequence of the use of disaster terminology in relation to the nexus is that advocacy documents are able to draw on (and indeed often open with) current statistics on disaster displacement in a way that is difficult for advocacy related to the nexus more broadly. As the opening passages of the Nansen Protection Agenda state:

> Between 2008 and 2014 a total of 184.4 million people were displaced by sudden-onset disasters, an average of 26.4 million people newly displaced each year. Of these, an annual average of 22.5 million people was displaced by weather- and climate-related hazards. (Nansen Initiative, 2015a: 6)

However, in an argument more typical for work on the migration and climate change nexus more generally where vague predictions of future movements are frequently employed, it continues as follows:

> [L]ooking to the future, there is high agreement among scientists that climate change, in combination with other factors, is projected to increase displacement in the future, with migration increasingly becoming an important response to both extreme weather events and long-term climate variability and change. (Nansen Initiative, 2015a: 6)

This therefore alters the timescale with which the 'problem' can realistically be considered. While efforts to combat climate change generally suffer from the malaise connected to a problem frequently conceptualised as playing out in the future and therefore largely posing a problem for future generations, disasters and the statistical information available on current displacements can function as a prompt for action on a faster time scale. Disaster terminology may therefore alter the level of urgency with which the nexus is conceptualised and acted on.

A surplus of meaning: plurality, contingency and the success of policy making on migration and climate change

As this chapter has illustrated, the 'phenomenon' of the migration and climate change nexus cannot be viewed singularly or in isolation. First, many different constructions of the migration and climate change nexus exist depending on the speaker. This is the case both in the sense of different meanings being applied to the same terms in different contexts (for example, IOM's divergent definition of migration) and to particular set phrases being the sole preserve of certain actors (for example, IOM's 'migration, environment and climate change' and the Nansen Initiative/ PDD's 'disaster displacement'). While the inability of those working on migration and climate change to reach consensus on accepted terminology, coupled with set definitions for those terms, is often maligned as a key difficulty of carrying out work on migration and climate change, various coexisting conceptualisations of the phenomenon may also be a factor that has contributed to its success in policy-making communities.

The malleability of the phenomenon allows a range of different advocacy actors to work on migration and climate change concurrently and even collaboratively within settings such as the Advisory Group. This is despite deeply rooted differences concerning how key concepts such as migration are understood. The coexistence of different, sometimes contradictory, conceptualisations of migration and climate change can therefore at times mean that documents on the nexus read rather circuitously, with discussions of terminology never reaching a satisfactory conclusion. However, at the same time this contestation over the phenomenon has arguably been vital for its success in policy making.

The phenomenon is also embedded in a much broader field of discursivity, elements of which influence its construction. Examples cited in this chapter that are particularly prominent are the concepts of mitigation, adaptation and loss and damage from the vocabulary of the UNFCCC, resilience and vulnerability, as well as the concepts of disaster and risk. While these are the most prominent examples from the documents analysed in the research for this book, an infinite number of different signifiers can be drawn into the policy-making discourse from the broad field of discursivity, with new concepts continuing to be drawn in as the discourse develops. Just as with the phenomenon of the migration and climate change nexus, concepts from the field of discursivity have their own genealogies, and in turn have complex links to even more concepts and ideas. A last point to make is that meanings of these concepts are also contingent, plural and perhaps even contradictory, and that these layers of complexity are an inescapable component of the phenomenon of migration and climate change.

All of this contention is also important for pursuing particular policy directions and forming policy outcomes, with the potential to both enable and constrain policy at the same time. On the one hand, the malleability of the phenomenon, and the links it has to a multitude of different discourses, means that there are a number of potential policy homes for migration and climate change. The phenomenon can be presented in a number of different guises depending on the occasion, whereby the preferred framing stresses compatibility with the relevant policy process. On the other hand, some formulations of the phenomenon may be constraining, limiting the policymaking arenas within which the nexus can be considered. For example, a framing of the phenomenon that is too heavily steeped in loss and damage politics of the UNFCCC is unlikely to gain a great amount of traction in the Global Compact for Migration. These enabling factors and constraints affect not only where migration and climate change can be talked about, but also what policy alternatives emerge as possible responses and the foreclosure of others as practical and political impossibilities.

6

Struggles to Locate Mobile People at the Centre of the Migration and Climate Change Nexus

'It's about people, like people, like the human face of climate change and they are not staying where they were expected to stay! And after that you can call them, I think however ... like, from many different things, whether you want to emphasise whether they were forced to move or whether they decided to move. But the basic point remains that we are talking about individuals, people, and not just things.' (IOM Interview 4, 2016)

The second nodal point in the policy-making discourse on migration and climate change is the people who are at the centre of the phenomenon analysed in Chapter 5 of this book. People are also central to this discourse, for without people whose mobilities are in some way being affected, the abstract phenomenon of the migration and climate change nexus would remain as such, an abstract phenomenon. However, this is not to say that an easily identifiable community of affected people exists or that the lives of those people who are perceived as being affected by the nexus can be slotted into existing systems for understanding and classifying people on the move. One commonality shared by the people at the centre of the migration and climate change nexus is the exceptionality that is created around them. To put it simply, they do not adhere to what is considered the norm or, to borrow from the quote at the opening of this chapter, "they are not staying where they were expected to stay!" (IOM Interview 4, 2016). The basis of this exceptionality being identified as movement reveals a sedentary bias underlying the conceptualisation of the migration and climate change nexus.

> It demands that we view the migrant and the refugee as the 'other', the constitutive outside or excess of what is otherwise imagined as the pairing of 'normal' even if fraught geopolitical and climatic conditions. It reinforces the belief, erroneous in our view, that life internal to the modern nation state is settled, sedentary and at some degree of remove from the transnational flows of labour, capital and technology, imagined to lie beyond state borders. (Baldwin and Bettini, 2017: 3)

At this point it is important to consider the agency of people moving in the context of climate change within the policy-making processes discussed in this book. Although the subjects of the discourse and the intended benefactors of policies thrashed out in high-level fora, the mobile people at the centre of the migration and climate change nexus are rarely the most dominant voice within the discourse that concerns itself with their fates. Indeed, even arguments for the protection of the rights of the vulnerable figure of the climate refugee tend to come from the perspective of Western researchers or advocacy organisations (Piguet et al, 2018). The position of the speaker in the policy-making discourse is therefore also important to interrogate. The speaker is predominantly placed in a non-exceptional position; they are placed external to the phenomenon and problematise it as an issue for international policy making from this perspective. The speaker is also ahistorical, and portrayed as a neutral observer. Particularly in policy documents and submissions, the speaker is not identified as a person, with recommendations being made in the imperative and frequently also in the third person and using passive constructions. These grammatical points are of great relevance for the way in which perceptions are set up within the discourse and therefore are worthy of attention.

Somewhat diverging from the quote used to open this chapter, the labels attached to people whose lives are entangled in the migration and climate change nexus are also highly relevant. This is not because these labels (which do not necessarily have one stable meaning) can provide great insights into the lives of the people being labelled, but because they can provide insights into the people and organisations that use them. Systems of classification can betray how the classifier views and tries to organise the world. Therefore, while it is incredibly important to retain awareness that the migration and climate change nexus is ultimately about people and that these people should not be reduced to the technical terms and bureaucratic labels that are so frequently applied to them, these terms and labels are also important. These considerations help us to understand the ways in which society is being moulded and the very production of the people at the heart of the migration and climate change nexus through the discourse within which they are entwined.

Struggles to identify and define mobile people

Identifying and defining mobile people caught up in the migration and climate change nexus is an ongoing discursive struggle. Although necessary for the 'phenomenon' to exist, the precise identification of the people implicated is difficult (perhaps even impossible) (Baldwin, 2017a). This, in turn, poses challenges for definition, which is frequently identified as one of the greatest challenges when working on the migration and climate change nexus. How does one define a figure that cannot be identified? But this figure persists and is consistently used to justify the need to consider the phenomenon. At the same time, this figure remains extremely imprecise and the nodal point is occupied by floating signifiers, whose meaning is shifting and contested.

This chapter deconstructs attempts in the policy-making discourse to identify and define mobile people, beginning with an examination of the greatest hegemonic closure visible in this part of the discourse, namely the rejection of the 'climate refugee' label by the policy-making community. The analysis then examines what conceptualisations are present to take the place of this rejected figure. While the discourse is explicitly dominated by people on the move being identified according to a forced–voluntary binary, this chapter digs deeper to examine implicit, latent, ways of conceptualising people in the migration and climate change nexus. The analysis of implicit classification below the surface is important for two reasons. First, this analysis represents an active problematisation of the forced–voluntary binary that has been widely recognised as a false dichotomy, with migration actually falling somewhere along a forced–voluntary continuum. However, as Marta Erdal and Ceri Oeppen argue:

> [The] distinction between forced and voluntary, as two very different forms of migration, has a tendency to stick around in the academic work and policy, [and] migration scholars must unpack the experienced, observed and labelled dimensions of this distinction. (Erdal and Oeppen, 2018: 982)

Despite significant critique, a 'categorical fetishism' exists, which 'continues to treat the categories "refugee" and "migrant" as if they simply exist, out there, as empty vessels into which people can be placed in some neutral ordering process' (Crawley and Skleparis, 2018). This is symptomatic of the discourse on mobilities more generally and has filtered into the discourse on migration and climate change. Second, escaping this dichotomy simply makes more analytical sense, with the forced–voluntary categories often being used in incredibly complex and circuitous ways in relation to the migration and climate change nexus, raising the suspicion that alternative ways of understanding people moving in the context of climate change may have more analytical purchase. The alternative discussion set out in this chapter is organised around the concept of potentiality (and its antonym of actuality). The second part of the chapter critiques the objectification of people who are mobile in the context of climate change. Both dividing practices and scientific classification are considered as ways in which people are objectified in work on the migration and climate change nexus.

Rejection of the 'climate refugee' label

The greatest degree of consensus regarding terminology to describe the people whose lives are entwined in the migration and climate change nexus is not around a particular term that either is being or should be employed; rather it is around the rejection of the 'climate refugee' or 'environmental refugee' label. For example, Antonio Guterres, then High Commissioner for Refugees, argued:

> UNHCR has refused to embrace the new terminology of 'climate refugees' or 'environmental refugees', fearing that this will complicate and confuse the organization's efforts to protect the victims of persecution and armed conflict. (Guterres, 2011a)

Advocacy actors have also highlighted an awareness of this position being shared by other actors, with a 'consensus' being identified as follows:

> Environmental migration terminology is still being refined. However, a consensus not to employ terms related to the refugee regime – such as climate refugee or environmental refugee – is emerging among key stakeholders, including the Office of the United Nations High Commissioner for Refugees (UNHCR). (IOM, 2014d: 21)

While this consensus does indeed appear to have been reached in the policy-making community, this does not necessarily mean that discursive struggles over the term have concluded. The consensus that has been detected by advocacy actors is based on the meaning laid out in the 1951 Refugee Convention being attached to the 'refugee' term. Following this definition, a refugee is someone who

> ... owing to well-founded fear of being persecuted for reasons of race, religion, nationality, membership of a particular social group or political opinion, is outside the country of his nationality and is unable or, owing to such fear, is unwilling to avail himself of the protection of that country. (UN General Assembly, 1951: A(2))

If this definition of 'refugee' is accepted, the argument follows that the mobile people at the centre of the migration and climate change nexus are not encapsulated by this term. Two frequently cited reasons why mobile people at the centre of the migration and climate change nexus should not be called refugees are the requirement of persecution and the need for movements to be cross-border while movements in the context of the nexus are predicted to be prominently internal.

However, this legal definition is by no means the only meaning that has been attached to the 'refugee' term. For example, a dictionary definition of a refugee is 'a person who has been forced to leave their country in order to escape war, persecution, or natural disaster' (Oxford Dictionaries, 2016). If this meaning is attached to the term, there is clearly room for it to be connected to climate change, although it would likely only partially apply, with the continuum of degree of compulsion towards movement again being relevant (only referring to forced movement), as well as the requirement of crossing international borders. Following this more popular definition, climate refugee terminology has not disappeared from the wider debate on migration and climate change and continues to be widely used in the media (for example, Dinshaw, 2015; Wendle, 2015; Schwartzstein, 2016), and academic arguments for the resurgence of the term have also been advanced (Gemenne, 2015).

Potentially mobile people

Central to the conceptualisation of people whose mobility is affected by climate change is their potentiality. Here, when I use the term potentiality, I simply refer to any possibility for mobility that a person is taken to have.

In contrast, actuality refers to a situation where this possibility becomes realised in its fullest sense and people are mobile. Given the future-conditional form of the majority of discussions on the migration and climate change nexus (Baldwin, 2012), this is incredibly important, with people overwhelmingly being identified because of the possibilities for their mobility rather than any actual materialisations of it. This potentiality has been portrayed in various ways, as both dangerous and endangering, and as both problematic and beneficial, depending on the different types of mobility involved.

Many analyses and policy interventions also conflate potentiality with actuality, not distinguishing between potential and actual movement, which as a result are often blurred into one category. However, analytically it makes sense to make this distinction, as potentiality cannot be divorced from uncertainty. Particularly given the uncertainties related to climate change impacts, where knowledge is based on simulations, predictions and scenarios, it is not surprising that this is also a feature of knowledge on the migration and climate change nexus. However, the centrality of the (potentially) mobile person in the policy-making discourse makes the acknowledgement of this inherent uncertainty difficult. In terms of advocacy work, not being able to point to the people affected by a phenomenon poses a challenge and reduces the possibilities for creating a legitimate policy priority.

Potentially mobile people is not a new category, and indeed potentiality has already been identified as a defining feature of the conceptualisation of people whose mobilities are affected by climate change (Baldwin, 2012). Methodologically, potentiality of movement has also been important for early academic literature on the nexus, with predictions of numbers of 'climate refugees' made in early contributions being attained by identifying areas where climate change impacts are anticipated to have strong negative consequences for populations and extrapolating predictions for numbers of 'climate refugees' from population data for these areas (for example, Myers, 1997; for a critique, see Gemenne, 2011). While methodologies have subsequently been refined, the potentiality of mobility remains central to conceptualisations of people moving in the context of climate change.

One of the terms that has been used to describe people who might (be forced to) move in the context of climate change is 'climate vulnerable populations'. For example, the Advisory Group on Climate Change and Human Mobility (hereafter Advisory Group) has argued the following:

> The Paris Agreement and decisions represent a unique opportunity for Parties to the UNFCCC to prevent and reduce

climate change-related displacement by encouraging and supporting the planning and implementation of mitigation and adaptation strategies. This includes measures that: strengthen the resilience of *climate vulnerable populations* to enable them to remain where they live; support or facilitate voluntary and dignified internal and cross-border migration as an adaptation strategy; and, as an option of last resort, plan for participatory and dignified relocation. (Advisory Group on Climate Change and Human Mobility, 2015a: 3, emphasis added)

Two concepts that come clearly to the forefront in this extract are resilience and its flip-side of vulnerability, two prominent components from the field of discursivity in which policy-making discourse on the nexus is located. As illustrated in this excerpt, potential forced mobilities are portrayed as stemming from vulnerability to climate change, with resilience able to prevent this potential mobility from actualising. Alternatively, other voluntary mobilities can be a reaction to this vulnerability, creating resilience.

This excerpt from the Advisory Group also highlights a split between potential mobilities that are perceived as either problematic or beneficial (for both the potentially mobile person and for society more broadly). For the figure of the climate-vulnerable person, this means that there is a hierarchy of potential scenarios, differentiated by types of movement located along the continuum of level of compulsion of movement. In another document, the Advisory Group underlines this conceptualisation by identifying displacement as preventable and alternative mobilities (signified as being more or less voluntary) as '*the right policies*': 'Climate change-induced displacement is not inevitable and may be mitigated where *the right policies* (migration, planned relocation) are developed and effectively implemented' (Advisory Group on Climate Change and Human Mobility, 2015b: 3, emphasis added).

The potential of these different types of movement therefore carries very different connotations. Movement that is located at the voluntary end of the spectrum, which can avoid displacement loaded with dangers for the person and linked to threats to security, is portrayed as virtuous and linked to the sphere of development (see also Bettini and Gioli, 2016). The potential of such migration is portrayed by the Advisory Group in the following example:

Migration is often assumed to result from a failure to adapt to a changing environment. However, migration can be a positive coping and survival strategy that, for example, allows rural household income sources to be diversified (i.e. remittances used to take resilience measures at household level), reduces pressures on fragile eco-systems, and leads to positive development impacts. (Advisory Group on Climate Change and Human Mobility, 2014a)

In itself, the separation of problematic or beneficial mobile people is no different from discourse on migration more generally, where people whose mobilities are conceptualised a certain way (overwhelmingly refugees) *can be* perceived as virtuous figures. Certain people are portrayed as endangered and therefore should be given protection and a specific legal status. Refugees can, of course, be, and frequently are, portrayed as threats, playing the role of a dangerous figure; however, in the hierarchy of mobilities, this figure carries more empathy and links to humanitarianism than the migrant. On the other hand, economic migrants are frequently singled out in popular discourse as people who have a choice of whether to move and who want to take advantage economically of receiving states. While the tendency of identifying problematic and beneficial movement persists, in the discourse on the migration and climate change nexus this attribution of virtuousness is turned on its head, with migrants becoming virtuous figures that are preventing alternative potential mobilities from materialising.

Actualised mobilities

Although the majority of narratives surrounding the people at the centre of the migration and climate change nexus portray people's mobilities as potentialities, the policy-making discourse also includes mobilities that are discussed in the present tense. This figure, whose mobility is no longer a potentiality but an actuality, is potentially powerful for policy making, shortening the timescales on which policy action is to be taken and removing the troublesome aspect of uncertainty from considerations.

Similarly to conceptualisations of the 'phenomenon' itself, the terms used to describe people who are actually mobile in the context of climate change are not homogenous. However, the terms mainly draw on exiting terms used in other contexts to denote different mobilities, with these terms being morphed to include the climate component. People are also frequently identified as being located somewhere along a continuum depending on the degree of compulsion that is present in decisions about whether to move. These movements are then identified as either forced (displacement or forced migration, which in this sense are used practically synonymously) or largely voluntary (migration).

In contrast to conceptualisations of the 'phenomenon' itself, which although often conflicting have a relatively easily identifiable list of semiotic components, it is difficult to locate clear, differentiated formulations to represent mobile people. Instead, terms are often used interchangeably, both with regard to the climate element (both 'climate change' and 'environmental' are used as signifiers) and the mobility element ('displacement', 'forced migration' and 'migration' are signifiers that are all used here).

One term to which a set definition has been proposed is 'environmental migrants', which was defined by the International Organization for Migration (IOM) in 2007 and has been frequently reproduced in other policy documents. According to the IOM definition:

> Environmental migrants are persons or groups of persons who, for compelling reasons of sudden or progressive changes in the environment that adversely affect their lives or living conditions, are obliged to leave their homes or choose to do so, either temporarily or permanently, and who move either within their country or abroad. (IOM, 2007: 1; see also, IOM, 2014d: 6)

This definition does not set particularly narrow parameters for the group of people who are being conceptualised here: any mobile people whose mobility decisions (however forced or voluntary) have been influenced by environmental factors (including climate change) are included. This is in line with IOM's definition of migration. It is also the broad nature of this definition, which is not related solely to climate change but also to environmental factors more generally, that makes it possible for IOM to move away from a description of migration based purely on potentiality. For example, elsewhere IOM has stated that:

(a) Environmental factors have always been a cause of migration;

(b) People flee to survive natural disasters or when faced with harsh and deteriorating environmental conditions;

(c) Climate change is expected to intensify sudden- and slow-onset disasters and gradual environmental degradation.... (IOM, 2014e: 1)

In this excerpt, a change can be noted after statements (a) and (b), which are made straightforwardly in the present tense, with statement (c) reverting to the future-conditional ('is expected'), which is a sign of potentiality rather than actuality.

Another aspect of mobilities in the context of climate change that makes a portrayal of mobilities as actualities difficult is the multi-causality of movement, something that the IOM definition does not take into account. This recognition of multi-causality has led to a cautious use of the environmental migrants term from other quarters. For example, the Foresight report places this term in inverted commas and emphasises the difficulty of actually distinguishing 'environmental migrants':

> Environmental change will affect migration now and in the future, specifically through its influence on a range of economic, social and political drivers which themselves affect migration. However, the range and complexity of the interactions between these drivers means that it will rarely be possible to distinguish individuals for whom environmental factors are the sole driver ('environmental migrants'). (Foresight, 2011b: 9)

In this example, mobility once again becomes a potentiality. Similarly, the United Nations High Commissioner for Refugees (UNHCR) emphasises that 'it is generally difficult to single out climatic and environmental factors as the sole, unilateral driver of population movements' (UNHCR, 2014: 13). Therefore, rather than denoting a specific term to people moving in the context of climate change, the organisation has pointed to the similarities to people moving for other reasons:

> Individuals and communities displaced by disasters and climate change and those displaced by conflicts often experience similar trauma and deprivation. They may have protection needs and vulnerabilities comparable to those whose flight is provoked by armed violence or human rights abuses. (UNHCR, 2014)

Although as vaguely identified as in the Foresight report (and even vaguer in failing to recognise a specific term for the people in question), UNHCR's use of the present tense gives an illusion of a figure who is at least identifiable even if they cannot be defined. This is illustrative of a tendency in the discourse to accept the actuality of mobile people, despite not being able to specifically identify or define them.

When the climate change component is removed from the terminology, this identification immediately becomes more straightforward (as IOM's statements on environmental migration have already shown). A sub-area of advocacy on the nexus where a term denoting mobile people whose mobilities are not based on potentiality has become a steady presence is work on disasters. Here, the category of 'disaster-displaced persons' is used by the Nansen Initiative and the PDD. This term creates a central node to the discourse that aligns with both organisational mandates.

The figure of the disaster-displaced person has the advantage of being much more easily identified than other people at the centre of the nexus, making the figure much easier to pin down. The Nansen Initiative has therefore been able to make the following statement about disaster-displaced persons:

> Every year, millions of people are displaced by disasters caused by natural hazards such as floods, tropical storms, earthquakes, landslides, droughts, salt water intrusion, glacial melting, glacial lake outburst floods, and melting permafrost. Between 2008 and 2014 a total of 184.4 million people were displaced by disasters, an average of 26.4 million people newly displaced each year. Of these, an annual average of 22.5 million people was displaced by weather- and climate-related hazards. Others have to move because of the effects of sea level rise, desertification or environmental degradation. (Nansen Initiative, 2015c: 24)

Although the initiative also recognises the multi-causality of movement and prominently refers to climate change, describing the phenomenon it is concerned with as 'forced displacement related to disasters, including the adverse effects of climate change (disaster displacement)' (Nansen Initiative, 2015a: 6), the focus on disasters provides an event that can be directly linked to movements of people. This focus therefore also creates a constituency of mobile people who can be fitted into the 'disaster displaced persons' category and whose mobility is not uncertain.

Immobile people

Seemingly contrary to the focus on mobility, or even potential mobility, in the context of climate change, a group of people that has emerged in the policy-making discourse since 2010 is that of immobile people, whereby persons are identified not by their (potential) mobility but in fact by the absence of potential for mobility. A prominent example of this can be found in the Foresight report:

> [I]n the decades ahead, millions of people will be unable to move away from locations in which they are extremely

vulnerable to environmental change. To the international community, this 'trapped' population is likely to represent just as important a policy concern as those who do not migrate. (Foresight, 2011b: 9)

The concept of 'trapped persons' has also moved beyond the Foresight report and has become an established part of the policy-making discourse (with organisations also frequently linking back to the Foresight report when using the concept). For example, IOM has argued:

[A]s highlighted in the UK Foresight report and somewhat counter-intuitively, climate change may actually put mobility out of reach as a coping strategy, as its cumulative impacts on livelihoods reduce the resources available for migration. There is a risk that populations could become trapped. (IOM, 2014d: 75)

While not reaching the same level of prominence as mobile, or potentially mobile, people, 'trapped persons' are now a category of people that cannot be legitimately ignored, sometimes seeming to be another caveat in a long list of aspects that add to the complexity of the 'phenomenon'. In a parallel to early work on human mobility in the context of climate change, the concept of trapped populations in this field also overwhelmingly isolates environmental factors as drivers of immobility, with other aspects such as the intensification of border security measures (Humble, 2014) being largely ignored.

What is interesting in the conceptualisation of immobile people at the centre of the migration and climate change nexus is how immobility has acquired negative connotations, with the 'quiet supposition' having emerged that trapped persons are 'maladaptive migrants [who] will be left behind and become "trapped", having failed in their individual responsibility to be resilient' (Ayeb-Karlsson et al, 2018: 559). This stands in stark contrast to mainstream discourse on migration, where mobility is seldom portrayed in a positive light. However, the notion of trapped populations is also frequently linked to types of mobility that are portrayed in the discourse on the nexus as beneficial. According to the Foresight report, 'planned and well-managed migration can be one important solution for this population of concern' (Foresight, 2011b: 9). Therefore, trapped populations can be transformed into potentially mobile people who employ a virtuous type of mobility to reduce their vulnerability and increase their resilience.

In a thread that runs through many of the conceptualisations of people at the heart of the migration and climate change nexus, the trapped populations concept also raises concerns surrounding the agency of people whose lives are the subject of the discourse:

> Referring to a person as 'sick' may lead to them being perceived as fragile, worthy of pity or infectious and thus treated differently by other people. In the same way, labelling a person as 'trapped' has the potential to reduce or remove an individual's agency, autonomy, and independence in determining their own destiny. (Ayeb-Karlsson et al, 2018: 570)

Objectification in the struggle to locate subjects of the migration and climate change nexus

One of the most important reasons behind examining the discursive construction of people is to question the effects that this has on the people themselves. In his work, Michel Foucault has identified three ways in which the subjects of a discourse can be objectivised. The first is dividing practices, whereby subjects are divided socially, and sometimes also spatially. The second is scientific classification, whereby people are identified as belonging to a particular category of subject. The third mode of objectification is subjectification and refers to processes by which humans turn themselves into subjects, a form of self-formation within which the person is active (Rabinow, 1984: 7–11; Foucault, 2006). The first two modes of objectification are particularly prevalent in international policy making on the migration and climate change nexus, and affect how we view people whose mobilities are or will be affected by climate change.

Dividing practices

Dividing practices, in which subjects are divided socially, are at play in the very identification of people at the centre of the migration and climate change nexus. By identifying people whose mobility is or will be affected by climate change (as opposed to those who are not), a social division is created. This division may also be spatial if people are physically divided according to this status. In the case of planned relocation, it is conceivable that entire communities could be spatially divided, if relocated as a distinct community in a different location where neighbouring communities have not had their mobility affected by climate change. The separation of people whose mobilities are affected by climate change from the masses is very vague, or often simply alluded to. As the previous section has set out, the potentiality of mobilities in the context of climate change is an important factor here, making it very difficult to identify people whose mobilities are affected on a contemporary timescale, and which can be traced back to climate change alone. For example, a compendium of policy briefings on environmental migration collated by the IOM poses the question 'What is environmental migration and who is an environmental migrant?', with only different aspects of the phenomenon being detailed in response, and despite the formulation of the question, no answer is proffered as to the identity of an environmental migrant (IOM, 2014d: 6). Here, the figure of the environmental migrant takes on the quality of a shadow lurking under the cover of the phenomenon, impossible to see but somehow assumed to be present. This supports the argument that the main group of people being considered as part of the migration and climate change nexus have been identified due to their *potential* mobility, with the unknown and future-oriented aspects of this group making identification of particular affected people especially problematic.

Despite this difficulty, the frequent use of images of people in policy documents concerned with the migration and climate change nexus suggests that, however abstract and vague this separation may seem, identifying the subjects of the migration and climate change nexus should be possible (for a fairly typical selection of images used in policy documents, see IOM, 2014d). By depicting people whose mobilities are presumably affected by climate change, these images suggest that it is possible to identify affected people.

One possible effect of dividing practices is the production of institutions aimed at intervening in the lives of the people who have been identified as a separate group. This can be seen in Michael Foucault's work, which has identified dividing practices surrounding the sick, the insane or the criminal and linked the identification of these groups to institutions such as the hospital, the psychiatric clinic and the prison (Rabinow, 1984: 7–8). In the run-up to the United Nations Framework Convention on Climate Change (UNFCCC) 21st Conference of the Parties (COP21) in Paris, a displacement coordination facility was proposed in the negotiating text; had this facility remained in the text and been created, an institution would also have been created, this time based around people divided because of their displacement due to climate change. Although it was vaguely formulated in the negotiating text, and it is therefore difficult to speculate about precisely what form this institution might have taken, the climate change displacement coordination facility could conceivably have had a role in intervening in the lives of displaced persons.

The dividing practices that this section has identified so far relate to the identification of individuals drawn from a rather undifferentiated mass. However, dividing practices are also at play in a second way. People who are affected by the migration and climate change nexus are not just identified in relation to an undifferentiated mass, but are also divided internally, creating differentiated categories. This has already been shown in the previous section in relation to the identification of problematic and beneficial mobilities largely based on a differentiation between forced and more or less voluntary mobility, as well as the differentiation between mobile people, potentially mobile people and immobile people.

While the effects of these differentiations are currently rather abstract, it is conceivable (based on comparison with international regimes on human mobilities more broadly) that categorisation along any of the axes identified earlier could have concrete effects on the people concerned through institutionalisation and/or legal codification of different categories. For example, the differentiation between refugees and migrants in describing broader mobility dynamics is important not only because of the meanings that are attached to these signs in different contexts, but also because international legal instruments and institutions have been developed in relation to these terms, meaning that the attribution of either term to a mobile person can have productive effects related to their legal status, rights and any protection that they may receive. The exceptionalism that is created for refugees because of the legal meaning attached to this term can therefore make division in the form of recognition as a refugee sought after. However, categorisation as a labour migrant, a term around which a legal regime has also been created, does not convey anything approaching the level of protection afforded to people designated as refugees.

Scientific classification

The second category of objectification refers to the domain of scientific inquiry, or rather modes of inquiry that give themselves this status (Rabinow, 1984: 8). A flourishing epistemic community has emerged around the migration and climate change nexus, which has a shared 'value-set, ontological beliefs, questions of interest, objects/domains of concern, methods of inquiry, the criteria favoured for determining worthy ideas, knowledge or information, and their chosen genre of communication' (Castree, 2014: 42). In an epistemic community where academics and policy makers rub shoulders very closely, the conventions that define the epistemic community are therefore a mixture of conventions of academic disciplines and of the international policy-making processes and institutions in which other actors are entrenched. As highlighted in previous chapters, particular policy language and institutional structures have become part of this community's lingua franca. However, the prominent presence of academics in the same epistemic community has also led to a central role for scientific classification in understanding people moving in the context of climate change and most advocacy work draws on scientific expertise to support and legitimise their work.

The following claim emphasising the weight of scientific knowledge in policy making is fairly typical for advocacy documents on the nexus:

> A growing body of research by academic institutions, international organizations, governments and other research institutions examines the complex relationship between climate change and human mobility, exploring not only negative impacts but also the potential for human mobility as an adaptation measure. (Kälin, 2015a: 3)

Particularly in the run-up to the UNFCCC negotiations in Paris, an emphasis was placed on the need to take scientific knowledge and transfer it into policy with the ultimate goal of concrete action based on this knowledge.

> ... a first generation of research, policy and advocacy work, as well as operational responses, were developed and initial recommendations identified. Further recognition in the Paris Agreement is now necessary to consolidate existing findings and recommendations and address the action gap, in order to effectively equip Sates with solid tools to guide their work in this area. (Advisory Group on Climate Change and Human Mobility, 2015b)

The portrayal of this pre-Paris research, policy and advocacy as a 'first generation' also implies an expectation of generations to follow. Therefore, much advocacy work contains a self-perpetuating call for more knowledge to be created (Nash, 2018c), sometimes (as in the following example) giving concrete suggestions for directions this knowledge creation could take:

> Many areas in relation to climate-related displacement remain to be studied, including further empirical research on: vulnerability to displacement; adaptation, relocation and migration responses; regional and national governance

schemes; and the inter-linkages between climate change, conflict and displacement. (UNHCR, 2011d)

The emphasis given in this discourse to knowledge that is generated through modes of academic inquiry is important. It has impacts on who can take on the role of the legitimate speaker in the discourse, with only those possessing appropriately formatted knowledge able to answer this call.

Within academic (or quasi-academic) work, classification usually serves the purpose of creating analytical categories that allow for simplification of an issue in order for an analysis to be possible. However, these categories are often adopted from political or legal categories. One danger of academic discourses is the portrayal of these categories as purely analytical or objective, when actually these categories have their own intricate genealogies. The analytical categories created in relation to the migration and climate change nexus often reflect different aspects of mobility dynamics (for example, distance and duration of migration), and whether mobility is forced or voluntary, as well as frequently drawing on established legal categories.[9]

Visualisations that are contained in documents that are more academically oriented are diametrically opposed to the images of people typically included in policy documents. Archetypal visualisations involve complex, abstract spiderwebs of text boxes and linking arrows, scales and colour coding. The most immediately obvious difference between these types of imagery is the absence of people in the more detached scientific visualisations, which convey a sense of academic objectivity. The effect is therefore the opposite to that created by photographs of people, with the complex, abstract approach of academic contributions often making these people invisible. One distinguishing feature of the knowledge-based academic discourse so revered by advocacy actors is therefore that people are less visible, with the focus being instead on the abstract complexity of the 'phenomenon' itself.

One of the challenges that is increasingly acknowledged in discussions surrounding migration and climate change is that posed by the complex nature of the nexus, coming not just from the fact that two issues are being linked (in a somewhat arbitrary manner), but also given that both issues are already saturated in complexities as stand-alone issues. Taking this argument into account, one aspect of the discourse discussed in the previous sections of this chapter in particular may account for the focus on abstract complexity, namely the potentiality of mobilities. The uncertainty inherent to potentiality is visible in questions on multiple levels: whether people are moving or will move; if so, what forms their mobility will take;

to what extent climate change will play a role in this movement; what impacts these mobilities will have. Therefore, once a nuanced portrayal of these uncertainties is given, emphasising the complexity of the issues involved as well as the mixed and multi-causal nature of mobility, it becomes increasingly difficult to not identify, define and also classify the people involved without using this level of abstractness. One result is that scientific classification in this way contributes to the objectification of the subjects of the nexus, not through a process of separating mobile people from each other, but rather by omitting an identifiable person from the discourse altogether.

An absent story: the voices of people on the move

In contrast to other policy and awareness-raising activities conducted by advocacy actors such as UNHCR and IOM in their broader, non-climate-specific, work, the voices of people on the move are glaringly absent from contributions made to the policy-making discourse on migration and climate change. In particular, the social media channels of both organisations frequently utilise videos of individuals and families who are either refugees or migrants to bring a human face to debates around human mobility. Even these highly selective, mediated snippets of the voices of people on the move are missing from the policy-making discourse on migration and climate change. Here, the lives of people on the move are mediated entirely by the words of experts, policy makers, academics and advocates. As a result, the lives of the people at the heart of the migration and climate change nexus are translated to conform with the conventions of policy-making arenas, a strategy that on the one hand allows the content to be deemed legitimate, but on the other hand disenfranchises people on the move and reduces the rawness of life to bureaucratic and technocratic policy positions.

The relegation from view of the voices of people whose mobilities are or will be affected by climate change has important consequences. Most importantly, people are removed from the discourse, which becomes impersonal and oriented around a phenomenon rather than people whose lives are being turned upside down by the adverse effects of climate change. This is cause for concern in itself, removing agency from people whose mobilities are affected. The coldness of a technical, policy-making bureaucracy comes into stark relief in institutions such as the UNFCCC, where phrasings, commas and the constitution of nebulous entities such as task forces are the focus of debate and agreement.

A side-effect of highly technical and bureaucratic policy making could be the spreading of tropes and generalisations about people on the move in the context of climate change in broader discourse in livelier but dangerous portrayals of people. Others have already critiqued the discourse on migration and climate change as containing and furthering gendered (Myrttinen, 2017; Rothe, 2017) as well as racialised (Telford, 2018) stereotypes. These tropes are not necessarily countered, and are sometimes even assimilated by the policy-making discourse.

However, the absence from policy-making spaces of the voices of people on the move is not a concern that can be addressed purely by distributing UN lanyards to a handful of people whose mobilities are affected by climate change and inviting them to make contributions to the process. In his critique of an Oxfam GB project 'Listening to the Displaced', Prem Kumar Rajaram makes the following warning:

> 'Listening' to refugee voices may have a less than remarkable effect on the workings of a humanitarian/development organization if the broader concept of development and of the purposes and agenda of aid organizations remain unproblematized. (Rajaram, 2002: 262)

This critique can also be applied to the inclusion in policy making of voices of people whose mobilities are affected by climate change. As Rajaram goes on to argue:

> In its claim to have empowered refugees (or having been a step in that direction), Oxfam's methodology of listening may obscure what amounts to an act of power in pre-emptively setting the boundaries wherein refugee identity is articulated. In this erasing of the trace of a forceful attempt to set boundaries that secure the positional leverage of the humanitarian agency, the refugee is subject to ever deepening abjection, one that appears to be all the more hazardous because the abjection is disguised as empowerment. (2002: 262)

The forum within which the voices of people on the move are heard, and the boundaries that are set around what can be said therefore influence whether inclusion is an empowering experience. Furthermore, following Rajaram, cursory inclusion of the voices of people on the move without interrogating these boundaries may prove more damaging than exclusion in the first place because it creates the illusion of inclusivity.

Any bids to include the voices of people whose mobilities are affected by climate change will also be faced with the challenge of recognising the plurality and diversity of experience among different (im)mobile people. Migration taking place in the context of, and influenced by, climate change is not homogenous, either in duration or distance of mobility. If migration in the context of climate change is approached intersectionally, to take into consideration race, gender and a multitude of other layered factors that make experiences of mobility even more diverse, it becomes even more apparent that it will not be possible to distil the experiences of people on the move into a compatible format. As Nando Sigona argues:

> [T]his plurality does not necessarily translate into humanitarian, academic, and media discourses, as these tend to privilege a one-dimensional representation of the refugee which relies heavily on feminized and infantilized images of 'pure' victimhood and vulnerability. (Sigona, 2014: 370)

Actively including the voices of people whose mobilities are affected by climate change into the policy-making discourse is a process that would move the policy-making discourse away from bureaucratic and technocratic language towards lived experience and modulate the narrator's voice away from advocacy actors. However, as warnings from studies on the representations of refugee voices have highlighted, inclusion in the discourse as a token gesture that does not explicitly consider the boundaries within which these voices are heard to speak or represent the plurality of experienced (im)mobility are more likely to bring only an illusion of inclusivity to policy making.

7

Interrogating a Notable Silence: Human Rights and the Migration and Climate Change Nexus

This chapter differs from the two preceding chapters in that it does not focus on prominent elements of the discourse on migration and climate change. Instead, it interrogates a silence – an idea or framing that is conspicuous in the discourse due to its (relative) absence. This is both an important element of genealogy and of critical scholarship, with a holistic analysis in this tradition needing to analyse both 'discursive tropes and silences' as part of its 'big picture analysis' (Death, 2014: 5). An infinite number of silences could be examined here; the absence of migrant voices in the discourse itself suggests a number of fitting ideas or framings might also be missing. To venture into the more far-fetched, the idea of space travel and an intergalactic framing are (somewhat unsurprisingly) also absent. But this chapter focuses on a silence that is all the more surprising because it is well established in elite policy making of the United Nations (UN) and the international community broadly, backed up with legal documents, norms and accepted parlance, but which prior to and indeed during the Paris Conference of the Parties (COP) of the United Nations Framework Convention on Climate Change (UNFCCC) remained on the margins of the policy-making discourse: human rights.

Climate change and human rights are not unusual bedfellows, with academics drawing on the utility of human rights as an analytical approach to the societal effects of climate change (for example, see Barry and Woods, 2009),[10] and the link also featuring frequently and prominently within UN fora (Human Rights Council, 2008, 2009, 2011, 2012, 2014, 2015; Knox, 2009). Against this background, it is notable that human rights does not have a more prominent position in the policy-making discourse on migration and climate change. For this analysis it is important to stress that human rights is a *relative* silence in the policy-making discourse on the migration and climate change nexus. It is described as such because human rights do actually feature in the discourse and have been very much present in broader debates surrounding the nexus (for a prominent example, see McAdam, 2012). However, prior to the Paris negotiations, human rights were not at all prominent in the policy-making discourse and advocacy documents in particular were often conspicuous by their lack of references to human rights. Post-2015, human rights are being gradually drawn into the discourse, a movement that this chapter will also explore.

Human rights in the policy-making discourse on the migration and climate change nexus

While the discourse in the broader epistemic community surrounding migration and climate change has included human rights (Manou et al, 2017), the pre-Paris policy-making discourse specifically has only paid very cursory attention to human rights. They are not a prominent part of the discourse, but appear rather perfunctorily at the edges. When they do appear, human rights are not drawn on homogeneously, and their usage in policy documents is threefold: as protection instruments in themselves; as standards against which to measure and align policy; and as something that can be damaged by the 'wrong' types of mobility.

In the first usage, human rights instruments are identified as potential protection instruments in themselves. For example, the International Organization for Migration (IOM) has argued that 'human rights remain the primary body of instruments that afford protection relevant to those who have to move due to environmental events or processes' (IOM, 2014d: 31). A series of UN Special Rapporteurs, actors who are very influential in the international human rights regime, have also attempted to draw the joint issues of migration and climate change into their spheres of authority. The then Special Rapporteur on the Human Rights of Internally Displaced Persons, Walter Kälin, included a thematic section on climate change in his annual report to the United Nations General Assembly in 2009 (Kälin, 2009), an act that was repeated by his successor Chaloka Beyani in 2011 (Beyani, 2011b), who also spoke on a human rights-based approach to protection of environmentally displaced persons during the Nansen Conference in 2011 (Beyani, 2011a). Although very much situated in the international human rights regime, this report shows awareness of some of the episodes that had been taking place in relation to the migration and climate change nexus, with both the United Nations High Commissioner for Refugees (UNHCR) expert meeting of 2011 and the Nansen Principles being referenced (Beyani, 2011b: paragraph 37).

A similar move was made by François Crépeau, Special Rapporteur on the Human Rights of Migrants, in 2012, when he also used his annual report to the General Assembly to include a thematic section on climate change (Crépeau, 2012). The fact that these particular individuals have used these fora to highlight the connections between human rights, climate change and migration is important. They are widely regarded as experts in their respective areas and the knowledge they produce therefore has great authority. Furthermore, the Special Rapporteurs are appointed by the Human Rights Council, thus occupying a privileged position in the UN system and enjoying a great deal of legitimacy with states, although retaining an independent position.

Despite this potential utility, the argument has also been made that changes may need to be made to human rights (referring here to the international human rights regime of the UN, including institutions and legal provisions) in order to respond to the challenges posed by the nexus:

> [T]he phenomenon of climate change-induced migration may require rethinking of the human rights categories afforded to migrants and the development of eventual protection mechanisms for persons on the move. (Crépeau, 2012: 16)

However, the international human rights regime, or its utility in addressing questions of migration and climate change, is not called into question here; the suggestion is rather that adjusting some of the categorisations by which people are ordered within it may be necessary.

This use of human rights as an existing system of ensuring protection (in this case for people migrating in the context of climate change) chimes with legal arguments that existing, general, non-group-specific human rights provisions (such as the Universal Declaration of Human Rights and International Covenants on Civil and Political, and Economic, Social and Cultural Rights respectively) provide relevant protections to people who may find themselves moving in the context of climate change (Mayer and Cournil, 2016). This has been used as an argument against developing new human rights provisions specifically in relation to those moving in the context of climate change (Mayer, 2017).

In the second usage in the policy-making discourse, human rights are mentioned as an aside, as a set of standards with which policy should be compatible or against which policy can be measured, but not necessarily portrayed as a policy avenue to be pursued in and of themselves. An example of this approach to human rights is in the documents of the Advisory Group on Climate Change and Human Mobility (hereafter Advisory Group), which has stated that it is 'essential to ensure that migration occurs in a manner that fully respects the dignity and human rights of those who move and those who stay behind' (Advisory Group on Climate Change and Human Mobility, 2015a: 7). In other examples, human rights are one of a list of principles with which policies must be compatible, such as in this excerpt from UNHCR:

> ... responses to climate-related displacement need to be guided by the fundamental principles of humanity, human dignity, human rights and international cooperation. They need furthermore to be guided by consent, empowerment, participation and partnership and to reflect age, gender and diversity aspects. (UNHCR, 2011d)

Although conceptualisations of human rights in relation to migration and climate change have been rather patchy and it is not clear what compatibility with human rights really means for migration and climate change policy, many organisations have labelled themselves as rights-based: for example, 'IOM promotes a rights-based approach to migration' (IOM, 2014d: 32); and 'as a rights-based and protection agency, UNHCR's concern relates to the enjoyment of human rights of people relocated or displaced by the effects of disasters and climate change, either within their own borders or across borders' (UNHCR 2014: 13). Coming from the two key organisations focused on human mobility in the advocacy community that has developed around the nexus, these are important statements. However, what is also notable is the lack of more specific statements about what is meant by rights-based. As no more than a passing reference, the rights-based aspect of the various approaches to the migration and climate change nexus do not take a central position.

The final way in which human rights feature in the policy-making discourse is as something that can be negatively affected by certain mobility scenarios. As the Nansen Initiative has argued, 'disaster displacement creates humanitarian challenges, affects human rights, undermines development and may in some situations affect security' (Nansen Initiative, 2015c: 15). That human rights are being affected can also be a signal of (negative) effects of displacement. The inclusion of human rights in the discourse in such a manner allows it to be used as a link between different categories of (more or less desirable) mobility outcomes. For example, the emphasis on human rights violations that occur in situations of displacement can build a part of the argument for migration as a form of adaptation.

Idiosyncrasies between the policy-making discourse and the international human rights regime

Two particular idiosyncrasies are apparent between the policy-making discourse on migration and climate change and the international human rights regime, both of which place hurdles in the way of human rights becoming a central lens through which migration and climate change can be thought about and acted on: the perceived weight of duties that human rights entail set against an area of policy making at pains to stress that new duties or legal standards are not being created; and the people-centred, human rights-based approach set against an area of policy making that does not have easily identifiable subjects.

In reporting on the links between climate change and human rights, the Special Rapporteur on the Human Rights of Internally Displaced Persons explicitly identified the positive duties that may be required from states in the context of migration and climate change:

> Some climate change-induced displacement however, such as movements triggered by slow-onset disasters, may require more emphasis on the positive obligations of States, with the support of regional bodies and the international community, to anticipate, plan ahead and take measures to prevent or mitigate conditions likely to bring about displacement and threaten human rights. This precautionary role to ensure conditions conducive to human rights, including rights related to an adequate standard of living which allow one to avoid displacement, is a standard of governmental, international governance and human rights protection which is based on positive obligations and actions, rather than the negative obligations of non-interference in human rights. (Beyani, 2011b: paragraph 54)

This is a position that is not frequently taken in advocacy documents, with Beyani's claims a rare example of emphasis being placed on potentially highly contentious and costly obligations that could be linked to the migration and climate change nexus if viewed through a human rights lens. In the broader policy-making discourse, the duties that human rights entail tend instead to be played down in order to avoid adding another layer of contention to policy-making discussions. Another exception that has broken this mould is the Peninsula Principles on Climate Displacement Within States (Displacement Solutions, 2013) (hereafter Peninsula Principles), which were developed by the non-governmental organisation Displacement Solutions and were intended to '[build] the foundations for a new normative framework to address climate displacement within States' (Displacement Solutions, 2013: 7). According to Displacement Solutions:

> [T]he Principles provide a comprehensive normative framework, based on principles of international law, human rights obligations and good practice, within which the rights of climate displaced persons within States can be addressed. The Principles set out protection and assistance provisions, consistent with the UN Guiding Principles on Internal Displacement (upon which they build and contextualise), to be applied to climate displaced persons. (Displacement Solutions, 2013: 8)

The approach taken by Displacement Solutions, which differs drastically from that of other advocacy actors, is interesting to note here and is highly likely to be one of the reasons why the Principles ultimately did not gain much traction in the policy community (indeed, the Principles are not included in the episodes set out in Part 1 of this book because of their absence in the policy discourse).

The policy-making discourse as a whole has tended to shy away from creating normative frameworks that are then presented to states as 'solutions' to the 'problem' of the nexus (which is here identified as internal displacement). For example, the Nansen Initiative has been at pains to emphasise that it is not aiming to create new legal standards (Nansen Initiative, 2013). The politics of human rights have therefore stood in the way of it becoming a central framing of migration and climate change. The layer of sensitivity that human rights is seen to add to policy debates, through the potential duties that are attached to certain rights claims due to the rights-holder/duty-bearer set-up of the human rights regime, has prompted caution.

A second idiosyncrasy that exists between a human rights lens to migration and climate change and policy making is the lack of an easily identifiable subject in the policy-making discourse, which is in turn a requirement for the very structuring of human rights claims. Human rights require both a rights-holder and a duty-bearer, moving discussions away from general statements of rectitude (whether something is morally 'right' or 'wrong') towards a narrower conception of entitlement (someone having a right). This is important as it creates concrete rights claims: to be a rights-holder is to be owed something and thus to be authorised to make claims on this right should it be threatened or denied (Donnelly, 2003: 7). However, in order for these concrete rights claims to be made, a subject of the nexus (whose human rights are being negatively affected) needs to be identified. As the previous chapter has illustrated, this is frequently a problem with which the migration and climate change nexus is faced; the subject of the nexus is often difficult to identify, and the potentiality of mobilities is often more of a focus.

However, in order to pursue a route that articulates the nexus in rights terms, this figure needs to be identified. For example, on the use of existing human rights mechanisms, François Crépeau, Special Rapporteur on the Human Rights of Migrants, has argued that:

> [A]lthough there is no one international human rights treaty designed to deal specifically with environmentally induced migrants, existing human rights law provides a range of situations that respond to their needs and rights. (Crépeau, 2012: 13)

While the content of this statement is not necessarily problematic, it does highlight the need for an identifiable subject in order to articulate rights claims (to respond to a person's needs and rights).

Human rights in Paris

The Paris negotiations of the UNFCCC provide an ideal opportunity to analyse the absence of a human rights framing on migration and climate change policy making. The negotiations are an example of an elite UN policy-making process, where all UN agencies tend to be present and bring in their perspectives to the issue at hand. Indeed, human rights actors were present at the Paris COP21 and were working to bring in a human rights framing of the issue of climate change. However, despite these background conditions, the discussions on migration and climate change that took place in Paris were not approached through the lens of human rights, taking place completely separately from these discussions. This section briefly sketches how human rights were brought into the negotiations in Paris, before the following section delves deeper into the mystery of the omission of human rights from the discussions on migration.

While the migration and climate change nexus has seldom been articulated in rights terms, the Geneva human rights community used a meeting of the Ad Hoc Working Group on the Durban Platform for Enhanced Action (ADP) in Geneva for pre-negotiations for the Paris conference as an opportunity to raise the profile of human rights and climate change. A 'climate justice dialogue' was also hosted by the Office of the High Commissioner for Human Rights (OHCHR) and the Mary Robinson Foundation – Climate Justice (MRFCJ) (MRFCJ, 2015; OHCHR, 2015) with climate change negotiators in attendance. In the closing plenary of the ADP negotiations in Geneva, a group of states[11] announced the Geneva Pledge on Human Rights in Climate Action, which emphasised the importance of taking heed of human rights in climate action and pledged to improve coordination between their involvement processes surrounding the UNFCCC and the Human Rights Council (Geneva Pledge, 2015).

During the Paris negotiations, human rights were a continued focus and a hard fought over reference to human rights is contained within the preamble to the Paris Agreement, which acknowledges that:

> [C]limate change is a common concern of humankind, Parties should, when taking action to address climate change, respect, promote and consider their respective obligations on human rights, the right to health, the rights of indigenous peoples, local communities, migrants, children, persons with disabilities and people in vulnerable situations and the right to development, as well as gender equality, empowerment of women and intergenerational equity. (UNFCCC, 2016a: Preamble)

Climate justice is also included in the preamble to the agreement (albeit heavily caveated), with the agreement

> ... noting the importance of ensuring the integrity of all ecosystems, including oceans, and the protection of biodiversity, recognized by some cultures as Mother Earth, and noting the importance for some of the concept of 'climate justice', when taking action to address climate change. (UNFCCC, 2016a: Preamble)

The Paris Agreement is the first occasion where human rights are explicitly mentioned in a multilateral environmental agreement (Savaresi, 2016), giving the preambular language, however weak, a 'political and moral value, drawing an explicit link between treaty obligations under the climate regime and those under the human rights instruments [States] have ratified' (Savaresi, 2016: 25).

Despite the inclusion of human rights in the preamble of the agreement, the inclusion of human rights within the text was not without controversy. Prior to the negotiations in Paris, human rights were included in Article 2 of the negotiating text:

[This Agreement shall be implemented on the basis of equity and science, in [full] accordance with the principles of equity and common but differentiated responsibilities and respective capabilities [, in light of national circumstances] [the principles and provisions of the Convention], while ensuring the integrity and resilience of natural ecosystems] [the integrity of Mother Earth, protection of health, a just transition of the workforce and creation of decent work and quality jobs in accordance with nationally defined development priorities] and the respect, protection, promotion and fulfilment of human rights for all, including the right to health and sustainable development, [including the right of people under occupation] and to ensure gender equality and the full and equal participation of women, [and intergenerational equity].] (ADP, 2015d: Article 2)

The sheer amount of bracketed text included in this excerpt highlights the controversy attached to this issue, providing a concrete illustration of the contestation surrounding human rights in the UNFCCC.

However, during the negotiations this strong wording was watered down and eventually disappeared completely from the draft text (ADP, 2015g), causing a group of state Parties, many of which had already been involved in the Geneva Pledge,[12] to write a letter calling on the French Presidency to 'ensure that the references in the preamble of the Agreement are kept and that the wording is consistent with international human rights Law' (Romson et al, 2015). This call was also supported by a large coalition of civil society actors, who released a statement backing up the position made in the state Party letter (Various authors, 2015).[13]

Explaining the silence on migration

Despite the flurry of activity surrounding human rights and climate change in Paris, the issue was not linked up with initial forays into a human rights perspective on the migration and climate change nexus and there were no concerted attempts in the run-up to or during the negotiations to link the issues. Speculatively, the lack of attempts from within formal human rights entities at the UN level could be attributed to the state-centric (and thus state-driven) structure of the international human rights regime and the same reluctance on the part of states that reportedly led to UNHCR being prevented from embracing work on the issue following the Nansen Conference.

Discussions regarding human rights were prominent during the Paris negotiations, with a coalition of human rights organisations actively carrying out advocacy work both in the run-up to and during the negotiations in order to ensure that human rights language was included in the text (OHCHR Interview, 2016). As the letter to the French Presidency supporting the inclusion of human rights language in the agreement highlights, certain state Parties were also on board with these advocacy goals. However, the focus of these groups was not on the narrow issue of migration and climate change. Instead, the core human rights advocacy groups were "really just focussing on a few sentences in the preamble and in Article 2" (OHCHR Interview, 2016).

One rather straightforward reason for a lack of engagement from human rights advocates with the issue of migration within the context of the Paris negotiations is simply a lack of resources (OHCHR Interview, 2016), with many of the organisations involved (from UN-based organisations through to non-governmental organisations) lacking staff members dedicated to work on climate change, never mind the capacity to carry out work on the migration and climate change nexus. John Knox, the Special Rapporteur on Human Rights and the Environment, also identified the size of his mandate and awareness of the work carried out by the Special Rapporteurs on the Human Rights of Migrants and Internally Displaced Persons as reasons for not engaging with the issue directly in his work:

'My mandate is so broad that I tend to focus on areas that are not being examined by other Special Rapporteurs or mandate holders and migration, because it was being examined both by the Special Rapporteur on migration and by the Special Rapporteur on Internally Displaced People, I have tended to just kind of refer to what they have done and borrow as much from it as I can.' (Knox Interview, 2016)

A lack of engagement by human rights advocates in the setting of the climate negotiations is, however, not synonymous with a lack of awareness of the issue and the international advocacy efforts that have been taking place. In particular, the Nansen Initiative enjoys the recognition of the human rights community, being cited by interview partners as an example of work being carried out on the migration and climate change nexus (OHCHR Interview, 2016; Knox Interview, 2016). Given the prominence of Walter Kälin, the Envoy of the Chairmanship of the Nansen Initiative within the human rights community, and his previous position as Special Rapporteur on the Human Rights of Internally Displaced Persons, this is not surprising.

As opposed to the largely capacity-based reasoning for a lack of engagement on the behalf of human rights advocates at COP21, the reasons cited by those carrying out advocacy work on human mobility are more tactical. This is already perceived by the human rights community, as John Knox has speculated:

> 'Some of these people may be choosing not to foreground human rights rhetoric, and they may be doing that because ... for the same reason that some people involved in development issues generally don't foreground human rights language because they don't think it will actually help the governments that they need to convince to do something about this to couch it in human rights terms.' (Knox Interview, 2016)

This is an opinion that is also mirrored by those who advocated on human mobility at COP21. Due to controversial discussions on human rights in the past, it is not utilised as a framing in relation to the climate change and human mobility nexus. The perceived danger here is that emphasis on climate justice could either result in the exclusion of migration concerns from an eventual climate change agreement or even in complete failure to reach an agreement. Also turning to the make-up of the Advisory Group (which represents the most coordinated advocacy effort on migration), no core human rights actors are represented, with most of the members coming from a migration perspective and academic institutions with a migration focus.

A distinction is drawn between closed-door meetings with governments and public fora:

> 'If you meet in closed doors governments will ... you know the ministry of representatives that are at those meetings, they embrace it, they get it, but the mandates, they don't get the mandates to embrace it in a public way or in a written document.' (Warner Interview, 2015)

It is this lack of mandates that leads to climate justice being "the first thing that gets bracketed when you're talking about government drafted texts" (Warner Interview, 2015).

Therefore, those involved in advocacy on the climate change and human mobility nexus, at the least on the part of international organisations and the Advisory Group, have become cautious in their messaging in order to pre-empt and also respond to direct concerns from states. The fear, on the part of some Parties is that an overreliance on human rights narratives "could hinder the negotiations" (UNHCR Interview 1, 2015).

For many working in the area, a pragmatic attitude sensitive to the delicate balance on which the climate change negotiations rests is at the core of their approach to advocacy. The attitude towards the climate justice framing is that "there's not much power behind it, other than saying it's the right thing. And the right thing, I think that's ultimately a humongous narrative question" (Warner Interview, 2015).

Walter Kälin, coming himself from the human rights community but now occupying a core position in the advocacy community surrounding the migration and climate change nexus, has speculated that the lack of a human rights framing in advocacy work on migration and climate change could have historical reasons:

> '... there is very little in the human rights mechanisms regarding the work of UNHCR and IOM. There is more language than we have on disaster displacement, climate change, and human rights. But in general there isn't that much. I don't know whether historically it was ... felt UNHCR with a protection mandate, that's good enough and ... we don't need to duplicate too much.' (Kälin Interview, 2016)

While able to speculate on the lack of adoption of human rights framing from the migration community, Kälin is unable to account for the absence of human rights actors in the issue. When asked why this partnership has not come about, he responded: "I ask myself that question repeatedly!" (Kälin Interview, 2016).

Ultimately it seems that in both advocacy communities different reasons are at play that have prevented the communities from coming together around the migration and climate change nexus. From the perspective of migration advocacy, this move appears to have been largely tactical, with a human rights or climate justice framing being actively avoided in order to increase the chances of human mobility being included in climate change agreements. However, from the perspective of the human rights community, the lack of integration of the two advocacy communities has not been tactical; indeed, different interviewees have declared an interest in the issue and wish they could have followed it more closely (OHCHR Interview, 2016; Knox Interview, 2016). Instead, capacity has been cited as a reason for not getting more closely involved, with recognition that others are already covering the issue also playing a role (Knox Interview, 2016).

Late to the party: human rights in policy making on migration and climate change post-Paris

Although human rights did not feature in the pre-Paris policy-making discourse on migration and climate change in any meaningful way, this has been changing in the years since the Paris negotiations. In 2017 and 2018, there was a flurry of activity from OHCHR with an intersessional panel discussion on 'human rights, climate change, migrants and persons displaced across international borders' (Human Rights Council, 2017d: 1) and the presentation of a summary report to the Human Rights Council which was to feed into both the Task Force on Displacement and the negotiations for the Global Compact on Migration (Human Rights Council, 2017d: 9), as well as a collaboration with the Platform on Disaster Displacement (PDD) on an expert meeting and report on slow-onset effects of climate change and the effects on the human rights protection of cross-border migrants (Human Rights Council, 2018).

This sudden uptake of migration and climate change as an area of work for OHCHR has been put down to two different developments: first, the Human Rights Council 2017 resolution on human rights and climate change specifically focused on human mobility and mandated OHCHR to carry out activities in this area (Human Rights Council, 2017b), and second, OHCHR had recently become a member of the advisory committee of the PDD. These two developments provided "two different reasons to, or two different things driving us to engage more on the issues of climate change, migration and human rights" (OHCHR Interview, 2018). An important link to other policy processes was also provided by the 2017 resolution, which explicitly mandated OHCHR to feed into both the Task Force on Displacement and the negotiations for the Global Compact for Migration with the report of the intersessional panel discussion.

A striking aspect of OHCHR's work on migration and climate change is that it does not advocate for change in the sense of a drive towards new policy, or, as many academic contributions from the field of law have done, advocating for new group-specific human rights provisions for people moving in the context of climate change. Instead, the key message that is frequently made by OHCHR is drawing attention to the existing 'obligations and responsibilities of States and other duty-bearers to address the human mobility challenges created by climate change' (OHCHR, no date: 1). The agency emphasises that:

> States must ensure that any measure or legislation that governs or affects migration is consistent with their human rights law obligations and does not adversely affect the full enjoyment of the human rights of migrants. (OHCHR, no date: 1)

Links are therefore drawn to existing sectoral agreements (for example on disaster risk reduction or climate change) as well as human rights law, which contains a catalogue of provisions that apply to and can be used to invoke protection for people who are on the move in the context of climate change:

> 'Why not work with what we have, I guess is … the approach we are trying to take. And why not look at the 2030 agenda, the Sendai Framework, the Paris Agreement, the Addis Ababa Action Agenda, all of which came out of, sort of, this massive international confab in 2015 and all of which have human rights at their core and can be sort of mobilised if you think of that as a package with international human rights law, you know, at its foundation.' (OHCHR Interview, 2018)

OHCHR's narrative therefore combines all three usages of human rights set out at the outset of this chapter: human rights as protection instruments in themselves; human rights as standards against which to measure and align policy; and human rights as something that can be damaged by the 'wrong' types of mobility. At the same time, OHCHR conforms with the dominant reticence towards the creation of new legislation or provisions on migration and climate change.

Another aspect of OHCHR's narrative that deserves highlighting in particular, as well as the human rights strand of the policy-making discourse on migration and climate change more broadly, is the (perceived) normative agenda-setting power of the agency and the international human rights regime. The ability to bring a new voice to proceedings and normatively influence the debate is something that OHCHR is aware of;

> 'I mean, I think we do have a sort of unique voice as well as moral authority that we can bring to the table and that

can be helpful in the context of these ongoing discussions and processes even if we were a little bit late to the game.' (OHCHR Interview, 2018)

This is not to say that human rights has instantly become an uncontroversial part of the discourse. Indeed, quite to the contrary, human rights remains an extremely contested way of framing the issue of climate change, especially in the UNFCCC context where it is frequently associated with questions of liability and compensation and the fear that a strong human rights framing will imply a new set of liability claims that many states are fixed on avoiding. A corollary that can be drawn from the controversies surrounding loss and damage and the difficulties that the formalisation of the area of work has come up against is that a human rights approach to migration and climate change is unlikely to be formalised or become the central way through which to conceptualise the nexus. Rather, human rights is likely to become part of a catalogue of relevant international agreements that are referenced by advocacy actors to provide weight and legitimacy to their thematic work. However, taking into consideration this flurry of activity from OHCHR, it is conceivable that OHCHR and the human rights framing that it brings to the table will continue to be an active part of the policy-making discourse on migration and climate change.

One way in which human rights may challenge and disrupt the status quo of the policy-making discourse is with the very regimented, person-oriented structure of human rights, which challenges the nebulousness of the figure at the centre of the phenomenon of the migration and climate change nexus. Indeed, the requirement of a rights-bearer for human rights claims to be made could provide impetus to clarify who the subjects of the discourse are and provide more shape to the shadowy figure of the people at the centre of the migration and climate change nexus.

Human rights: depoliticising and sanitising climate justice in the policy-making discourse

Human rights is increasingly being identified as a vital element of climate justice, with most definitions of climate justice containing a reference to human rights, such as that invoked by the MRFCJ:

> The Principles of Climate Justice are founded in legal and moral imperatives of human rights and respect for the dignity of the person, making them the indispensable foundation for action on climate justice. (MRFCJ, 2014: 1)

In the policy-making discourse on migration and climate change, references to climate justice are overwhelmingly made through the lens of human rights, which at times appears to be subsuming the broader climate justice concept.

However, the tone in which human rights are overwhelmingly discussed, at least in the context of the human rights architecture of the UN, is at odds with the genealogy of climate justice. The concept is inextricably linked to the environmental justice movement in the US in the 1980s and 1990s, which was concerned with how poor, African-American communities were disproportionately adversely affected by environmental hazards, in particular the disposal of toxic waste in close proximity to their communities. The movement brought together both civil rights and environmental activists, and as a result 'the movement's idea of environmental justice combined notions of environmental sustainability and everyday environments with demands for social justice' (Schlosberg and Collins, 2014: 361).

As such, the concerns of the environmental justice movement transgressed a narrow consideration of environmental factors in isolation. Instead, 'environmental conditions were seen as yet another indicator, another symptom, of the larger reality of social and economic inequity many communities lived with every day' (Schlosberg and Collins, 2014: 361). This articulation of climate justice is situated, referring to lived experiences in specific locales, with the focus not only on climate issues, but on an interrelated range of structural factors that affect communities. A human rights framing can serve to remove the focus from these structural factors. The focus on the rights claim that a situation must be rectified can often mask the roots of the situation in the first place.

As with other concepts that have become commonplace in the policy-making discourse on migration and climate change, from resilience and vulnerability, disaster and risk, to mitigation, adaptation, and loss and damage, human rights is a contingent concept, and a normative lens through which migration and climate change is understood. The decision to employ a human rights framing, the ways in which human rights-based approaches affect the discourse, and the productive effects that this may have on policy making are all fair game for analysis, indeed introducing a political gaze on human rights and the role they play in the policy-making discourse. Overwhelmingly depoliticised human rights-based approaches have implications for policy responses that are conceived as an answer to migration in the context of climate change. As Andrew Baldwin has argued:

> [d]isplacing considerations of power from the terrain of human rights delimits the very terms of responsible action.

> For example, it limits responsible action to ensuring the human rights of those who are forced to relocate from climate change, rather than including within the scope of responsible action efforts to expose how power functions in relation to knowledge claims about human rights, climate change and migration. (Baldwin, 2017c: 221)

There is an inherent difficulty in approaching migration in the context of climate change as a human rights issue. This is due to a large extent to the difficulty of identifying the people whose mobilities are affected by climate change, a necessary component of a human rights logic and of rights-holders in the rights-holder/duty-bearer structure at the heart of human rights. However, since the Paris climate change negotiations, human rights advocacy actors have decided to join the party on migration and climate change. Given the institutional environment within which policy making has been taking place, and the other actors involved, the increasing presence of actors from the international human rights regime is hardly surprising and the approach does show some potential for centring people in the discourse rather than an abstract phenomenon. Nevertheless, the subsumption of climate justice claims within a discourse of human rights could run the risk of depoliticising and sanitising climate justice, shutting out another potential direction for policy making that does not have its roots in UN institutions.

8

Conclusion: Closing
the Policy Circle

This book has told as complete as possible a story of mainstream policy making on migration and climate change between the Cancun negotiations of the United Nations Framework Convention on Climate Change (UNFCCC) in 2010 and its 2018 Conference of the Parties (COP) in Katowice. On the one hand, the book serves as a reference tool, detailing the main happenings during this time (see Part I), focusing on the Paris COP21 in extra detail in a stand-alone chapter (Chapter 3). On the other hand, the book works with critique to offer an analysis of policy making on migration and climate change that calls some of the very foundations of policy making in the area into question and pushes us to move beyond existing boundaries of the thinkable (Part II). The level of detail on policy making included in the first part of this book, as well as the overarching critical theoretical approach, set this volume apart from other recent book-length contributions to the literature that have addressed policy and governance on migration and climate change. Important contributions have been made on mandate change in selected organisations that have integrated the climate change and migration nexus into their work (Hall, 2016) and whether IGOs are expanding as a result (Simonelli, 2016), as well as on the prospects of a series of narratives on migration and climate change to influence global governance (Mayer, 2016b). The contribution contained within these pages aims to complement such volumes by providing a fresh perspective on the policy-making process, exploring its emergence and how different aspects of its genealogy influence how policy is being made on migration and climate change today.

Each half of the book has a distinct argument running through its core. The first half argues that migration and climate change has come of age as an area of policy making, having undergone many changes since the

Cancun Adaptation Framework was thrashed out in 2010. The second half deconstructs a series of boundary-marking processes that are creating the 'phenomenon' of the migration and climate change nexus and influencing the policies emerging as possible responses. In the following two sections, this chapter will pull these arguments together, before turning to the future, extrapolating what the arguments made in this book could mean for future work on the migration and climate change nexus.

The coming of age of policy making on migration and climate change

The preceding chapters have told a story of the coming of age of an area of policy making that has, during the writing of the book, gained acceptance on the global stage. From a policy field that was just emerging tentatively on to the global policy-making scene in 2010, the migration and climate change nexus has since become a part of the policy establishment. The nexus between migration and climate change has been inserted into a number of policy processes, new entities have been created, and advocacy actors have dedicated people and entire divisions to working on it. It is no longer out of the ordinary for migration and climate change to be discussed in relation to one another in the throes of high-profile policy making. Therefore, while a neat and tidy convention on the rights of 'climate refugees' has not been created, a policy framework of sorts has been erected around migration and climate change, composed of agreements stretching from climate change, through migration, to disaster risk reduction, development, and latterly the international human rights regime. In none of these agreements is migration and climate change the headline issue on which policy is being made, but is instead a sub-topic, offshoot or tangential issue that is given some space and recognition in the relevant agreements. Some of these agreements do not even explicitly mention the relation between migration and climate change, but have been drawn into this loose framework because of their perceived relevance by people working on the nexus. Taken together, these different agreements have been harnessed to put forward a comprehensive case for addressing migration and climate change together, as a recognised phenomenon.

This situation can be seen in stark contrast to the state of affairs in 2010 when, at COP16 in Cancun, advocacy actors were pushing for the inclusion of migration concerns into the document that was to become the Cancun Adaptation Framework without any other policy hooks on which to build their argument. On the one hand, in 2010 the boundaries of the thinkable were much more open, with few predefined boundaries already set out on how to think and communicate about migration and climate change in the policy sphere. On the other hand, advocacy actors were almost entirely focused on agenda setting, ensuring that migration made its way into final decision documents but not working on policy content. The question of whether migration and climate change would take off as an area of policy making on the international stage was still very much open.

Fast forward to 2019, and the policy basis that has emerged on migration and climate change together as a recognised phenomenon is accompanied by a sense of completion and achievement, now that nearly a decade of policy work is coming to an end and policy foundations have been put in place. As one interviewee put it, "I think with the two Global Compacts now and maybe with the Task Force on Displacement presenting its recommendations to the COP, I think the policy circle is kind of closed now" in the sense of having relevant global policy frameworks in place (PDD Interview, 2018). The outlook is therefore for more programmatic work that uses the established policy framework as its foundations. This perspective chimes with the work of Koko Warner, who argues that

> [F]or the next stage, a yardstick of efficacy in coordinating responses to large-scale movements of people will be the degree to which both state and non-state actors take up the recommendations of the Task Force on Displacement, how the Global Compact for Migration is negotiated, and the degree to which the states utilize the Comprehensive Refugee Response Framework as climate and other dynamics unfold in future years. (Warner, 2018: 398)

This is interesting, as the policy regime is created from a number of different puzzle pieces that were never intended to create a framework on migration and climate change, but have been appropriated by people working on the migration and climate change nexus to provide one. This poses the question of purpose. Why does this framework need to exist? Is it a question of needing tools with which to help people in distress? Or is it a question of needing policy levers with which to justify the continuation of particular policy agendas? The intention undoubtedly exists to utilise the policy framework to help people whose lives are being endangered and most severely disrupted by climate change. On the other hand, mandate-bound organisations are working to define themselves in relation to the challenge posed by climate change, and a policy framework that can be applied to legitimise migration and climate change as a valid area of work can help them do this.

Further questions therefore emerge. What does this loose policy framework do? What are its productive effects? Most obviously, this framework provides a springboard for work on the issue. This can be most clearly seen in written contributions from advocacy actors to policy processes that open by listing all of the separate policy components as justifications for this area of work to set the stage for their input. This is already a norm in many different UN policy arenas, where decision documents begin with verbs such as 'recalling', 'noting' and 'recognising' and a list of existing decisions from that policy area, serving as a reminder of the current state of affairs and setting the groundwork on which new decisions are built. However, the listing of policy frameworks in this way, reminiscent of UN decisions, is also restrictive for how policy making can be done. By tying the issue to particular existing policy and institutional structures, it also ties policy making to their logics; to give a purposely provocative example, it would be mightily difficult to follow a listing of relevant UN decisions and global migration policies with an argument for open borders as a response to climate change. The policy framework that advocacy actors have constructed and are using to legitimise and further their work is therefore at the same time subtly limiting in terms of what policy might be able to entail.

As with any captivating story, it is not just the ending alone that is interesting, but the twists and turns that have led to that point and the various mechanisms that have led to one particular ending as opposed to a range of possible alternatives. These alternatives, the fan fiction endings of the story of the emergence of migration and climate change as an area of policy making, are multiple; an alternative where the issue complex did not manage to find a foothold in international policy-making processes is not a difficult reality to imagine. The current situation was therefore far from inevitable; indeed, imagining these alternatives actually makes the coming of age of migration and climate change on the global policy stage seem all the more unlikely. This in turn makes the examination of the process of emergence all the more interesting.

It is important to realise that as well as being a process of policy making (of meetings, of discussions, of documents, of track-changes, of bracketed text, of debating paragraphs, words, and even commas), this process of emergence has also been a process of attempting to understand and articulate the migration and climate change nexus. The conceptual discussions in the first chapter of this book highlighted the essentially contested, future-oriented construction of the phenomenon of the migration and climate change nexus, presenting a somewhat wobbly foundation for concrete policy action. It is against this background that the area of policy making has somewhat defiantly emerged and become established.

Two key components of this process have been language and knowledge, neither of which is neutral. Language is not a neutral mode of communication; knowledge is not a presentation of an objective truth. And both need to be situated to be understood. One of the threads running through this book is that language on migration and climate change is complex, contested and often confused. However, the simultaneously polyphonic and polysemic terminology that is used to talk about migration and climate change has not necessarily hindered work on the conceptual couplet. Indeed, linguistic openness allows for multiple conceptualisations of the phenomenon of the migration and climate change nexus and the people at its core to sit side by side. Advocacy actors with different mandates are therefore able to approach the nexus from different perspectives while working on the same advocacy issues. Discursive struggles over both the semiotic and ideational components of the language used to talk about the migration and climate change nexus have not been settled, but, in settings such as the Advisory Group on Climate Change and Human Mobility (hereafter 'Advisory Group') have temporarily been put aside in order to allow collaboration on the topic to continue. A shared conviction of the existence and importance of the migration and climate change nexus has therefore been strong enough to allow for differences in how to talk about and conceptualise the nexus, with these differences in turn strengthening the area of work by allowing parallel work on the nexus with different word choice and conceptualisation. At times the facade of an apparently unified discourse has been erected, although discourse analysis reveals that underlying discursive contestation prevails.

Contention regarding language, both in terms of the semiotic components to use to describe migration and climate change and the ideational components that are attached to these terms, is overcome in part by the weight of knowledge that has been created to bolster the phenomenon of the migration and climate change nexus. This has evolved from a shared perception of more knowledge being required on migration and climate change in 2010 (illustrated by the call for more knowledge in the Cancun and Doha decisions from the UNFCCC as well as the mandate of the Nansen Initiative) to a position where recommendations are being made (the mandate of the Task Force on Displacement) and implementation of findings is being strived for (the mandate of the Platform on Disaster Displacement (PDD)). The increasing corpus of knowledge on which this shift is based is therefore actually a complex web of knowledge, with knowledge creation influencing policy-making decisions, as well as policy demands influencing the knowledge that is being created.

Furthermore, due to the presence of particular knowledge producers carrying out advocacy work during policy-making processes, a self-reinforcing relationship has evolved. Advocacy actors involved in policy making on migration and climate change are supporting calls for greater understanding of the phenomenon as well as creating knowledge in order to respond to the calls they have had a hand in creating. This both justifies their existence in the policy-making community that has built up around the nexus and allows them to function as a filter for knowledge into policy processes. Continuing to feed this cycle of knowledge and policy is not necessarily 'because of empirical evidence or with malicious intent', but, as Kayly Ober and Patrick Sakdapolrak have argued, 'because it is part and parcel of existing practices of positioning themselves within the system and playing the rules of the game' (2017: 366). It is therefore not just a case of problematising the linguistic and ideational constructions that are apparently beyond question, but looking afresh at the seemingly self-evident practices of advocacy actors in the discourse.

Policy making on migration and climate change as a performative boundary-marking process

The discourse on migration and climate change does not just regulate and constrain the migration and climate change nexus, but also plays a role in producing the very phenomenon itself (see performativity following Judith Butler). The foreclosure of certain ways of viewing the migration and climate change nexus within the policy-making discourse due to the roadblocks that are erected in the structures of certain institutions is therefore problematic not just because a particular policy alternative is no longer possible (for example, compensation for forced migration in the context of climate change through the loss and damage mechanisms of the UNFCCC), but because this feeds into broader conceptualisations of migration and climate change (which become disassociated with the concept of compensation as a result).

Knock-on effects are possible. For example, academics pursuing policy-relevant research may present their results so as to be compatible with the conventions (and biases) of policy processes, mirroring the language of the policy forum but also pre-emptively avoiding policy suggestions that are not going to be possible within current boundaries. Furthermore, knowledge is being created (commissioned) according to certain prerequisites (for example, the mandates of the Task Force on Displacement, studies commissioned by the Nansen Initiative or the PDD, reports mandated by the Human Rights Council and produced by the Office of the High Commissioner for Human Rights (OHCHR)), with the prerequisites that are given for these knowledge products effectively setting out the boundaries of the thinkable. Knowledge that is based on different premises that are incompatible with the institutional structures and assumptions of policy making may therefore have a harder time being accepted.

A useful way of understanding the restrictions placed on policy on migration and climate change is by understanding the policy-making discourse as a boundary-marking process. Boundary marking is not only a process of delineation of space in a geographical sense, for example through the demarcation of state borders or the identification of particular geographical spaces. Rather, boundaries are being created in relation to the nature and subject of the 'phenomenon', the legitimate forum for policy making, and the legitimate voices to speak in policy-making processes. In marking out these boundaries, a great deal of influence is wielded on the development of policy-making processes, the power relations that are present within them, and ultimately any policy mechanisms that are agreed as a result.

It is important to note that boundary marking is not a process unique to policy making on the migration and climate change nexus. Indeed, policy making always involves the marking of boundaries to some extent; after all, it is impossible to make a policy without demarcating the phenomenon to be addressed, as well as the desired aims and beneficiaries of the policy. Despite the universality of boundary marking, it is a useful lens through which to explore the conclusions of this book. By setting out boundary marking in policy making on the migration and climate change nexus as a process, it questions whether the categories that have emerged are as objective, natural or self-evident as they may appear. Understanding the demarcations that have been made therefore assists not just with understanding how the 'phenomenon' has emerged as a policy issue but also with opening up space to call into question further attempts to create policy.

Different sets of boundaries are being demarcated. Perhaps most obviously, boundaries are being marked around the actual 'phenomenon' of the migration and climate change nexus, as such identifying the very issue on which policy making is concentrated. As the analysis has highlighted, the polyphonic and polysemic nature of terminology and configurations of the phenomenon are continuing, even though the phenomenon has already become a concrete object of policy making, particularly in the UNFCCC. There are continued attempts to draw and refine the boundaries of the conceptual couplet as a phenomenon rather than simply an arbitrary pairing, and a strong reliance on knowledge in order to do this.

Also concerned with the content of what is understood when the relations between migration and climate change are discussed, a parallel boundary-marking process is the identification, definition and categorisation of the subjects of the nexus. Again, although central to the policy-making discourse on the nexus, the subject is a shadowy figure, actually overwhelmingly marked out by the potentiality of mobilities. Rather than being a tangible group of people, the subjects are marked out by their intangible potential mobilities. At this stage of policy making on the migration and climate change nexus, the impact of being classified as belonging to this group of people at the heart of the nexus is not yet clear. If policy mechanisms are developed to confer particular rights on this group of people, or provide particular financial resources, for example via funds for climate change adaptation, being recognised as belonging to this group may be an advantageous position. Looking in particular to initiatives rooted in protection, such as the Nansen Initiative, the identification of people as subjects of the nexus and categorisation into a particular category (based on mobilities being at the forced end of the continuum) could be an attempt to create privileges. Of course, when considering anti-migrant sentiment and attempts being made around the world to make (international) migration more difficult, being classified as belonging to this group may also be a disadvantage, where the physical boundaries of border security mechanisms are activated to prevent people's potential mobilities from becoming actualised.

Boundary-marking processes are also evident in terms of defining the area of work that is policy making on migration and climate change. The marking of boundaries of the 'phenomenon' of the subjects of the migration and climate change nexus is a process that is generally not undertaken by (potentially) affected people themselves. Instead a group of individuals, organisations, and to a certain extent states, has emerged that has been involved in making systematic efforts to further policy making on the nexus. These actors have access not only to the high-profile, outward-facing plenary discussions or sessions where proclamations of new policies are made, but also to the back rooms, corridors and closed-door meetings where the details of policy are thrashed out and where shared understandings of migration, climate change and the social world within both of these phenomena are honed and will influence policy making for decades to come.

A good example of an organisation that has self-defined as a legitimate group to work on migration and climate change is the Advisory Group, a purposely small group of advocacy actors that delegates particular voices as legitimate by granting them membership of the group. The self-designation of this group of actors as advisers to the UNFCCC creates an air of legitimacy that in turn affords the members a certain status and marks them out as particularly legitimate advisers in relation to other voices. The presence of other United Nations (UN) agencies in the group (such as the United Nations High Commissioner for Refugees (UNHCR) and the International Organization for Migration (IOM)) is also likely to be an advantage, with these agencies bringing experience of UN etiquette, language and protocols as well as helping smooth the way with the not trifling issue of access.

As the UNFCCC has emerged as the primary forum for policy making on the nexus, this is particularly important. This policy-making forum automatically creates another boundary-marking process around legitimate actors, with access to the UNFCCC being highly controlled, often difficult and bureaucratic. The provision of the Paris decision relating to the establishment of a dedicated Task Force on Displacement also explicitly sets out the group of actors to be drawn into the process. According to the decision, the task force should

> ... complement, draw upon the work of and involve, as appropriate, existing bodies and expert groups under the Convention including the Adaptation Committee and the Least Developed Countries Expert Group, as well as relevant organizations and expert bodies outside the Convention.... (UNFCCC, 2016a: 49)

These boundaries leave room for manoeuvre, with the caveat of 'as well as relevant organizations and expert bodies outside the Convention' allowing for actors that have already been working on the nexus to also fall within these boundaries and gain explicit legitimation for their (continued) presence in the policy space. However, this provision does also raise the question of which organisations and bodies are considered to be 'relevant' and what criteria relevance is to be judged against. Therefore, while relatively open, these boundaries are also incredibly opaque and it remains in the hands of UNFCCC insiders to decide which actors are invited into the inner circle.

Visions for a transformative future

The existing loose policy framework that has emerged on migration and climate change and the boundaries that have been drawn around it constitute what Todd Miller (2017: 163) has described as 'scaffolding for the status quo'. Attachments to existing policy instruments and fora, organisations, mandates, accepted terminologies, and ways of creating knowledge function as metal uprights, joining brackets and wooden boards, intricately fitted together and combining to bear the load of policy making on migration and climate change, allowing workers to carry out maintenance on a number of relevant areas and join the dots between migration and climate change in a number of key policy documents. However, the bones of the structure under the scaffolding remain the same. This structure, global governance surrounding both migration and climate change respectively, has a number of in-built difficulties that make it hard to move away from the status quo, be they the carefully protected mandates of international organisations, the reticence of states (particularly in the Global North) to allow particular human bodies to cross their state borders, the complex dynamics that prevent meaningful action to address greenhouse gas (GHG) emissions and reverse the trend on climate change, or the uneven power relations between actors operating within this system.

The work that is being carried out from the scaffold therefore contributes to supporting this status quo, working from the fringes of the system to make small changes that at the same time reinforce conventional ways of thinking and making policy. This does not detract from the importance of this work, be it to improve global efforts to mitigate GHG emissions to avoid the worst adverse effects of climate change, to ensure that migration is recognised as a consequence of climate change and thus open doors for climate change programmes to work on migration, or to fight for the human rights of people whose mobilities are driven by and disrupted in the context of climate change. However, visions for a transformative future, beyond the status quo, will not be developed within these boundaries.

The moral, so to speak, of this story is therefore that changing policy making on migration and climate change does not just imply coming up with new policy ideas, populating a new policy domain with mentions of migration and climate change, or being open to a sprinkling of new faces in policy arenas. Instead, it entails reconsidering how we understand and talk about migration and climate change and undertaking a process of self-reflection: what perspective do we (people talking about migration and climate change) have on the issue complex and why? This does not necessarily involve interrogating the reasons why people are moving, or the extent to which people connect changes in weather patterns to their decisions to move or their inability to do so. Rather, this involves a process of critical reflection of the motives, both explicit and implicit, of the policy juggernaut.

This perspective is really important if the migration and climate change nexus is going to exist as anything but a dire warning of the realities of climate change, and if policy responses are going to be transformative rather than buttresses for the current global state of affairs. To quote Andrew Baldwin:

'When we bring climate and migration together as two distinct areas, the question we need to ask is not what can we do to prevent, you know, cataclysm, but it's how can we put these two things together to cultivate some really transformative vision for the world that we live in?' (Baldwin, 2017b)

As the world continues to hurtle towards an uncertain but increasingly certainly dire climate future as global GHG emissions fail to decrease, and established institutional frameworks do not appear to be up to the task of reversing the trend, the time has come for transformative visions of the future to take hold. Since early 2019, children and young people the world over have been skipping school to take to the streets and demand serious action against climate change. Uninhibited by the often unspoken rule of pushing for gradual change that allows for action so long as it does so hand in hand with economic growth and existing structures, the movement of young people is a refreshing and unapologetic confrontation with the bureaucratic, technocratic world of both state-level and international policy making. The power of this movement to disrupt the status quo became apparent when the initiator of the global movement, Greta Thunberg, addressed the UNFCCC at its 2018 COP in Katowice. In a forum known for its double-speak and endless debates over the finer points of grammar and vocabulary, Thunberg's frank tone and refusal to conform to diplomatic niceties when addressing global leaders captured attention worldwide and has led to the Swedish teenager being nominated for the Nobel Peace Prize and included on countless lists of the world's most influential young people and most influential climate leaders.

The tenacity and honest straight-talking of the global youth movement is gaining traction exactly because it does not adhere to expected rules of engagement. Sparks of something similar can be seen in pro-migration movements, such as 'rebel cities' and 'sanctuary cities', which create moments and spaces of welcoming in challenge to a larger national or regional context of anti-migrant sentiment (Turhan and Armiero, 2017), or in the Dutch church that held a continuous religious service for 96 days to prevent a family from being deported from the Netherlands, utilising a law that prevents police from interrupting religious services to perform arrests (Kingsley, 2019). These moments fundamentally challenge the status quo, utilising spaces that can be created within it to call into question the underlying dynamics of global governance.

These movements and the energy for change that is created by them are the polar opposite of the bureaucracy of policy making that takes place on the international stage. A transformative vision for the future of migration taking place in the context of climate change therefore cannot be one that is confined within the processes of the UNFCCC, a cumbersome colossus that is often technocratic and bureaucratic. Phrases such as the 'adverse effects of climate change' anchored in the UNFCCC (UNFCCC, 1992: Preamble) also function to dehumanise the effects that climate change is having and will continue to have on people's lives (and mobilities), unlikely to deliver a people-centred approach to migration and climate change. As argued by Giovanni Bettini in a comment piece published shortly before the COP21 in Paris:

> A 2, 3 or even 4°C warmer planet is a largely unknown place, where people will understand, plan and fight for their (im)mobility in ways different than today's. Visualizing and acting through such transitions requires a radical imaginative openness, which is a precondition for a politics striving for solidarity and just approaches to the changes, able to go beyond business-as-usual. Can we expect this from the UNFCCC? (Bettini, 2015)

Despite the broadening of the boundaries around acceptable fora for conducting policy making on migration and climate change post-Paris, initiatives such as the Warsaw International Mechanism for Loss and Damage associated with Climate Change Impacts (WIM) and the arguably even more problematic Global Compact for Migration continue to strive for action on migration and climate change. The advocacy juggernaut involved with negotiating mobilities in the context of climate change, however, has displayed little room for alternative analyses that question the utility of the processes at hand and unnecessarily complicate their advocacy messages. A similar lack of imagination to look beyond existing monoliths of policy and global governance is highlighted by a lack of flexibility with terminology, which is holding firmly to the categories of human mobility, displacement, migration and planned relocation, despite the questionable utility of this system of understanding and categorising current movement in the context of climate change.

Both the restriction of policy making on migration and climate change to selected policy fora and the constraints placed on the ways that migration and climate change can be talked about in policy discourse limit the possibilities for responding to the issue complex. For example, the limitation placed on work on loss and damage under the UNFCCC explicitly excludes responses involving compensation or liability for losses or damages that occur due to the adverse effects of climate change (UNFCCC, 2016a: Article 8). As migration is currently considered under this work stream, these avenues are excluded as policy responses to migration. The conceptualisation of migration and climate change predominantly as an abstract phenomenon also affects possible responses; for example, the possibility of approaching the migration and climate change nexus from a human rights perspective is limited by the difficulty of identifying the people at the centre of the nexus, a necessity for person-centred approaches.

What next? The future of research and policy on migration and climate change

In previous work, I have critiqued the self-perpetuating circle of research, policy and knowledge creation that sustains work on the migration and climate change nexus (Nash, 2018c). This presents obvious challenges for sketching out future directions for research and policy on migration and climate change, as the specification of research and policy agendas is a central component of this circle. Furthermore, the prophesying of agendas for policy is often based on two assumptions; first, that the issue complex of migration and climate change is a problem that requires solutions, and second, that global policy communities are where we should be looking for these solutions.

A different approach is taken in closing this book, which has set out the genealogy of policy making and also deconstructed and critiqued many of these components. It does not assume the need for more research on migration and climate change, nor does it assume the necessity for the global policy-making juggernaut to continue apace. What the following paragraphs present are perspectives that could be added to the research and policy that will almost inevitably occur (for whatever reasons) to address some of the critiques this book has elucidated.

As Benoît Mayer argued back in 2013 (Mayer, 2013), the field does not need more research for research's sake. Whether it is case studies of over-studied small island states, or research projects that continue to recognise the conceptual difficulties with climate migration as a phenomenon, yet discard these difficulties and continue to draw on the concept regardless, a certain repetitiveness can be identified. I suggest therefore that work that aims to further the research area needs not only to acknowledge the conceptual difficulties but also to question the very ontological and epistemological foundations of the field. This is not a suggestion made simply to satisfy personal interests in theoretical and conceptual work, but a necessary step to recentre the people whose mobilities are being linked to climate change in the discourse. As Andrew Baldwin has argued:

> [W]hen we talk about 'climate migrants' or 'climate refugees' we are in effect inventing a category that corresponds with how we imagine the world to be, not one that describes the world as it really is. In this sense, we can say that the figures of the climate migrant or climate refugee are socially constructed phenomenon. The political underpinnings of this disjuncture between image and reality are legion. Most notably, the actual everyday experiences of those deemed to be climate migrants and refugees become masked, in turn, obscuring the real political contexts that mark daily life in those places. (Baldwin, 2017a: 3)

These theoretical discussions are therefore far from being purely of theoretical interest. For scholars whose research is motivated by improving the lives of people feeling the adverse effects of climate change very concretely and often violently in their everyday lives (I would argue that this group comprises the majority of scholars working on the issue), these theoretical discussions can contribute to unmasking experiences and exposing the political contexts marking daily life in places that also bear the brunt of climate change.

This perspective calls for research that pushes the boundaries of not just *what* we know about migration and climate change, but *how* we know it and *why* we want to know it. It also involves more exploration of how the boundaries of the thinkable are being erected around migration and climate change as a phenomenon, and how to critique and move these boundaries if they are not fit for purpose.

For policy agendas, this is perhaps trickier to initiate than for research communities. While researchers may have the freedom to break free of policy relevance (at least to some extent), those operating within policy communities are bound by institutional mandates, member states' interests, and the rulebooks for international engagement, both explicit and implicit. However, if policy making is also to push the boundaries of what is thinkable, this will require thinking beyond the strict confines set by existing institutions and ways of categorising people on the move. A transformative vision for mobility in the context of climate change will be forced to go beyond tinkering at the edges of existing policy structures and find ways to address fundamental underlying structural issues that are behind many of the inequalities exposed and exacerbated by climate change and influencing migration worldwide.

A commonality across both research and policy work that pushes the boundaries of the thinkable on migration and climate change is that this work will be expressly political. A purely technocratic search for solutions compatible with and continuing to buttress the status quo will not suffice. One only has to cast an eye over the political situation in states across the Global North to see the necessity of being openly and expressly political on these issues. Across Europe, populist parties are not only making a lot of noise about migration, but are also gaining traction with their anti-migrant sentiment. The populist right now sits on the government benches in a number of EU countries and forms an increasingly formidable share of the opposition in others, often pushing centrists to the right on migration issues in particular in an attempt to appease. As well as being unified by a desire to prevent migration, many of these parties share, at best, a disinterest in addressing climate change, and at worst an active denial of the realities of climate change. One only needs to glance across the Atlantic to the Trump administration in the US for a dramatic example of anti-migrant and anti-climate politics going hand in hand.

For those who are grappling with the space where migration and climate change converges, this presents a whole host of challenges. A delicate balancing act is required that on the one hand pushes for action on climate change in order to prevent some of the worst 'adverse effects' from coming to pass, and on the other hand does not play into or stoke fears on migration. Cultivating a transformative vision for climate and migration futures also slides further down priority lists as capacities are taken up with preventing backsliding on issues across the board, not just on migration or climate change, but on membership of international organisations, social security nets, and human rights protections more broadly. Engaging with this political context, and the multitude of intricately interlinked issues that are gaining political traction, will be an essential component of the debate on migration and climate change in years to come.

Notes

1   UNHCR has a narrow mandate, with the role of the agency defined in the UNHCR statute as follows: 'The United Nations High Commissioner for Refugees, acting under the authority of the General Assembly, shall assume the function of providing international protection, under the auspices of the United Nations, to refugees who fall within the scope of the present Statute and of seeking permanent solutions for the problem of refugees by assisting Governments and, subject to the approval of the Governments concerned, private organizations to facilitate the voluntary repatriation of such refugees, or their assimilation within new national communities' (UN General Assembly, 1950).

2   In 2011, UNHCR created the position of Senior Technical Advisor on Climate Change. The position was for one year and largely funded by the Norwegian Refugee Council (Hall, 2013).

3   A further mention is made in the work plan of the WIM: SBSTA and SBI (2014).

4   Nepal's original submission was worded as follows: 'The purpose of the international climate change displacement coordination support mechanism is to provide assistance to people displaced by the impacts of climate change including measures to provide support for: – emergency relief; – assistance in providing organised migration and planned relocation – compensation measures' Nepal (2014) .

5   'Annex 1 Parties include the industrialized countries that were members of the OECD (Organisation for Economic Co-operation and Development) in 1992, plus countries with economies in transition (the EIT Parties), including the Russian Federation, the Baltic States, and several Central and Eastern European States' (UNFCCC, 2018a). 'Non-Annex 1 Parties are most developing countries. Certain groups of developing countries are recognized by the Convention as being especially vulnerable to the adverse impacts of climate change, including countries with low-lying coastal areas and those prone to desertification and drought. Others (such as countries that rely heavily on income from fossil fuel production and commerce) feel more vulnerable to the potential economic impacts of climate change response measures' (UNFCCC, 2018a).

6   The word 'phenomenon' is placed in inverted commas here to emphasise that the 'phenomenon' of the migration and climate change nexus is not considered here simply as a naturally occurring 'fact' of 'reality', but that it has instead been constructed as a phenomenon comprising of two different elements (migration and climate change), the combination of which into one entity was by no means inevitable and therefore cannot be taken for granted.

7   The text of the Cancun Adaptation actually reads 'climate change induced displacement, migration and planned relocation' (UNFCCC, 2010) and the text

of the Doha decision actually reads 'migration, displacement and human mobility' (UNFCCC, 2013).

8   The term 'natural disasters' is not used here, following critiques that this terminology emphasises the 'natural' elements of disasters while disguising other political and structural factors such as weak or corrupt governance, inequalities, discrimination, and legacies of colonialism.

9   It is important to note that while these are *established* legal categories, they are also constructed of, and able to encapsulate, different meanings, rather than being naturally existing categories incapable of change (Zetter, 2007).

10 For a comprehensive list, see the Global Network for the Study of Human Rights and the Environment at gnhre.org.

11 Initial signatories of the Geneva Pledge were: Costa Rica, Chile, France, Guatemala, Ireland, Kiribati, Maldives, Marshall Islands, Micronesia, Mexico, Palau, Panama, Peru, Philippines, Uganda, Uruguay, Samoa and Sweden.

12 The letter was signed by representatives (Ministers and Heads of Delegations) for the following countries: Sweden, Belgium, Chile, Costa Rica, Dominican Republic, Finland, Guatemala, Ireland, Luxembourg, Mexico, the Netherlands, the Philippines, Switzerland and Uruguay.

13 The statement had a total of 323 signatories (civil society constituencies and networks, and individual organisations).

References

ADP (Ad Hoc Working Group on the Durban Platform for Enhanced Action) (2014a) 'Non-Paper on elements for a draft negotiating text. Updated Non-Paper on Parties' views and proposals, 1 November 2014', ADP.2014.11.Non-Paper, https://unfccc.int/resources/docs/2014/adp2/eng/11nonpap.pdf [Accessed 7 October 2018].

ADP (2014b) 'Parties' views and proposals on the elements for a draft negotiating text. Non-Paper, 7 July 2014', ADP.2014.6.NonPaper, https://unfccc.int/resource/docs/2014/adp2/eng/6nonpap.pdf [Accessed 7 October 2018].

ADP (2015a) 'Ad Hoc Working Group on the Durban Platform for Enhanced Action Second Session, Part Eight, Geneva, 8–13 February 2015, negotiating text', FCCC/ADP/2015/1, http://unfccc.int/files/bodies/awg/application/pdf/negotiating_text_12022015@2200.pdf [Accessed 29 October 2018].

ADP (2015b) 'Draft agreement and draft decision on workstreams 1 and 2 of the Ad Hoc Working Group on the Durban Platform for Enhanced Work of the ADP contact group, edited version of 6 November 2015', ADP.2015.11.InformalNote, http://unfccc.int/resource/docs/2015/adp2/eng/11infnot.pdf [Accessed 7 October 2018].

ADP (2015c) 'Draft agreement and draft decision on workstreams 1 and 2 of the Ad Hoc Working Group on the Durban Platform for Enhanced Action. Work of the ADP Contact Group incorporating bridging proposals by the co-facilitators, version of 4 December 2015@10.00', htpps://unfccc.int/sites/default/files/compared_adp_compilation_bridging_4dec_clean.pdf [Accessed 7 October 2018].

ADP (2015d) 'Draft agreement and draft decision on workstreams 1 and 2 of the Ad Hoc Working Group on the Durban Platform for Enhanced Action. Work of the ADP contact group, version of 23 October 2015 @23:30hrs', https://archive.org/details/Ws1and22330/page/n0 [Accessed 7 October 2018].

ADP (2015e) 'Draft Paris outcome', FCCC/ADP/2015/L.6/Rev.1, https://unfccc.int/files/bodies/awg/application/pdf/draft_paris_outcome_rev_5dec15.pdf [Accessed 7 October 2018].

ADP (2015f) 'Draft text on COP21 agenda item 4(b) Durban Platform for Enhanced Action (decision 1/CP.17) Adoption of a protocol, another legal instrument, or an agreed outcome with legal force under the Convention applicable to all Parties, version 1 of 9 December 2015 at 15:00', https://unfccc.int/resource/docs/2015/cop21/eng/da01.pdf [Accessed 7 October 2018].

ADP (2015g) 'Draft text on COP21 agenda item 4(b) Durham Platform for Enhanced Action (decision 1/CP.17) Adoption of a protocol, another legal instrument, or an agreed outcome with legal force under the Convention applicable to all Parties, version 2 of 10 December 2015 at 21:00', Draft decision -/CP.21, https://reproterre.net/IMG/pdf/texte-brouillon_accord_paris_10_dec_21_h.pdf [Accessed 7 October 2018].

ADP (2015h) 'Working document, Ad Hoc Working Group on the Durban Platform for Enhanced Action, second session, part nine', https://unfccc.int/files/bodies/awg/application/pdf/adp_2_9_wd_11062015@1645.pdf [Accessed 29 October 2018].

Adger, W.N. (2000) 'Social and ecological resilience: are they related?' *Progress in Human Geography* 24(3): 347–364.

Advisory Group on Climate Change and Human Mobility (2014a) 'Human mobility in the context of climate change. Recommendations from the Advisory Group on Climate Change and Human Mobility COP20 Lima, Peru', www.iom.int/files/live/sites/iom/files/pbn/docs/Human-Mobility-in-the-context-of-Climate-Change.pdf [Accessed 5 October 2015].

Advisory Group on Climate Change and Human Mobility (2014b) 'Joint submission on activities for the Nairobi Work Programme', www.uncclearn.org/sites/default/files/inventory/unhcr02.pdf [Accessed 29 October 2018].

Advisory Group on Climate Change and Human Mobility (2014c) 'Joint submission to the Excom of the Warsaw International Mechanism for Loss and Damage associated with Climate Change on the Excom's draft initial two-year workplan for the implementation of the functions of the Mechanism, in accordance with paragraph 5 of Decision 2/CP.19', www.unhcr.org/542e94e69.pdf [Accessed 7 October 2018].

Advisory Group on Climate Change and Human Mobility (2014d) 'Joint submission to the United Nations Convention on Climate Change (UNFCCC) on National Adaptation Plans (NAPs) for consideration at SBI40', www.environmentalmigration.iom.int/sites/default/files/NAPs2014.pdf [Accessed 7 October 2018].

Advisory Group on Climate Change and Human Mobility (2014e) 'Joint submission to the United Nations Convention on Climate Change (UNFCCC) on the Nairobi Work Programme on impacts, vulnerability and adaptation to climate change. For consideration at SBSTA41', https://unfccc.int/sites/default/files/160.pdf [Accessed 7 October 2018].

Advisory Group on Climate Change and Human Mobility (2015a) 'Human mobility in the context of climate change UNFCCC-Paris COP-21, recommendations from the Advisory Group on Climate Change and Human Mobility (November 2015)', www.unhcr.org/protection/environment/565b21bd9/human-mobility-context-climate-change-unfccc-paris-cop-21-recommendations.html [Accessed 29 October 2018].

Advisory Group on Climate Change and Human Mobility (2015b) 'Human mobility in the context of climate change, elements for the UNFCCC Paris Agreement (March 2015)', www.unhcr.org/5550ab359.pdf [Accessed 7 October 2018].

Advisory Group on Climate Change and Human Mobility (2015c) 'Human mobility in the context of climate change. Recommendations from the Advisory Group on Climate Change and Human Mobility (October 2015)', https://reliefweb.int/sites/reliefweb/int/files/resources/201510-human-mobility-advisory-group-bonn.pdf [Accessed 7 October 2018].

Andersson, R. (2014) *Illegality, Inc.* Oakland, CA: University of California Press.

Ayeb-Karlsson, S., Smith, C.D. and Kniveton, D. (2018) 'A discursive review of the textual use of "trapped" in environmental migration studies: the conceptual birth and troubled teenage years of trapped populations' *Ambio* 47(5): 557–573.

Baldwin, A. (2012) 'Orientalising environmental citizenship: climate change, migration and the potentiality of race' *Citizenship Studies* 16(5–6): 625–640.

Baldwin, A. (2014) 'Pluralising climate change and migration: an argument in favour of open futures' *Geography Compass* 8(8): 516–528.

Baldwin, A. (2017a) 'Climate change, migration, and the crisis of humanism' *Wiley Interdisciplinary Reviews: Climate Change* 8(3): e460.

Baldwin, A. (2017b) Speaking in video with Nash, S.L., Turhan, E. and Fröhlich, C. (2017) 'Workshop: Beyond Climate Migration', Istanbul: Istanbul Policy Center, https://vimeo.com/225525742 [Accessed 25 October 2018].

Baldwin, A. (2017c) 'Conclusion. On the politics of climate change, migration and human rights' in Manou, D., Baldwin, A., Cubie, D., Mihr, A. and Thorp, T. (2017) *Climate Change, Migration and Human Rights. Law and Policy Perspectives* Abingdon: Routledge, pp. 219–225.

Baldwin, A. and Bettini. G. (2017) *Life Adrift: Climate Change, Migration, Critique* London and New York, NY: Rowman & Littlefield.

Baldwin, A., Methmann, C. and Rothe, D. (2014) 'Securitizing "climate refugees": the futurology of climate-induced migration' *Critical Studies on Security* 2(2): 121–130.

Barry, J. and Woods, K. (2009) 'The environment' in Goodhart, M. (2009) *Human Rights Politics and Practice* Oxford: Oxford University Press, pp. 316–333.

Bettini, G. (2013) 'Climate barbarians at the gate? A critique of apocalyptic narratives on climate refugees' *Geoforum* 45: 63–72.

Bettini, G. (2014) 'Climate migration as an adaptation strategy: de-securitizing climate-induced migration or making the unruly governable?' *Critical Studies on Security* 2(2): 180–195.

Bettini, G. (2015) 'What can and should we expect from COP21 on climate migration?', TransRe Blog, www.transre.org/en/blog/what-can-and-should-we-expect-cop21-climate-migration/ [Accessed 29 October 2018].

Bettini, G. and Gioli, G. (2016) 'Waltz with development: insights on the developmentalization of climate-induced migration' *Migration and Development* 5(2): 171–189.

Bettini, G., Nash, S.L. and Gioli, G. (2017) 'One step forward, two steps back? The fading contours of (in)justice in competing discourses on climate migration' *The Geographical Journal* 183(4): 348–358.

Bevir, M. and Rhodes, R.A.W. (2016) 'Interpretive political science: mapping the field' in Bevir, M. and Rhodes, R.A.W. (2016) *Routledge Handbook of Interpretive Political Science*, Abingdon and New York, NY: Routledge.

Beyani, C. (2011a) 'A human rights-based approach to protection of environmentally displaced persons', *Brookings* [online], www.brookings.edu/research/speeches/2011/06/07-beyani-nansen [Accessed 29 October 2018].

Beyani, C. (2011b) 'Protection of an assistance to internally displaced persons. Note by Secretary-General', A/66/285, https://reliefweb.int/sites/reliefweb.int/files/resources/full_report_83.pdf [Accessed 29 October 2018].

Biermann, F. and Boas, I. (2010) 'Preparing for a warmer world: towards a global governance system to protect climate refugees' *Global Environmental Politics* 10(1): 60–88.

Black, R., Bennett, S.R.G., Thomas, S.M. and Beddington, J.R. (2011) 'Climate change: migration as adaptation' *Nature* 478(7379): 447–449.

Boas, I. and Rothe, D. (2016) 'From conflict to resilience? Explaining recent changes in climate security discourse and practice' *Environmental Politics* 25(4): 613–632.

Butler, J. (1993) *Bodies That Matter: On the Discursive Limits of "Sex"* London and New York, NY: Routledge.

CARE International and UNU-EHS (2012) *Where the Rain Falls* [online], http://wheretherainfalls.org/mission/ [Accessed 5 October 2015].

Castree, N. (2014) *Making Sense of Nature* Abingdon: Routledge.

Chan, S. (2015) 'Paris Accord considers climate change as a factor in mass migration', *New York Times* [online], www.nytimes.com/2015/12/13/world/europe/paris-accord-considers-climate-change-as-a-factor-in-mass-migration.html?_r=0 [Accessed 26 October 2018].

Chaturvedi, S. and Doyle, T. (2015) *Climate Terror: A Critical Geopolitics of Climate Change* Basingstoke: Palgrave Macmillan.

Crawley, H. and Skleparis, D. (2018) 'Refugees, migrants, neither, both: categorical fetishism and the politics of bounding in Europe's "migration crisis"' *Journal of Ethnic and Migration Studies* 44(1): 48–64.

Crépeau, F. (2012) 'Human rights of migrants. Note by the Secretary-General', A/67/299, https://documents-dds-ny.un.org/doc/UNDOC/GEN/N12/460/71/PDF/N1246071.pdf?OpenElement [Accessed 29 October 2018].

Dean, M, (2010) *Governmentality. Power and Rule in Modern Society* London: Sage.

Death, C. (2014) *Critical Environmental Politics* Abington and New York, NY: Routledge.

Dimitrov, R.S. (2016) 'The Paris Agreement on climate change: behind closed doors' *Global Environmental Politics* 16(3): 1–11.

Dinshaw, F. (2015) 'This is what a climate refugee looks like', *National Observer* [online], www.nationalobserver.com/2015/09/04/news/what-climate-refugee-looks [Accessed 29 October 2018].

Displacement Solutions (2013) 'The Peninsula Principles on climate displacement within States', http://displacementsolutions.org/peninsula-principles [Accessed 29 October 2018].

Donnelly, J. (2003) *Universal Human Rights in Theory and Practice* New York, NY: Cornell University Press.

Dunn Cavelty, M., Kaufmann, M. and Søby Kristensen, K. (2015) 'Resilience and (in)security: practices, subjects, temporalities' *Security Dialogue* 46(1): 3–14.

Environmental Justice Foundation (2009) 'No place like home – where next for climate refugees?', https://ejfoundation.org//resources/downloads/no-place-like-home.pdf [Accessed 29 October 2018].

Erdal, M.B. and Oeppen, C. (2018) 'Forced to leave? The discursive and analytical significant of describing migration as forced and voluntary' *Journal of Ethnic and Migration Studies* 44(6): 981–998.

European Cooperation in Science and Technology Secretariat (2011) 'Memorandum of Understanding for the implementation of a European Concerted Research Action designated as COST Action IS1101: Climate Change and Migration: Knowledge, Law and Policy and Theory', https://www.cost.eu/actions/IS1101/#tabs|Name:overview [Accessed 29 October 2018].

Evans, B. and Reid, J. (2013) 'Dangerously exposed: the life and death of the resilient subject' *Resilience: International Policies, Practices and Discourses* 1(2): 83–98.

Executive Committee of the WIM (Warsaw International Mechanism for Loss and Damage associated with Climate Change Impacts) (2016) 'Draft Terms of Reference: Task Force on Displacement', https://unfccc.int/files/adaptation/groups_committees/loss_and_damage_executive_committee/application/pdf/22092016_task_force_on_displacement_-_revised_version.pdf [Accessed 23 June 2018].

Executive Committee of the WIM (2017) 'Terms of Reference: Task Force on Displacement', https://unfccc.int/files/adaptation/groups_committees/loss_and_damage_executive_committee/application/pdf/tor_task_force_final.pdf [Accessed 29 October 2018].

Executive Committee of the WIM (2018) 'III Recommendations. Advanced unedited version', https://unfccc.int/sites/default/files/resource/Recommendations_21_Sep-1600hrs.pdf [Accessed 13 October 2018].

Faber, D. and Schlegel, C. (2017) 'Give me shelter from the storm: framing the climate refugee crisis in the context of neoliberal capitalism' *Capitalism Nature Socialism* 28(3): 1–17.

Falstrom, D.Z. (2001) 'Stemming the flow of environmental displacement: creating a convention to protect persons and preserve the environment' *Colorado Journal of International Environmental Law and Policy* 1(1–19).

Felli, R. (2013) 'Managing climate insecurity by ensuring continuous capital accumulation: "climate refugees" and "climate migrants"' *New Political Economy* 18(3): 337–363.

Foresight (2011a) 'Annual review 2010', www.gov.uk/government/uploads/system/uploads/attachment_data/file/276536/11-p91-foresight-annual-review-2010.pdf [Accessed 29 October 2018].

Foresight (2011b) *Final Project Report. Foresight: Migration and Global Environmental Change* London: Government Office for Science.

Foresight (no date) 'Reports and publications', http://webarchive. nationalarchives.gov.uk/20140108140803/ [Accessed 3 August 2016].

Foucault, M. (1977) 'Nietzsche, genealogy, history' in Bouchard, D.F. (1980) *Language, Counter-Memory, Practice: Selected Essays and Interviews by Michel Foucault* Ithaca, NY: Cornell University Press, 139–164.

Foucault, M. (1980) 'Two lectures' in Colin, G. (1980) *Power/Knowledge: Selected Interviews and Other Writings 1972–1977* New York, NY: Pantheon Books, 78–108.

Foucault, M. (1994) 'Polemics, power, and problematizations' in Faubion, J.D. (2000) *Ethics: Essential Works of Foucault 1954–1984* London: Penguin, 112–119.

Foucault, M. (2006) *History of Madness* Abingdon: Routledge.

Geddes, A., Adger, N.W., Arnell, N.W., Black, R. and Thomas, D.S.G. (2012) 'Migration, environmental change, and the "challenges of governance"' *Environment and Planning C: Government and Policy* 30: 951–967.

Gemenne, F. (2011) 'Why the numbers don't add up: a review of estimates and predictions of people displaced by environmental changes' *Global Environmental Change* 21(1): 41–49.

Gemenne, F. (2015) 'One good reason to speak of "climate refugees"' *Forced Migration Review* 49: 70–71.

Geneva Pledge (2015) 'The Geneva Pledge', *Freidrich Ebert Foundation* [online] https://carbonmarketwatch.org/wp-content/uploads/2015/02/ The-Geneva-Pledge-13FEB2015.pdf [Accessed 12 May 2019].

Georgi, F. (2010) 'For the benefit of some: the International Organization for Migration and its global migration management' in Geiger, M. and Pécoud, A. (2010) *The Politics of International Migration Management* Basingstoke: Palgrave Macmillan, pp. 45–72.

Global Compact for Migration (2018) 'Global Compact for Safe, Orderly and Regular Migration. Final draft', https://refugeesmigrants.un.org/ sites/default/files/180711_final_draft_0.pdf [Accessed 12 October 2018].

Gottweis, H. (2003) 'Theoretical strategies of poststructuralist policy analysis: towards an analytics of government' in Hajer, M.A. and Wagenaar, H, (2003) *Deliberative Policy Analysis: Understanding Governance in the Network Society* Cambridge: Cambridge University Press, pp. 247–265.

Government of Norway (2011) 'Statement by Norway', Geneva UNHCR Ministerial Meeting, www.norway-geneva.org/humanitarian/Statements/UNHCR-Ministerial-Meeting-2011/Statement-at-UNHCR-Ministerial-Meeting/#.V-T5vPmLRD8 [Accessed 3 August 2016].

Guadagno, L. (2015) 'Migration and disaster risk reduction in the Sendai Framework', Trans Re Blog, www.transre.org/en/blog/migration-and-disaster-risk-reduction-sendai-framework/ [Accessed 29 October 2018].

Guterres, A. (2011a) 'Nansen Conference on Climate Change and Displacement: statement by António Guterres, United Nations High Commissioner for Refugees', www.unhcr.org/4def7ffb9.html [Accessed 16 August 2016].

Guterres, A. (2011b) 'Statement by Mr António Guterres, United Nations High Commissioner for Refugees, intergovernmental Meeting at ministerial level to mark the 60th anniversary of the 1951 Convention relating to the Status of Refugees and the 50th anniversary of the 1961 Convention on the Reduction of Statelessness', www.unhcr.org/4ecd0cde9.html [Accessed 29 October 2018].

Guterres, A. (2011c) 'UNHCR intergovernmental meeting at ministerial level: closing remarks by the United Nations High Commissioner for Refugees', www.unhcr.org/print/4ef094a89.htlm [Accessed 16 August 2016].

Hall, N. (2013) 'Moving beyond its mandate? UNHCR and climate change displacement' *Journal of International Organizational Studies* 4(1): 91–108.

Hall, N. (2016) *Displacement, Development, and Climate Change: International Organizations Moving Beyond their Mandates* Abingdon: Routledge.

Haraway, D. (1988) 'Situated knowledges: the science question in feminism and the privilege of partial perspective' *Feminist Studies* 14(3): 575–599.

Holling, C.S. (1973) 'Resilience and stability of ecological systems' *Annual Review of Ecology and Systematics* 4: 1–23.

Hulme, M. (2009) *Why We Disagree about Climate Change: Understanding Controversy, Inaction and Opportunity* Cambridge: Cambridge University Press.

Human Rights Council (2008) 'Human rights and climate change', UN.Doc.A/HRC/RES/7/23, http://ap.ohchr.org/documents/e/hrc/resolutions/a_hrc_res_7_23.pdf [Accessed 29 October 2018].

Human Rights Council (2009) 'Human rights and climate change', UN.Doc.A/HRC/RES/10/4, https://ap.ohchr.org/documents/E/HRC/resolutions/A_HRC_RES_10_4.pdf [Accessed 29 October 2018].

Human Rights Council (2011) 'Human rights and climate change', UN.Doc.A/HRC/RES/18/22, http://www.ohchr.org/Documents/Issues/ClimateChange/A.HRC.RES.18.22.pdf [Accessed 29 October 2018].

Human Rights Council (2012) 'Human rights and the environment' UN.Doc.A/HRC/RES/19/10, https://documents-dds-ny.un.org/doc/RESOLUTION/GEN/G12/131/59/PDF/G1213159pdf?OpenElement [Accessed 29 October 2018].

Human Rights Council (2014) 'Human rights and climate change', UN.Doc.A/HRC/RES/26/27, https://documents-dds-ny.un.org/doc/UNDOC/GEN/G14/083/51/PDF/G1408351.pdf?OpenElement [Accessed 29 October 2018].

Human Rights Council (2015) 'Human rights and climate change', A/HRC/RES/29/15, https://documents-dds-ny.un.org/doc/UNDOC/GEN/G15/163/60/PDF/G1516360.pdf?OpenElement [Accessed 29 October 2018].

Human Rights Council (2016) 'Human rights and climate change', A/HRC/RES/32/33, https://documents-dds-ny.un.org/doc/UNDOC/GEN/G16/157/72/PDF/G1615772.pdf?OpenElement [Accessed 6 July 2018].

Human Rights Council (2017a) 'Addressing human rights protection gaps in the context of migration and displacement of persons across international borders resulting from the adverse effects of climate change and supporting the adaptation and mitigation plans of developing countries to bridge the protection gaps', A/HRC/38/21, https://documents-dds-ny.un.org/doc/UNDOC/GEN/G18/116/26/PDF/G1811626.pdf?OpenElement [Accessed 9 July 2018].

Human Rights Council (2017b) 'Human rights and climate change', A/HRC/RES/35/20, https://documents-dds-ny.un.org/doc/UNDOC/GEN/G17/184/52/PDF/G1718452.pdf?OpenElement [Accessed 6 July 2018].

Human Rights Council (2017c) 'Intersessional panel discussion on human rights, climate change, migrants and persons displaced across international borders (Concept Note as of 28 September 2017)', www.ohchr.org/Documents/Issues/ClimateChange/ClimateChangeMigration/CNPanelDiscussion_CCandMigration.pdf [Accessed 6 July 2018].

Human Rights Council (2017d) 'Summary of the panel discussion on human rights, climate change, migration and persons displaced across international borders', A/HRC/37/35, https://reliefweb.int/sites/reliefweb.int/files/resources/G1734080.pdf [Accessed 9 July 2018].

Human Rights Council (2018) 'The slow onset effects of climate change and human rights protection for cross-border migrants', A/HRC/37/CRP.4, www.ohchr.org/Documents/Issues/ClimateChange/SlowOnset/A_HRC_37_CRP_4.pdf [Accessed 9 July 2018].

Humble, A. (2014) 'The rise of trapped populations' *Forced Migration Review* 45.

IOM (International Organization for Migration) (2007) 'Migration and the environment, ninety-fourth session, discussion note', MC/INF/288, https://www.iom.int/jahia/webdav/shared/shared/mainsite/about_iom/en/council/94/MC_INF_288.pdf [Accessed 29 October 2018].

IOM (2014a) '2013 survey on environmental migration' https://publications.iom.int/system/files/pdf/mecc_infosheet_survey_27may2014.pdf [Accessed 29 October 2018].

IOM (2014b) 'Capacity-building activities on migration, environment and climate change', https://publications.iom.int/system/files/pdf/mecc_infosheet_climatechange_8oct2014.pdf [Accessed 29 October 2018].

IOM (2014c) 'Focus on migration, environment and climate change (MECC) at the 105th IOM Council', https://publications.iom.int/system/files/pdf/mecc_thematic_global_report.pdf [Accessed 29 October 2018].

IOM (2014d) 'IOM outlook on migration, environment and climate change', http://publications.iom.int/system/files/pdf/mecc_outlook.pdf [Accessed 29 October 2018].

IOM (2014e) 'IOM perspectives on migration, environment and climate change', http://publications.iom.int/system/files/pdf/meccinfosheet_climatechangeactivities.pdf [Accessed 29 October 2018].

IOM (2014f) 'Programmatic activities on migration, environment and climate change', http://publications.iom.int/system/files/pdf/meccinfosheet_programmatic_activities.pdf [Accessed 29 October 2018].

IOM (2014g) 'What is at stake on migration and for IOM at COP20? 20th Conference of the Parties (COP), United Nations Framework Convention on Climate Change (UNFCCC) Lima Peru, 1–12 Dec 2014', www.iom.int/sites/default/files/press_release/file/What-is-at-stake-on-Migration-and-for-IOM-at_COP20.pdf [Accessed 6 July 2018].

IOM (2015a) 'IOM Environmental migration newsletter – March 2015' *Environmental Migration Portal Newsletter* [online], https://us10.campaign-archive.com/home/?u=de24e8e8ad97c261502582454&id=277f364351 [Accessed 6 July 2018].

IOM (2015b) 'Human mobility at COP21', *Environmental Migration Portal* [online], https://environmentalmigration.iom.int/human-mobility-cop21 [Accessed 29 October 2018].

IOM (2015c) 'Infographics: MECLEP infographics on migration as adaptation to environmental and climate change', *Environmental Migration Portal* [online], https://environmentalmigration.iom.int/infographics [Accessed 13 October 2018].

IOM (2015d) 'IOM contributions to the "Year of Climate" – Paris 2015, 21st Conference of Parties of the United Nations Framework Convention on Climate Change (UNFCCC)', http://publications.iom.int/system/files/pdf/mecc_cop_21.pdf [Accessed 29 October 2018].

IOM (2015e) 'UNFCCC COP21 ONE UN high-level roundtable, human mobility and climate change', *Environmental Migration Portal* [online], https://environmentalmigration.iom.int/one-un-high-level-roundtable-human-mobility-and-climate-change [Accessed 29 October 2018].

IOM (2016a) 'Climate migration events at COP22', *Environmental Migration Portal* [online], www.environmentalmigration.iom.int/human-mobility-cop22 [Accessed 29 October 2018].

IOM (2016b) 'Environmental migration portal, human mobility in the UNFCCC', *Environmental Migration Portal* [online], https://environmentalmigration.iom.int/human-mobility-unfccc, [Accessed 29 October 2018].

IOM (2016c) 'Environmental Migration Portal. Knowledge Platform on People on the Move in a Changing Climate', www.environmentalmigration.iom.int [Accessed 29 October 2018].

IOM (2016d) 'Recommendations, draft 1 – September 2016', http://unfccc.int/files/adaptation/groups_committees/loss_and_damage_executive_committee/application/pdf/technical_meeting_recommendations.pdf [Accessed 23 June 2018].

IOM (2016e) 'Synthesis of relevant information, good practices and lessons learned in relation to Pillar 3: Enhancing Action and Support', http://unfccc.int/files/adaptation/groups_committees/loss_and_damage_executive_committee/application/pdf/excom_iom_technical_meeting_pillar_3.pdf [Accessed 23 June 2018].

IOM (2016f) 'Technical meeting – Concept Note', http://www.environmentalmigration.iom.int/sites/default/files/EXCOM%2010M_Technical%20Meeting_AA6%20%28migration%29%20Concept%20Note%20%2829July2016%29.pdf [Accessed 23 June 2018].

IOM (2017) 'Migration, Environment and Climate Change: Evidence for Policy (MECLEP)', https://environmentalmigration.iom.int/iom-publications [Accessed 11 July 2018].

IOM (2018a) 'Environment and Climate Change in the GCM', https://environmentalmigration.iom.int/iom-publications [Accessed 12 October 2018].

IOM (2018b) 'Experts meet to scale up efforts to tackle climate change displacement', www.iom.int/news/experts-meet-scale-efforts-tackle-climate-change-displacement [Accessed 11 July 2018].

IOM, Hugo Observatory, Norwegian Refugee Council and UNU-EHS (2016) 'Synthesis of relevant information, good practices and lessons learned in relation to Pillar 1: Enhancing Knowledge and Understanding', https://unfccc.int/files/adaptation/groups_committees/loss_and_damage_executive_committee/application/pdf/excom_iom_technical_meeting_pillar_1.pdf [Accessed 9 July 2019].

IOM, UNHCR, UNU, NRC and RSG on the HR of IDPs (2009) 'Climate change, migration, and displacement: impacts, vulnerability, and adaptation options, 5th session of the Ad Hoc Working Group on Long-Term Cooperative Action under the Convention (AWG-LCA 5). Bonn, March 29– April 8, 2009', https://unfccc.int/resource/docs/2008/smsn/igo/031.pdf [Accessed 29 October 2018].

IPCC (Intergovernmental Panel on Climate Change) (2007) *Climate Change 2007: Synthesis Report. Contribution of Working Groups I, II and III to the Fourth Assessment Report of the Intergovernmental Panel on Climate Change* Geneva: IPCC.

IPCC (2014) *Climate Change 2014: Impacts, Adaptation, and Vulnerability. Part A: Global and Sectoral Aspects. Contribution of Working Group II to the Fifth Assessment Report of the Intergovernmental Panel on Climate Change* Cambridge and New York, NY: Cambridge University Press.

IPCC (no date) 'Organization', https://www.ipcc.ch/about/ [Accessed 12 May 2019].

Jäger, J., Frühmann, J., Grünberger, S. and Vag, A. (2009) 'EACH-FOR Environmental Change and Forced Migration Scenarios Synthesis Report', www.ccema-portal.org/article/read/each-for-project-publications [Accessed 7 March 2016; no longer available].

Jakobeit, C. and Methmann, C. (2012) '"Climate refugees" as dawning catastrophe? A critique of the dominant quest for numbers' in Scheffran, J., Brzoska, M., Link, M. and Schilling, J. (2012) *Climate Change, Human Security and Violence Conflict: Challenges for Societal Stability* New York, NY: Springer, pp. 301–314.

Kälin, W. (2009) 'Protection of an assistance to internally displaced persons', A/64/214, https://documents-dds-ny.un.org/doc/UNDOC/GEN/N09/437/86/PDF/N0943786.pdf?OpenElement [Accessed 29 October 2018].

Kälin, W. (2012) 'From the Nansen Principles to the Nansen Initiative' *Forced Migration Review* 41: 48–49.

Kälin, W. (2015a) 'Discussion Paper on the relationship between climate change and human mobility. Professor Walter Kaelin, Envoy of the Chairmanship of the Nansen Initiative 27 April 2015', https://unfccc. int/files/science/workstreams/the_2013-2015_review/application/pdf/ cvf_submission_annex_3_migration.pdf [Accessed 29 October 2018].

Kälin, W. (2015b) 'Sendai Framework: an important step forward for people displaced by disasters', *Brookings* [online], www.brookings.edu/ blog/up-front/2015/03/20/sendai-framework-an-important-step-forward-for-people-displaced-by-disasters [Accessed 29 October 2018].

Keane, D. (2004) 'The environmental causes and consequences of migration: a search for the meaning of "environmental refugees"' *Georgetown International Environmental Law Review* 16: 209–223.

Kingsley, P. (2019) '90 days later, nonstop church service to protect refugees finally ends', *New York Times* [online], www.nytimes.com/2019/01/30/ world/europe/netherlands-church-vigil-refugees.html [Accessed 24 March 2019].

Knox, J. (2009) 'Linking human rights and climate change at the United Nations' *Harvard Environmental Law Review* 33, 477–498.

Laclau, E. and Mouffe, C. (1985) *Hegemony and Socialist Strategy: Towards a Radical Democratic Politics* London: Verso.

Lynch, C. (2014) *Interpreting International Politics* New York, NY: Routledge.

Mahon, M. (1992) *Foucault's Nietzschean Genealogy: Truth, Power, and the Subject* New York, NY: State University of New York.

Manou, D., Baldwin, B., Cubie, D., Mihr, A., Thorp, T. (2017) *Climate Change, Migration and Human Rights. Law and Policy Perspectives* Abingdon: Routledge.

Martin, S. (2010) 'Climate change, migration and governance' *Global Governance* 16: 397–414.

Mayer, B. (2013) 'Constructing "climate migration" as a global governance issue: essential flaws in the contemporary literature' *McGill International Journal of Sustainable Development Law and Policy* 9(1), 90–117.

Mayer, B. (2014) '"Environmental migration" as advocacy: is it going to work?' *Refuge* 29(2): 27–41.

Mayer, B. (2016a) 'Migration in the UNFCCC Workstream on Loss and Damage: an assessment of alternative framings and conceivable responses' *Transnational Environmental Law* FirstView: 1–23.

Mayer, B. (2016b) *The Concept of Climate Migration: Advocacy and its Prospects* Cheltenham: Edward Elgar.

Mayer, B. (2017) 'Critical perspective on the identification of "environmental refugees" as a category of human rights concern' in Manou, D., Baldwin, B., Cubie, D., Mihr, A., Thorp, T. (2017) *Climate Change, Migration and Human Rights. Law and Policy Perspectives* Abingdon: Routledge, pp. 28–42.

Mayer, B. and Cournil, C. (2016) 'Climate change, migration and human rights: towards group-specific protection?' in Quirico, O. and Boumghar, M. (2016) *Climate Change and Human Rights: An International and Comparative Law Perspective* London and New York, NY: Routledge, pp. 173–188.

McAdam, J. (2011a) 'Climate change displacement and international law: complementary protection standards', UNHCR PPLA/2011/03, www.unhcr.org/4dff16e99.pdf [Accessed 29 October 2018].

McAdam, J. (2011b) 'Swimming against the tide: why a climate change displacement treaty is not the answer' *International Journal of Refugee Law* 23(1): 2–27.

McAdam, J. (2012) *Climate Change, Forced Migration and International Law* Oxford: Oxford University Press.

McLeman, R. (2014) *Climate and Human Migration: Past Experiences, Future Challenges* Cambridge: Cambridge University Press.

McNamara, K.E. (2014) 'Exploring loss and damage at the international climate change talks' *International Journal of Disaster Risk Science* 5(3): 242–246.

Melde, S., Laczko, F. and Gemenne, F. (2017) *Making Mobility Work for Adaptation to Environmental Changes: Results from the MECLEP Global Research* Geneva: IOM.

Methmann, C. and Oels, A. (2014) 'Vulnerability' in Death, C. (2014) *Critical Environmental Politics* Abingdon and New York, NY: Routledge pp. 277–286.

Methmann, C. and Oels, A. (2015) 'From "fearing" to "empowering" climate refugees: governing climate-induced migration in the name of resilience' *Security Dialogue* 46(1): 51–68.

Methmann, C., Rothe, D. and Stephan, B. (2013) *Interpretive Approaches to Global Climate Governance: (De)constructing the Greenhouse* Abingdon: Routledge.

Miller, T. (2017) *Storming the Wall. Climate Change, Migration, and Homeland Security* San Fransisco, CA: City Lights Books.

MRFCJ (Mary Robinson Foundation – Climate Justice) (2014) 'Position Paper: human rights and climate justice', www.mrfcj.org/wp-content/uploads/2015/09/PositionPaperHumanRightsandClimateChange.pdf [Accessed 29 October 2018].

MRFCJ (2015) 'A climate justice dialogue in Geneva', www.mrfcj.org/resources/climate-justice-dialogue-geneva/ [Accessed 29 October 2018].

Myers, N. (1997) 'Environmental refugees' *Population and Environment* 19: 2.

Myrttinen, H. (2017) 'The complex ties that bind: gendered agency and expectations in conflict and climate change-related migration' *Global Policy* 8(S1): 48–54.

Nabers, D. (2015) *A Poststructuralist Discourse Theory of Global Politics* Basingstoke: Palgrave Macmillan.

Nansen Initiative (2013) *The Nansen Initiative: Towards a Protection Agenda for Disaster-Induced Cross-Border Displacement. Information Note* Geneva: Nansen Initiative.

Nansen Initiative (2014a) 'About us', www.nanseninitiative.org/secretariat [Accessed 8 March 2016].

Nansen Initiative (2014b) 'Integrating disaster–induced displacement within the post-2015 Framework for Disaster Risk Reduction. Position Paper by the Envoy of the Nansen Initiative on the occasion of the Preparatory Committee of the Third United Nations World Conference on Disaster Risk Reduction', www.preventionweb.net/publications/view/38482 [Accessed 29 October 2018].

Nansen Initiative (2015a) 'Agenda for the Protection of Cross–Border Displaced Persons in the Context of Disasters and Climate Change: Volume 1', https://nanseninitiative.org/wp-content/uploads/2015/02/PROTECTION-AGENDA-VOLUME-1.pdf [Accessed 29 October 2018].

Nansen Initiative (2015b) 'Fleeing floods, earthquakes, droughts and rising sea levels. 12 lessons learned about protecting people displaced by disasters and the effects of climate change', https://nanseninitiative.org/wp-content/uploads/2015/10/12-LESSONS-LEARNED.pdf [Accessed 12 October 2018].

Nansen Initiative (2015c) 'Global Consultation Conference Report, Geneva 12–13 Oct 2015', www.nanseninitiative.org/wp-content/uploads/2015/02/GLOBAL-CONSULTATION-REPORT.pdf [Accessed 29 October 2018].

Nansen Initiative (2015d) 'More than 100 governments affirm broad support to better protect people displaced across borders by disaster and the effects of climate change', Press release, www.nanseninitiative.org/more-than-100-governments-affirm-broad-support-to-better-protect-people-displaced-across-borders-by-disasters-and-the-effects-of-climate-change [Accessed 19 January 2016].

Nansen Initiative (2015e) 'Side event: World Conference on Disaster Risk Reduction, Sendai', www.nanseninitiative.org/side-event-world-conference-on-disaster-risk-reduction-sendai [Accessed 29 October 2018].

Nash, S.L. (2016) 'Towards an "environmental migration management" discourse: a discursive turn in environmental migration advocacy?' in Rosenow-Williams, K. and Gemenne, F. (2016) *Organizational Perspectives on Environmental Migration* Abingdon: Routledge.

Nash, S.L. (2018a) 'Between rights and resilience: struggles over understanding climate change and human mobility' in Labonte, M. and Mills, K. (2018) *Human Rights and Justice. Philosophical, Economic, and Social Perspectives* London: Routledge pp. 123–144.

Nash, S.L. (2018b) 'From Cancun to Paris: an era of policy making on climate change and migration' *Global Policy* 9(1): 53–63.

Nash, S.L. (2018c) 'Knowing human mobility in the context of climate change: the self-perpetuating circle of research, policy, and knowledge production' *Movements* 4(1), 67–81.

Nepal (2014) 'Submission by Nepal on behalf of the Least Developed Countries Group on the ADP Co-Chairs' Non Paper of 7 July 2014 on Parties' views and proposal on the elements for a draft negotiating text', www4.unfccc.int/submissions/Lists/OSPSubmission Upload/39_99_130584499817551043-Submission%20by%20Nepal%20 ADP_21%20Oct%202014.pdf [Accessed 29 October 2018].

Norwegian Refugee Council (2011) 'The Nansen Conference, Climate Change and Displacement in the 21st Century', www.nrc.no/ globalassets/pdf/reports/the-nansen-conference---climate-change-and-displacement-in-the-21st-century.pdf [Accessed 29 October 2018].

Ober, K. and Sakdapolrak, P. (2017) 'How do social practices shape policy? Analysing the field of "migration as adaptation" with Bourdieu's "theory of practice"' *The Geographical Journal* 183: 359–369.

OHCHR (1996–2018) 'Mandate', www.ohchr.org/EN/AboutUs/Pages/ Mandate.aspx [Accessed 6 July 2018].

OHCHR (2015) 'Climate change impacts enjoyment of human rights', www. ohchr.org/EN/NewsEvents/Pages/Climatechangeimpactsenjoyment. aspx [Accessed 29 October 2018].

OHCHR (2017a) 'Expert Meeting. Slow onset effects of climate change and human rights protection for cross-border migrants', www.ohchr. org/Documents/Issues/ClimateChange/SlowOnset/Programme.pdf [Accessed 9 July 2018].

OHCHR (2017b) 'OHCHR stakeholder input to Task Force on Displacement', https://unfccc.int/sites/default/files/ohchr.pdf [Accessed 23 June 2018].

OHCHR (no date) 'OHCHR's key messages on human rights, climate change and migration', www.ohchr.org/Documents/Issues/ClimateChange/Key_Messages_HR_CC_Migration.pdf [Accessed 6 July 2018].

Olsson, L., Jerneck, A., Thoren, H., Persson, J. and O'Byrne, D. (2015) 'Why resilience is unappealing to social science: theoretical and empirical investigations of the scientific use of resilience' *Science Advances* 1(4).

Oxford Dictionaries (2016) [online] www.oxforddictionaries.com/de/definition/englisch/refugee [Accessed 31 August 2016].

Park, S. (2011) 'Climate change and the risk of statelessness: the situation of low-lying island states', UNHCR PPLA/2011/04, www.unhcr.org/protection/globalconsult/4df9cb0c9/20-climate-change-risk-statelessness-situation-low-lying-island-states.html [Accessed 29 October 2018].

PDD (Platform on Disaster Displacement) (2017) 'PDD fact sheet', https://disasterdisplacement.org/the-platform/our-response [Accessed 2 April 2018].

PDD (2018) 'Task Force on Displacement – stakeholder meeting: "Recommendations for integrated approaches to avert, minimize and address displacement related to the adverse impacts of climate change"', https://disasterdisplacement.org/task-force-on-displacement-stakeholder-meeting [Accessed 11 July 2018].

PDD and UNHCR (2016) 'Synthesis of relevant information, good practices and lessons learned in relation to Pillar 2: Strengthening Dialogue, Coordination, Coherence and Synergies', http://unfccc.int/files/adaptation/groups_committees/loss_and_damage_executive_committee/application/pdf/excom_iom_technical_meeting_pillar_2.pdf [Accessed 23 June 2018].

Piguet, E., Kaenzig, R. and Guélat, J. (2018) 'The uneven geography of research on "environmental migration"' *Population and Environment* 39(4): 357–383.

Pilath, A. (2016) 'International epistemic organizations and their role in shaping the politics of environmental migration' in Rosenow-Williams, K. and Gemenne, F. (2016) *Organizational Perspectives on Environmental Migration* Abingdon: Routledge, pp. 216–235.

Rabinow, P. (1984) *The Foucault Reader* New York, NY: Pantheon Books.

Rajaram, P.K. (2002) 'Humanitarianism and representations of the refugee' *Journal of Refugee Studies* 15(3): 247–264.

Reid, J. (2012) 'The disastrous and politically debased subject of resilience' *Development Dialogues* 58: 67–79.

Republic of Maldives Ministry of Environment, Energy and Water (2006) *Report of the First Meeting on Protocol on Environmental Refugees: Recognition of Environmental Refugees in the 1951 Convention and 1967 Protocol Relating to the Status of Refugees* Male: Government of the Maldives.

Roberts E. and Huq S. (2015) 'Coming full circle: the history of loss and damage under the UNFCCC' *International Journal of Global Warming* 8:141–157.

Roberts, E. and Pelling, M. (2018) 'Climate change-related loss and damage: translating the global policy agenda for national policy processes' *Climate and Development* 10(1): 4–17.

Romson, Å, Marghem, M.C., Magnette, P., Mena, M., Gutierrez, E.E., Ramirez, O., Tiilikainen, K., Lehnoff, A., Kelly, A., Dieschbourg, C., Alaman, R.P., Dijksman, A.M., de Guzman, E.M., Perrez, F.X., de León, E. (2015) Letter, Paris [on file with the author].

Rosenow-Williams, K. and Gemenne, F. (2016) *Organizational Perspectives on Environmental Migration* Abingdon: Routledge.

Rothe, D. (2017) 'Gendering resilience: myths and stereotypes in the discourse on climate-induced migration' *Global Policy* 8(S1): 40–47.

Saussure, F. (1960) *Course in General Linguistics* London: Peter Owen.

Savaresi, A. (2016) 'The Paris Agreement: a new beginning?' *Journal of Energy & Natural Resources Law* 34(1): 16–26.

SBSTA (Subsidiary Body for Scientific and Technological Advice) and SBI (Subsidiary Body for Implementation) (2014) 'Report of the Executive Committee of the Warsaw International Mechanism for Loss and Damage associated with Climate Change Impacts', FCCC/SB/2014/4, https://unfccc.int/resource/docs/2014/sbsta/eng/04.pdf [Accessed 29 October 2018].

Schlosberg, D. and Collins, L.B. (2014) 'From environmental to climate justice: climate change and the discourse of environmental justice' *WIREs Climate Change* 5(May/June 2014): 359–374.

Schwartzstein, P. (2016) 'The climate-change refugee crisis is only just beginning', *Quartz* [online] https://qz.com/605609/the-climate-change-refugee-crisis-is-only-just-beginning/ [Accessed 29 October 2018].

Sendai Framework for Disaster Risk Reduction (2015) 'Sendai Framework for Disaster Risk Reduction 2015–2030', www.preventionweb.net/files/43291_sendaiframeworkfordrren.pdf [Accessed 29 October 2018].

Sigona, N. (2014) 'The politics of refugee voices: Representations, narratives, and memories' in Fiddian-Qasmiyeh, E., Loescher, G., Long, K. and Sigona, N. (2014) *The Oxford Handbook of Refugee and Forced Migration Studies* Oxford: Oxford University Press, pp. 369–382.

Simonelli, A.C. (2016) *Governing Climate Induced Migration and Displacement. IGO Expansion and Global Policy Implications* Basingstoke: Palgrave Macmillan.

Surminski, S. and Lopez, A. (2015) 'Concept of loss and damage of climate change – a new challenge for climate decision-making? A climate science perspective' *Climate and Development* 7(3): 267–277.

Swiss Confederation (2011) 'Statement of Switzerland in the plenary session', www.unhcr.org/ministerial-meeting.html [Accessed 29 October 2018].

Task Force on Displacement (2017a) 'Summary of proceedings of the first meeting of the Task Force on Displacement, the Executive Committee of the Warsaw International Mechanism for Loss and Damage', https://unfccc.int/sites/default/files/tfd_1_summary_of_proceedings.pdf [Accessed 23 June 2018].

Task Force on Displacement (2017b) 'Workplan of the Task Force on Displacement', https://unfccc.int/sites/default/files/tfd_workplan.pdf [Accessed 23 June 2018].

Task Force on Displacement (2018) 'Report of the Task Force on Displacement', https://unfccc.int/sites/default/files/resource/2018_TFD_report_17_Sep.pdf [Accessed 12 October 2018].

Telford, A. (2018) 'A threat to climate-secure European futures? Exploring racial logics and climate-induced migration in US and EU climate security discourses' *Geoforum* 96: 268–277.

Toles, T. (2015) 'Climate future will be the Syria refugee crisis times 100', *Washington Post* [online], www.washingtonpost.com/news/opinions/wp/2015/10/27/climate-future-will-be-the-syria-refugee-crisis-times-100/?utm_term=.d8cd8c55fada [Accessed 26 October 2018].

Trent, S. (2016) 'COP22: As Paris promises become law, focus turns into action', https://ejfoundation.org/news-media/2016/cop22-as-paris-promises-become-law-focus-turns-to-action [Accessed 3 March 2017].

Turhan, E. and Armiero, M. (2017) 'Cutting the fence, sabotaging the border: migration as a revolutionary practice' *Capitalism Nature Socialism* 28(2): 1–9.

UKCCMC (UK Climate Change and Migration Coalition) (2014) 'Migration as adaptation: exploring mobility as a coping strategy for climate change', http://climatemigration.org.uk/wp-content/uploads/2014/02/migration_adaptation_climate.pdf [Accessed 29 October 2018].

UKCCMC (2015) 'Not optimistic, but not pessimistic', http://climatemigration.org.uk/not-optimistic-but-not-pessimistic [Accessed 29 October 2018].

UN General Assembly (1950) 'Statute of the Office of the United Nations High Commissioner for Refugees', General Assembly Resolution 428 (V) of 14 December, www.unhcr.org/3b66c39e1.pdf [Accessed 29 October 2018].

UN General Assembly (1951) 'Convention Relating to the Status of Refugees', www.refworld.org/docid/3be01b964.html [Accessed 29 October 2018].

UN General Assembly (2016) 'New York Declaration for Refugees and Migrants', A/RES/71/1, www.un.org/en/ga/search/view_doc. asp?symbol=A/RES/71/1/1 [Accessed 10 July 2018].

UNFCCC (United Nations Framework Convention on Climate Change) (1922) 'United Nations Framework Convention on Climate Change', FCCC/INFORMAL/84, http://unfccc.int/key_documents/the_convention/items/2853.php [Accessed 29 October 2018].

UNFCCC (2008) 'Report of the Conference of the Parties on its thirteenth session, held in Bali from 3 to 15 December 2007', FCCC/CP/2007/6/ADD.1, https://unfccc.int/resource/docs/2007/cop13/eng/06a01.pdf [Accessed 29 October 2018].

UNFCCC (2010) 'The Cancun Agreements: outcome of the work of the Ad-Hoc Working Group on Long-term Cooperative Action under the Convention', FCCC/CP/2010/7/Add.1, https://unfccc.int/resource/docs/2010/cop16/eng/07a01.pdf [Accessed 29 October 2018].

UNFCCC (2012) 'A literature review on the topics in the context of thematic area 2 of the work programme on loss and damage: a range of approaches to address loss and damage associated with the adverse effects of climate change', FCCC/SBI/2012/INF.14, https://unfccc.int/resource/docs/2012/sbi/eng/inf14.pdf [Accessed 29 October 2018].

UNFCCC (2013) 'Report of the Conference of the Parties on its eighteenth session, held in Doha from 26 November to 8 December 2012', FCCC/CP/2012/8/Add.1, http://unfccc.int/resource/docs/2012/cop18/eng/08a01.pdf [Accessed 25 October 2018].

UNFCCC (2014) 'Report of the Conference of the Parties on its nineteenth session, held in Warsaw from 11 to 23 November 2013', FCCC/CP/2013/10/Add.1, http://unfccc.int/resource/docs/2013/cop19/eng/10.pdf [Accessed 29 October 2018].

UNFCCC (2016a) 'Report of the Conference of the Parties on its twenty-first session, held in Paris from 30 November to 13 December 2015', FCCC/CP/2015/10/Add.1, http://unfccc.int/sites/default/files/resource/docs/2015/cop21/eng/10a01.pdf [Accessed 12 October 2018].

UNFCCC (2016b) 'Technical meeting on Migration, Displacement and Human Mobility. In the context of Action Area 6 of the initial two-year workplan of the Executive Committee of the Warsaw International Mechanism for Loss and Damage. Presentation by Ms Pepetua Latasi and Ms Scheren D'Souza Co-chairs of the Executive Committee', http:// unfccc.int/files/adaptation/application/pdf/excom_aa6_technical_ meeting.pdf [Accessed 29 October 2018].

UNFCCC (2017) 'Report of the Conference of the Parties on its twenty-second session, held in Marrakech from 7 to 18 November 2016' FCCC/ CP/2016/10, https://unfccc.int/resource/docs/2016/cop22/eng/10. pdf [Accessed 29 October 2018].

UNFCCC (2018a) 'Parties and observers', https://unfccc.int/parties-observers [Accessed 12 October 2018].

UNFCCC (2018b) 'Report of the Conference of the Parties on its twenty-third session, held in Bonn from 6 to 18 November 2017' FCCC/ CP/2017/11/Add.1, https://unfccc.int/sites/default/files/resources/ docs/2017/cop23/eng/11a01.pdf [Accessed 25 October 2018].

UNFCCC (2019) 'Report of the Conference of the Parties on its twenty-fourth session, held in Katowice from 2 to 15 December 2018, part two: actions taken by the Conference of the Parties at its twenty-fourth session', FCCC/CP/2018/10/Add.1, https://unfccc.int/sites/default/ files/resource/cp2018_10_add1_advance.pdf [Accessed 21 March 2019].

UNHCR (United Nations High Commissioner for Refugees) (2011a) 'Additional Guidance Note to support the State pledges process', www. unhcr.org/events/commemorations/4dedf5719/additional-guidance-note-support-state-pledges-process.html [Accessed 29 October 2018].

UNHCR (2011b) 'Climate change and displacement: identifying gaps and responses, expert roundtable Concept Note', www.unhcr. org/4d1c92bb9.pdf [Accessed 29 October 2018].

UNHCR (2011c) 'Ministerial Communiqué', HRC/ MINCOMMS/2011/6, www.unhcr.org/501fd0739.pdf [Accessed 29 October 2018].

UNHCR (2011d) 'Summary of deliberations on climate change and displacement', www.unhcr.org/4da2b5e19.pdf [Accessed 29 October 2018].

UNHCR (2011e) 'UNHCR marks 60th anniversary of Refugee Convention', www.unhcr.org/4e3106fa6.html [Accessed 29 October 2018].

UNHCR (2014) 'UNHCR, the environment and climate change: an overview', www.unhcr.org/540854f49.pdf [Accessed 29 October 2018].

UNHCR (2015) 'Prepare and adapt: climate change and human mobility – in COP21 and beyond', Press briefing. Paris, France, 2 December, https://unfccc6.meta-fusion.com/cop21/events/2015-12-02-17-00-united-nations-high-commissioner-for-refugees-unhcr-prepare-and-adapt-climate-change-and-human-mobility-in-cop21-and-beyond [Accessed 29 October 2018].

UNHCR, IOM and NRC (2009a) 'Submission. Climate change and statelessness: an overview, to the 6th session of the Ad Hoc Working Group on Long-Term Cooperative Action (AWG-LCA 6) under the UN Framework Convention on Climate Change (UNFCCC) 1 to 12 June 2009, Bonn, Germany', https://unfccc.int/resource/docs/2009/smsn/igo/048.pdf [Accessed 29 October 2018].

UNHCR, IOM, NRC, UNU and RSG on HR of IDPs (2009b) 'Comments and proposed revisions to the negotiating text prepared by the Chair of the UNFCCC Ad Hoc Working Group on Long-Term Cooperative Action to the 6th session of the Ad Hoc Working Group on Long-Term Cooperative Action under the Convention (AWG-LCA 6) from 1 until 12 June in Bonn', https://unfccc.int/resource/docs/2009/smsn/igo/055.pdf [Accessed 29 October 2018].

UNHCR, NRC, RSG on HR of IDPs and UNU (2009c) 'Submission. Forced displacement in the context of climate change: challenges for states under international law, to the 6th session of the Ad Hoc Working Group on Long-Term Cooperative Action under the Convention (AWG-LCA 6) from 1 until 12 June in Bonn', https://unfccc.int/resource/docs/2009/smsn/igo/049.pdf [Accessed 29 October 2018].

UNHCR, UNU, NRC/IDMC, SR on the HR of IDPs and IOM (2012) 'Submission. Human mobility in the context of loss and damage from climate change: needs, gaps, and roles of the Convention in addressing loss and damage', http://unfccc.int/resource/docs/2012/smsn/igo/106.pdf [Accessed 29 October 2018].

UNHCR, NRC/IDMC, UNU, UNDP, IOM, ILO, OHCHR, Sciences Po (CERI) and Refugees International (2013) 'Contributions and potential elements related to human mobility in the context of a Warsaw COP 19 decision on loss and damage', https://environmentalmigration.iom.int/sites/default/files/November2013.pdf [Accessed 29 October 2018].

UNISDR (United Nations Office for Disaster Risk Reduction) (2005) 'Hyogo Framework for Action 2005–2015: building the resilience of nations and communities to disasters. Extract from the final report of the World Conference on Disaster Reduction', A/CONF.206/6, www.unisdr.org/files/1037_hyogoframeworkforactionenglish.pdf [Accessed 29 October 2018].

UNISDR (2009) 'Terminology', www.unisdr.org/we/inform/terminology#letter-r [Accessed 29 October 2018].

United Nations Climate Change Secretariat (2016) 'WIM ExCom letter on Action Area 6, Activity a', EXCOM/MK/cma, http://unfccc.int/files/adaptation/groups_committees/loss_and_damage_executive_committee/application/pdf/excom_invitation_letter_aa6a.pdf [Accessed 29 October 2018].

United Nations General Assembly (2015) 'Transforming our world: the 2030 Agenda for Sustainable Development', A/RES/70/1, http://www.un.org/ga/search/view_doc.asp?symbol=A/RES/70/1&Lang=E [Accessed 29 October 2018].

Various authors (2015) 'A call to action to defend humanity and the planet', www.ciel.org/wp-content/uploads/2015/12/A-Call-to-Action-to-Defend-Humanity-and-the-Planet-11-Dec-2015.pdf [Accessed 29 October 2018].

Vucetic, S. (2011) 'Genealogy as a research tool in international relations' *Review of International Studies* 37(3): 1295–1312.

Warner K. (2011) 'Climate Change Induced Displacement: Adaptation Policy in the Context of the UNFCCC Climate Negotiations'. Available at: http://www.unhcr.org/4df9cc309.pdf [Accessed 12 June 2019].

Warner, K. (2012) 'Human migration and displacement in the context of adaptation to climate change: the Cancun Adaptation Framework and potential for future action' *Environment and Planning C: Government and Policy* 30: 1061–1077.

Warner, K. (2018) 'Coordinated approaches to large-scale movements of people: contributions of the Paris Agreement and the Global Compacts for migration and on refugees' *Population and Environment* 39(4): 384–401.

Warner, K. and Zakieldeen, S.A. (2011) 'Loss and damage due to climate change: an overview of the UNFCCC negotiations', European Capacity Building Initiative, www.oxfordclimatepolicy.org/publications/documents/LossandDamage.pdf [Accessed 29 October 2018].

Warner, K. and Afifi, T. (2014a) 'Special Issue: Connections between (changing) rainfall patterns, food and livelihood security, and human mobility: evidence and a new analytical framework' *Climate and Development* 6.

Warner, K. and Afifi, T. (2014b) 'Where the rain falls: evidence from 8 countries on how vulnerable households use migration to manage the risks of rainfall variability and food insecurity' *Climate and Development* 6(1): 1–17.

Warner, K., Afifi, T., Henry, K., Rawe, T., Smith, C. and De Sherbinin, A. (2012) *Where the Rain Falls: Climate Change, Food and Livelihood Security, and Migration: Global Policy Report* Bonn: UNU-EHS.

WIM (Warsaw International Mechanism for Loss and Damage associated with Climate Change Impacts) (2016) 'Third meeting of the Executive Committee of the Warsaw International Mechanism for Loss and Damage associated with Climate Change, Impacts Agenda item 4(f) Action Area 6: Migration, displacement and human mobility', http://unfccc.int/files/adaptation/groups_committees/loss_and_damage_executive_committee/application/pdf/aa6_intro.pdf [Accessed 29 October 2018].

Wendle, J. (2015) 'The ominous story of Syria's climate refugees', *Scientific American* [online] www.scientificamerican.com/article/ominous-story-of-syria-climate-refugees [Accessed 16 August 2016].

White, G. (2011) *Climate Change and Migration: Security and Borders in a Warming World* Oxford: Oxford University Press.

Williams, A. (2008) 'Turning the tide: recognizing climate change refugees in international law' *Law & Policy* 30(4): 502–529.

Williams, A. and Black, R. (2012) 'The Nansen Initiative, UNHCR and the Foresight report on migration and global environmental change', www2.nanseninitiative.org/wp-content/uploads/2015/03/3.-FINAL-Foresight-Nansen-paper-270912.pdf [Accessed 29 October 2018].

Wrathall, D., Oliver-Smith, J.A., Fekete, A., Gencer, E., Reyes, M.L. and Sakdapolrak, P. (2015) 'Problematising loss and damage' *International Journal of Global Warming* 8(2): 274–294.

Zetter, R. (2007) 'More labels, fewer refugees: remaking the refugee label in an era of globalization' *Journal of Refugee Studies* 20(2): 172–192.

Zetter, R. (2011) 'Protecting environmentally displaced people: developing the capacity of legal and normative frameworks', www.rsc.ox.ac.uk/files/publications/other/rr-protecting-environmentally-displaced-people-2011.pdf [Accessed 29 October 2018].

Zolli, A. (2012) 'Learning to bounce back', *New York Times* [online], www.nytimes.com/2012/11/03/opinion/forget-sustainability-its-about-resilience.html [Accessed 29 October 2018].

Index

Page numbers in italics refer to figures; those in bold refer to tables.